A Sacramental Life

Marquette Studies in Theology
Andrew Tallon, editor

Frederick M. Bliss. *Understanding Reception*

Martin Albl, Paul Eddy, and Renee Mirkes, OSF, editors. *Directions in New Testament Methods*

Robert M. Doran. *Subject and Psyche*

Kenneth Hagen, editor. *The Bible in the Churches. How Various Christians Interpret the Scriptures*

Jamie T. Phelps, O.P., editor. *Black and Catholic: The Challenge and Gift of Black Folk. Contributions of African American Experience and Thought to Catholic Theology*

Karl Rahner. *Spirit in the World.* CD

Karl Rahner. *Hearer of the Word.* CD

Robert M. Doran. *Theological Foundations. Vol. 1 Intentionality and Psyche*

Robert M. Doran. *Theological Foundations. Vol. 2 Theology and Culture.*

Patrick W. Carey. *Orestes A. Brownson: A Bibliography, 1826-1876*

Patrick W. Carey, editor. *The Early Works of Orestes A. Brownson.* Volume I: *The Universalist Years, 1826-29*

Patrick W. Carey, editor. *The Early Works of Orestes A. Brownson.* Volume II: *The Free and Unitarian Years, 1830-35*

Patrick W. Carey, editor. *The Early Works of Orestes A. Brownson.* Volume III: *The Transcendentalist Years, 1836-38*

John Martinetti, S.J. *Reason to Believe Today*

George H. Tavard. *Trina Deitas: The Controversy between Hincmar and Gottschalk*

Jeanne Cover, IBVM. *Love: The Driving Force. Mary Ward's Spirituality. Its Significance for Moral Theology*

David A. Boileau, editor. *Principles of Catholic Social Teaching*

Michael Purcell. *Mystery and Method: The Other in Rahner and Levinas*

W.W. Meissner, S.J., M.D. *To the Greater Glory: A Psychological Study of Ignatian Spirituality*

Virginia M. Shaddy, editor. *Catholic Theology in the University: Source of Wholeness*

Thomas M. Bredohl. *Class and Religious Identity: The Rhenish Center Party in Wilhelmine Germany*

William M. Thompson and David L. Morse, editors. *Voegelin's **Israel and Revelation**: An Interdisciplinary Debate and Anthology*

Donald L. Gelpi, S.J. *The Firstborn of Many: A Christology for Converting Christians.* Volume 1: *To Hope in Jesus Christ*

Donald L. Gelpi, S.J. *The Firstborn of Many: A Christology for Converting Christians.* Volume 2: *Synoptic Narrative Christology*

Donald L. Gelpi, S.J. *The Firstborn of Many: A Christology for Converting Christians.* Volume 3: *Doctrinal and Practical Christology*

Stephen A. Werner. *Prophet of the Christian Social Manifesto. Joseph Husslein, S.J.: His Life, Work, & Social Thought*

Gregory Sobolewski. *Martin Luther: Roman Catholic Prophet*

Matthew C. Ogilvie. *Faith Seeking Understanding: The Functional Specialty, "Systematics" in Bernard Lonergan's* **Method in Theology**

Timothy Maschke, Franz Posset, and Joan Skocir, editors. *Ad fontes Lutheri: Toward the Recovery of the Real Luther: Essays in Honor of* Kenneth Hagen's Sixty-Fifth Birthday

William Thorn, Phillip Runkel, and Susan Mountin, editors. *Dorothy Day and The Catholic Worker Movement: Centenary Essays*

Michele Saracino. *On Being Human: A Conversation with Lonergan and Levinas*

Ian Christopher Levy. *John Wyclif: Scriptural Logic, Real Presence, and the Parameters of Orthodoxy*

Michael Horace Barnes & William P. Roberts, editors. *A Sacramental Life: A Festschrift Honoring Bernard Cooke*

Roger Aubert. *Catholic Social Teaching: An Historical Perspective*

A Sacramental Life

A Festschrift Honoring Bernard Cooke

Michael Horace Barnes
William P. Roberts

Editors

Marquette University Press

Marquette Studies in Theology No. 37
Series Editor, Andrew Tallon

Library of Congress Cataloguing-in-Publication Data

A sacramental life : a festschrift honoring Bernard Cooke / by Michael
Horace Barnes, William P. Roberts, editors.
  p. cm. — (Marquette studies in theology ; no. 37)
Includes bibliographical references.
  ISBN 0-87462-689-7 (pbk. : alk. paper)
  1. Cooke, Bernard J. 2. Catholic Church—Doctrines.
I. Cooke, Bernard J. II. Barnes, Michael Horace. III. Roberts, William P., 1931- IV. Marquette studies in theology ; #37.
  BX1751.3.S23 2003
  230'.2—dc22

2003020759

Marquette University Press
Member, American Association of University Presses
Association of Jesuit University Presses

MARQUETTE UNIVERSITY PRESS
MILWAUKEE

The Association of Jesuit University Presses

Table of Contents

Foreword

It has been some four decades since both of us, as doctoral candidates at Marquette University, first met Bernard Cooke, then chair of the theology department and founder of its Ph.D. program. In the years since, we have had a number of occasions to work with Bernard, and to express privately to him our appreciation for the effect he has had on our lives. It is beyond our furthest dreams that we would have the opportunity to show that gratitude publicly through this well deserved Festschrift. We know in doing so we speak not only for ourselves, but for the thousands of students, colleagues and faithful at large, whose lives Bernard has touched.

Others in this volume will speak of his brilliance as a scholar and a theologian, his extraordinary talent as a teacher and a writer, and his contributions to the Catholic Theological Society of America and the College Theology Society, both of which organizations he has been past president. Equally, if not more impressive are three qualities that Bernard possesses to an unusual degree and that go far beyond what can appear on a resume. He is totally unassuming, fully respectful of even the slowest or most obstinate student, and absolutely generous with his time. He taught us lifelong lessons not only through the insightful content of his theology classes, but also, at least as deeply, through the kind of person and teacher he is. In countless ways this has affected our own teaching and our own way of relating to others.

The essays in this Festschrift celebrate Bernard's life, and the major themes of his theological work. As Bernard Cooke is recognized as the leading American sacramental theologian over the past four and a half decades, this volume is fittingly entitled, *A Sacramental Life*. The authors of this volume have explored diverse aspects of Bernard's major theological focus, drawn from them, and directly and indirectly addressed them in a variety of topics.

We have divided these contributions into three general categories: biographical, speculative theology, and applied theology. While there can be some room for argument regarding which heading a particular essay might best come under, we trust this threefold framework will serve as a convenient guide to the reader.

We wish to extend our personal thanks to Pauline Turner and Gary Macy who conceived this project, and to each of the contributors who took time out of extremely busy schedules to commit themselves to this Festschrift. Their expressed willingness to do so is a testimony to their own personal esteem of Bernard Cooke, and their gratitude for all he has accomplished on behalf of the Church and the field of Theology.

Michael H. Barnes
William P. Roberts
University of Dayton
November 15, 2002

I. Biographical

1 Highlights of Bernard Cooke's Career

Education and degrees

1935-39 Our Lady of Lourdes High School, Marinette, WI
1939-43 A.B. St. Louis University (classics)
1943-46 M.A. St. Louis University (philosophy)
1949-53 S.T.L. St. Mary's College, St. Marys, Kansas
1953-54 Specialized graduate study, Muenster, Germany
1954-56 S.T.D. Institut Catholique de Paris, France

Professional Activity

1946-49 Instructor in classical languages, Marquette High
School, Milwaukee WI
1954-56 Lecturer in pastoral theology, Grand Seminaire de Saint
Sulpice, Paris
1956-69 Professor theology, chair of department, Marquette University, Milwaukee, WI
1962-70 Consultant and examiner, North Central Association
1969-70 Research fellow, Yale Divinity School
1970-76 Professor of Religious Studies, University of Windsor,
Windsor, Ontario
1973-74 Bernard Hanley Visiting Professor, University of Santa
Clara, Santa Clara, CA
1976-80 Professor of Religious Studies, University of Calgary,
Calgary, Alberta
1980-92 Professor of Theology, College of the Holy Cross,
Worcester, MA
1983-84 Fellow, Woodrow Wilson Center for International
Scholars, Washington, D.C.

1986-88 Chair, Department of Religious Studies, College of the
    Holy Cross
1992 Loyola Professor of Theology Emeritus, College of the
    Holy Cross
1992-97 Monsignor French Chair in Theology, Incarnate Word
    University, San Antonio,
1998 Knapp Visiting Professor, University of San Diego, San
    Diego, CA
1999-01 Adjunct professor of theology, University of San Diego
1957- present. Numerous lectures, workshops, professorships in
    summer graduate programs (Boston College, Loyola University
    in New Orleans, Loyola Marymount University in Los Ange-
    les, Incarnate Word in San Antonio), in US and abroad
Areas of Professional Specialization
Religious symbolism (sacramental theology), Christian ministry,
    New Testament, Christology, religious psychology, history of
    theological method
Membership in Professional Societies
Catholic Theological Society of America, 1958- ; President, 1982-
    83
College Theology Society, 1957- ; Board of Directors, 1960-64;
    President,1962-64
American Academy of Religion, 1970-
Society for Scientific Study of Religion, 1966-80
Council for the Study of Religion, 1972-; Board of Directors,
    1976-78; Vice-Chairman 1979-80
Academy of Catholic Hispanic Theologians of the United States,
    1997-

Academic Honors

Honorary Doctorate (Litt.D.), University of Detroit, 1968
    (Th.D), Loyola University, New Orleans, 1993
Research Fellowship, Yale Divinity School, 1969
John Courtney Murray Award of CTSA, 1979
Fellow, The Wilson Center, Washington DC, 1983-4

Presidential Award of the College Theology Society, 1997

Publications: Books

Christian Sacrament and Christian Personality, New York, 1965.
Formation of Faith, Chicago, 1965.
Christian Involvement, Chicago, 1966.
Response to Vatican II, Chicago, 1966.
Vatican Council II, Study Week, 1966, (private publication Sogang College, Seoul).
New Dimensions in Catholic Life, Wilkes-Barre, 1968.
Beyond Trinity, Milwaukee, 1969.
The God of Space and Time, New York, 1969.
The Eucharist, Mystery of Friendship, Dayton, 1969.
Christian Community, Response to Reality, New York, 1970.
Theology in an Age of Revolution, Wilkes-Barre, 1971.
Rethinking the Faith, Chicago, 1972.
Ministry to Word and Sacrament, Philadelphia, 1976.
Sacraments and Sacramentality, Mystic CT, 1983 (2nd edit., 1994).
Reconciled Sinners, Mystic CT, 1986.
Alternative Futures for Worship, vol. 5 (*Christian Marriage*), editor and contributor, Collegeville, 1988.
The Papacy and the Church in the United States (editor and introductory essay), Mahwah NJ, 1989.
The Distancing of God, Minneapolis, 1992.
Why Angels? Mystic CT, 1995.
The Future of Eucharist, Mahwah NJ, 1997.

Publications:
Periodical Articles and Essays in Books

"The Mutability-Immutability Principle in St. Augustine's Metaphysics." *The Modern Schoolman*, 23(1946):181-194; 24(1947):37-49.

"Developments in Dogma," *Perspectives,* 4 (1959):11-18.

"Faith and the Human Personality," Catholic Mind, 57 (1959): 450-458.

"The Catholic Press and the Role of the Laity," *Catholic School Editor* 28 (1959): 3-12.

"The Psalms and Christian Prayer," *A.P.I. Bulletin,* 24 (1959).

"Synoptic Presentation of the Eucharist as Covenant Sacrifice," *Theological Studies* 21(1960):1-44. (reprinted in Spanish—"La Eucharistia como Sacrificio de la Alianza en los sinopticos," *Seleciones de la Teologia,* Barcelona, 1964.

"Teaching Christ from Scripture," *Perspectives* 5 (1960): 11-16.

"Nature, the Basis of Right and Law," *Human Rights* 18 (1960): 3-10.

"New Perspectives in Dogmatic Theology," *Theology Digest* 8 (1960): 69-73.

"The Problem of Sacred Scripture in the College," *Modern Catechetics* (ed. G. Sloyan), New York, 1960, 267-290.

"The Sacraments as the Continuing Acts of Christ," *Proceedings of the Catholic Theological Society of America,* 1961, 41-68 (reprinted in Sullivan, *Readings in Sacramental Theology,* Englewood Cliffs, 1964, 31-51).

Personal Development through Sacramental Life," *Catholic World* 194 (1961): 157-162.

The Theology of Person," *Spiritual Life* 7 (1961): 11-20 (reprinted as "The Biblical Theology of Person" in R. Ryan, *Contemporary New Testament Studies,* Collegeville, 1965, 83-89)

"The Sacraments, Encounters with Mystery," *Perspectives* 6 (1961): 7-10.

"The Core of the Christian Message," *Proceedings of Midwestern Institute of Pastoral Theology,* Detroit, 1961, 77-89.

"Awareness of Christianity as Mystery," *Proceedings of the SCCTSD* 7 (1961), 14-20.

"The Resurrection in Christian Life," *Perspectives* 7 (1962): 168-172.

"Christianity and the Unity of Faith," *Country Beautiful* 2 (1962): 22-25.

"The Hour of Temptation," *The Way* 2 (1962): 177-187.

"College Theology and the Ecumenical Spirit," *NCEA Bulletin* 59 (1962): 14-20.

"A Catholic Response" (to Ernest Koenker, "Church and Sacraments in Lutheranism"), *Continuum* 1 (1963): 62-67.

"Use of Symbol in Sacred Doctrine," *Proceedings of the SCCTSD*, 1963, 147-153.

"Religious Education as Fidelity," *The Renewal of Christian Education* (National Liturgical Week 1963), 50-55.

"St. Thomas' Theology of Sacrifice," *Catholic Messenger*, April 1963, 5-6.

"What's Ahead for the Churches? America's Catholic Community," *Christian Century* 80 (1963), 360-362.

"Concept of the Church as Body of Christ in Contemporary Roman Catholic Theology," *The Church as the Body of Christ* (ed. R. Pelton), Notre Dame, 1963, 105-124.

"Catechesis of the Church," *Perspectives* 8 (1963): 138-145 (reprinted in *Religious Education* 59 (1964): 136-145).

"Personal Development through Grace," *Catholic World* 199 (Sept. 1964): 371.

Introduction to *The Prophets and the Word of God* by Carroll Stuhlmueller, Notre Dame, 1964.

Introduction to *From Baptism to the Act of Faith* (ET) by Jean Mouroux, Boston, 1964.

Theology and Catechetical Renewal," *Pastoral Catechetics* (ed. J. Hofinger and T. Stone), New York, 1964, 88-104.

"'De Sacramentis' and the Seminary Course," *Apostolic Renewal in the Seminary* (ed. R. Armstrong, New York, 1964, 185-193.

"A Roman Catholic Look at the Lutherans," *Arena* 73 (1964), 4-7.

"Word of God: Scripture and Sacrament," *Proceedings of the SCCTSD* 10 (1964), 122-138.

"The Eucharistic Mystery," *Bible Today* 14 (1964): 936-941.

"The Core of the Christian Message," *Guide* 186 (1964): 3-9.

"The Task of Ecumenicity," *Ecumenism and Vatican II* (ed. C. O'Neill), Milwaukee, 1964, 1-66.

"Spirituality of Involvement," *Cross and Crown* 17 (1965): 342-345.

"Christian Sacrifice," *The Way* 5 (1965): 118-125.

"The Theology of the Liturgy," *Church Architecture: The Shape of Reform*, Washington, 1965, 3-11.

"Steps Toward Unity," *Journal of Ecumenical Studies* 1 (1964): 518-520.

"Eucharistic Action of the Word," *The Scotist* 21 (1965): 5-16.

"Can Sinful Man Be the Holy People of God?," *Proceedings of the National Liturgical Week*, 1965, 3-11.

"Catechetics and Social Structures," *The Living Light* 2 (1965): 76-81.

"The Place of Theology in the Curriculum of the Catholic College," *NCEA Bulletin* 1966, Washington, 210-214.

"The Layman, His Translation of Christ," 6-27; "Faith and Sanctity in the Layman," 28-45; "Transformation of the Contemporary World," 46-67 in *The Layman, His Christian Witness* (Proceedings of the 5th Midwestern Pastoral Institute), Detroit, 1966.

"The Pilgrim Church," *The Way* 6 (1966): 284-288.

"Christ's Eucharistic action and History," *Wisdom in Depth* (ed. V. Daues) Milwaukee, 1966, 51-67.

"Responsibility of the Religious Communities in the United States," *Graduate Journal* (of the Univ. of Texas) 7 (1966)): 104-114.

"Theological Education of Seminarians," *Chicago Studies* 5 (1966): 41-52.

"Theology of Imagination," *Focus* 3 (1966): 7-16.

"Existential Pertinence of Religion," *Spirituality in the Secular City* (ed. C. Duquoc), vol. 19 of *Concilium*, N.Y., 1966, 32-43.

"The New Dimensions in the Apostolate of the Religious Woman," *Revolution in Missionary Thinking* (ed. W. Richard son), Maryknoll, 1966, 164-171.

"Eucharist: Source or Expression of Community," *Worship* 40 (1966): 339-348.

"Principles for Formation of Community," 82-97; "Formation of the Individual Religious in Community," 98-113 in *Proceedings of Conference of Major Religious Superiors*, Washington, 1966.

"What is Community?," 126-154; "The Vows," 155-179; "What is it to be a Christian within a Religious Community?," 180-214 in

Problems that Unite Us (Proceedings of the B.V.M. Institute), Dubuque, 1966.

"Intercommunion with the Orthodox," *Diakonia* 1 (1967): 256-262 (reprinted in Holy Cross Magazine 78 (1967): 13-18.

"Ecumenism and the Unbeliever," 38-49; "The Holy Spirit and Authority," 170-182 in *Ecumenism, the Spirit, and Worship* (ed. L. Swidler), Pittsburgh, 1977.

"Religious Chastity," *Vows But No Walls*, (ed. F. Grollmes), St. Louis, 1967, 71-86.

"The Church Always Undergoing Reform," *Lutheran Quarterly*, 1967, 249-256.

"The 'Presence' of Jesus," *Commonweal* 87 (1967): 264-269.

"The Social Aspects of the Sacrament of Penance," *Proceedings of the C.T.S.A.*, 22 (1967): 173-184.

"Holiness and the Bible," *Religion in Life* 37 (1968): 8-17.

"The Relevance of Philosophy for the New Theology," *New Themes in Christian Philosophy* (ed. R. McInerny), Notre Dame, 1968, 152-163.

"Theologians as Teachers in the Church," *Theology in Revolution* (ed. G. Devine), New York, 1970, 267-276.

"Theology of the Word: Implications for Religious Education," *Towards a Future for Religious Education* (ed. J. Lee), Dayton, 1970, 138-153.

"Ministering in Tomorrow's Church," *Commonweal* 101 (1974): 150-153.

"The War-myth in 2nd Century Christianity," *No famine in the Land*, (ed. J.Flanagan), Missoula, 1975, 235-250.

"Living Liturgy: Life as Liturgy," *Emerging Issues in Religious Education* (ed. G. Durka), New York, 1976, 116-126.

"The Paradox of Doing Theology Together and Doing Theology Apart," *Doing Theology Today* (ed. Choon-Seng Song), Madras, 1976, pp. 90-100.

"Wie vertregen sich Gemeinschaft und Individualitat in der Theologie?," *Theologie im Enstehen* (ed. L. Vischer—original manuscript in English), Munich 1976, 33-44.

"Women and Catholic Priesthood," *Worship* 51(1977): 400-407.

"Whither American Catholic Theology," *Commonweal* 105 (1978): 520-524.

"The Ministering Community," Series of twenty taped lectures published by *National Catholic Reporter*, Kansas City, 1978.

Series of twenty articles on sacraments in *Religion Teachers Journal*, 1978.

"Horizons of Christology in the Seventies," *Horizons* 6 (1979):193-217.

"Truly Human Dreams," *The Denigration of Capitalism* (ed. M. Novak), 1979, 39-46.

"The Church: Catholic and Ecumenical," *Theology Today* 36 (1979): 353-367.

"The Current State of Theological Reflection," *Bulletin of the Council on the Study of Religion* 10 (1979): 37-41.

"The Experiential Word of God," *Consensus in Theology* (ed. L. Swidler) Philadelphia, 1980, 69-74.

"Contraception and the Synod," *Commonweal* 107 (1980): 649-650.

"Has the Ecumenical Movement Almost Run Its Course?," *Ecumenical Trends* 10 (1981): 149-151.

"Fullness of Orders: Theological Reflections," *The Jurist* 41(1981): 405-421.

"Spiritual Renewal and Professionalism," *St. Luke's Journal of Theology* 25 (1982): 105-121.

"Discipleship and Ministry: Early Christianity's View," *New Catholic World* 225 (1982): 28-31.

"Feminist Thought and Systematic Theology" (with Pauline Turner), *Horizons* 11(1984): 125-135.

"The Vatican and the U.S. Church," *America* 156 (1986): 206-208.

"Are They Christian? Are They the Future?," *Woodstock Report*, Washington, 1986, 3-6.

"Prophetic Experience as Revelation," *Philosophy and Theology* 1 (1987): 214-224.

"Indissolubility: Guiding Ideal or Existential Reality," *Commitment to Partnership* (ed. W. Roberts), New York, 1987, 64-80.

"Response to Daniel Maguire: Catholicism and Modernity," *Horizons* 13 (1986): 381-383.

"Ecclesiology: Implicit but Influential," *Tensions between Citizenship and Discipleship* (ed. N. Slater), New York, 1989, 69-83.

"Basic Christian Understandings," *Education for Citizenship and Discipleship* (ed. M. Boys), New York, 1989, 79-97.

"The Consciousness of Christ," *Warren Lecture* 9, Unversity of Tulsa), 1989.

"Sacramentality of Second Marriages," *Divorce and Remarriage* (ed. W. Roberts), Kansas City, 1990, 70-77.

"Eucharist, A Threatened Species," series of three articles in *National Catholic Reporter*, (vol. 26), May 11, 18, 25, 1990.

"Charism, Power and Community," *That They May Live* (ed. M. Downey), New York, 1991, 77-88.

2 Bernard Cooke: Pioneer in Theology

"Let us now praise famous men and our fathers in their generation."
Ben Sirach [44:1]

(Rev.) William J. Kelly, S.J.

One of the most influential figures in getting proper theological studies into the curriculum of Catholic colleges and universities is Bernard J. Cooke. My relationship with Bernard Cooke dates from 1941 when, as a novice in the Missouri Province of the Society of Jesus at Florissant, Missouri, he, two years my senior, had a reputation even then for excellence in studies. His preparation in Greek, Latin, and other literatures at Florissant prepared him for continued success in the three years of professional studies in the College of Philosophy and Letters at Saint Louis University. He generously and modestly assisted others by spending endless hours tutoring those who had difficulty grasping either the languages or the issues. His nickname through his years of training in the Jesuits was Barney; later and, generally for others, it became Bernie, but it was always spoken with overtones of admiration and respect.

In addition to an attraction to the texts of Saint Thomas Aquinas, Barney also cultivated a love of Saint Augustine, which would surface once again after his three years of teaching at Marquette University High School in Milwaukee, Wisconsin. These three years of "regency" in Milwaukee proved him an outstanding teacher and a gifted guide for young men. The four years of professional studies in theology that followed at Saint Mary's College in Kansas (1949-1952), although taught in what was then called tract theology, revealed his ambition to shape a curriculum in theology for the colleges and universities administered by the Society of Jesus. In this rural setting he did not waste time pining for the more active life of engagement in the cities, but threw himself into theological studies with the same vigor that he showed in his philosophical studies. He appreciated the connection of philosophy and theology. And once again he became the master tutor of many of his fellow students who found the years long and the studies difficult.

While still at Saint Mary's College, at that time the Divinity School of St. Louis University, he worked closely with Rev. Gerald Van Ackeren, S.J., and collaborated in the founding of *Theology Digest*. With others, he developed many of the details of his future project of introducing theology into the colleges. Catholic institutions of higher learning, including Marquette, were discovering from the reactions of many of their graduates that something important was missing in their education. In the years after World War II many graduates, certainly grateful for their general and professional education, soon discovered that a mere repetition of catechism and apologetics was not a satisfactory response to the need and desire of a deeper intellectual and critical grasp of the Christian faith. When called upon to explain, defend, or even discuss their faith with others in their culture, they found themselves insufficiently equipped.

There were, however, changes being gradually introduced. Many of the regular faculty at Saint Mary's College in Saint Mary's, Kansas, were invited to Marquette University to teach during the summers. These members were aware of the changes needed in the colleges and some were active in planning and executing them. In 1952 there were a few significant changes that had already taken place. The Religion Department, under the direction of the Rev. Cyril Donohue, S.J., had changed its name to the Theology Department. The requirement in theology was ten credit hours distributed over the four years and obligatory for all Catholic students. The courses all carried two credit hours. Freshmen took one course in each semester. Sophomores took one course in either of the two semesters. These were Lower Division courses. Once sophomore standing was achieved, juniors and seniors were required to take two more obligatory Upper Division courses. The reasoning behind the change of the name Religion to that of

Theology was that the approach would be more solidly academic and would provide for the students an intellectual and critical appropriation of their faith commitment. These courses then would be on a par with the other college courses. A minor concentration in Theology was introduced. In 1953 a graduate program was inaugurated with a possibility of gaining an MA in Theology over a period of several summers. This was to accommodate many women religious and lay teachers of religion in other colleges and secondary schools who were not free for higher studies in the course of the academic year. A faculty for these graduate courses was arranged with the help of Saint Mary's College faculty who appreciated being in Milwaukee for the summer months. Many of these summer faculty persons were also instrumental in the establishment of the College Theology Society (Carey 1996, 14).

Although much of this was begun and put in place before Bernard Cooke came to Marquette University, he was kept informed of this progress through his contact with members of the Saint Mary's College faculty, including Rev. Cyril Vollert, S.J., Rev. Gerald Van Ackeren, S.J., Rev. Gerald Kelly, S.J., Rev. G. Augustine Ellard, S.J., Rev. Gerald Ellard, S.J., Rev. Francis Korth, S.J. He was not alone in these efforts, but he did provide a certain drive and optimistic enthusiasm to what may be called a movement.

To determine how best to shape the future of theological education in the Colleges, Barney, while still a theological student at Saint Mary's College in Kansas, worked in seminars and other less formal discussions with those faculty members who had taught at Marquette during the summers. With the encouragement of the Rev. Gerald Van Ackeren, S.J., and others in the Jesuit Educational Association, Barney went to France in 1954 to enroll at the Catholic University of Paris [*Institut Catholique de Paris*] to obtain the Doctorate in Theology but also to undertake a program aimed not at teaching in the seminary but specifically oriented to the colleges and universities. In addition to obtaining the Doctorate in Theology, he also profited from a renewed catechetical program at Saint Sulpice and had contact with the Catechetical Institute in Brussels, Belgium [*Lumen Vitae*]. He was searching for a way of communicating theological learning to the laity through a pedagogy, which formerly had been provided only for seminary students in what were called Divinity schools or programs. He planned to accomplish this objective in the ordinary structure of colleges that had no Divinity School attached.

At that time, the Jesuit mid-Western Provinces were planning to divide. There was an increase in the number of novices—too many for one Director of Novices. Likewise, the number of institutions was too great for one Provincial Superior to oversee. The Wisconsin Province was created out of the Missouri Province, and the Detroit Province was created out of the Chicago Province. These new divisions were somewhat geographical, but more importantly, were arranged around commitments to secondary and higher education. The Wisconsin Province was committed to Creighton University in Omaha, Nebraska, and Marquette University in Milwaukee. Although Barney's first responsibility was to the institutions of higher learning, he was also influential in shaping the curricula in the high schools of the province. These institutions were imitating the colleges by changing the name of the Department of Religion to that of Theology. The change was all done with the intention of emphasizing not only formation, but also solid information and critical reflection. (This change of name from Religion to Theology would be oddly reversed later on when the first doctoral program in theology was approved for Marquette University.)

Barney returned from Paris in 1956 and began to implement his plans at Marquette University. In the meantime, the Missouri and Wisconsin Provinces had already begun sending men for special studies in theology. The plan was to send these men to different centers with the same aim—a special preparation for college theology. One followed Barney's choice of Paris; another was sent to Innsbruck; two others to Rome; another to Minnesota for American Studies. It was hoped that all would direct their theological preparation to the perceived needs of a special curriculum for college theology. It was further hoped that all would return after their studies to share their insights and integrate what they had mastered into this new and, at that time, exciting venture. But it was Barney who had the vision and it was Barney who set the pace.

He took over the direction of the Theology Department at Marquette University in 1958, succeeding Rev. Floyd Stanton, S.J., and immediately went to work on the reshaping of the curriculum. He patiently awaited those who were sent to special studies aimed at the preparation for teaching theology in the colleges. He inherited the curriculum requirement of ten hours of theology: two hour courses, six Lower Division and four Upper Division. Because of the two hour courses, Fridays were free for his other planning and organization. It was on these days and weekends that he tirelessly spread his plans and his influence to other schools, to convents and seminaries, to other religious orders, and to many lay organizations. His influence was immediate and effective.

He joined the Catholic Theological Society although at that time it was generally populated by seminary professors. He participated actively in the College Theology Society. His goal was not tract theology, with dogma first, morality second, scripture third, and history last, but an integrated theology rooted in the Biblical Renewal. He made this look so easy, so second nature, that one wondered why it had not been accomplished before.

Barney was not quite a year in the Chair of the Department of Theology when on January 25, 1959, Pope John XXIII announced his desire to convoke the twenty-first Ecumenical Council. Technically, the First Council of the Vatican was prorogued and so this 20th century council was an attempt to bring to completion what had been launched in 1869. The Pope, however, envisioned more than a completion of the 19th century efforts. He had a positive and optimistic view that the Christian Church had to open up and offer its treasures to a world in need. Under his inspiration the Council was to bring a much more pastoral concern for the Church and the world. Barney shared that vision.

I would like to list some of his accomplishments in various areas, but first I want to point out what I would call the mystery of the 3 x 5 card. It never ceased to amaze me how this man could lecture, whether to a small class or a large audience, with only an index card in front of him on the desk or in his hand. The lecture would flow smoothly for the hour's time with a seemingly effortless development and come to a conclusion faithful to the announced topic. The question and answer period was even more satisfying. He had a way of understanding the question, relating it to the lecture, giving a satisfying answer, and yet pointing to the need for further questioning in the area. To the questioner who misunderstood, he patiently explained again; to the hostile questioner, he remained calm and dignified. All of this occurred without citations given, yet with a reassuring tone that the sources were there.

Here are a few specific areas in which his competence enlightened others and inspired them to go further in study and research.

Social Justice: Years before the tensions of the Student Revolution, the Black Revolution, and the Resistance to the Vietnam War surfaced in Milwaukee, Barney was awakening the social consciousness of the students. He was a friend and counselor to the Rev. James Groppi in the early days of that movement. Together with members of the philosophy faculty, he worked for the integration of the Milwaukee Schools.

Scripture: From his training in Paris, he made the Scriptures the foundation of the Theology Program and hired specialists in both Old and New Testament writings.

Liturgy: He revised the syllabus for courses on the liturgy and developed courses on the Eucharist and the other Sacraments. These courses eventually were developed into the important book he published years later, *Word and Sacrament.* He implemented much of the content of Vatican Council's *Decree on the Liturgy* [1963]. In a practical way, he regularly celebrated the 7:00 A.M. Mass in the Lower Gesu and gave simple but solid homilies explaining the Scriptures. In many campus gatherings, undergraduate and graduates listened appreciatively to the new path to Christian spirituality he opened up for them. Without dramatic flair or oratory his message got through to them. He developed a course on Christian Life and Worship and another on Christian Personality Development, which was an adaptation for the laity of the content of the seminary courses in ascetical and spiritual theology.

Ecumenism: In my judgment, it was in the area of ecumenism that Barney had the most lasting influence. Aggiornamento, the desire of Pope John XXIII, became a guideline for Barney and he followed it very faithfully. In the Vatican II *Decree on Ecumenism* (Abbott 1996, 336), the Council fathers looked to the teaching of theology and gave some directions with regard to method and procedure: "Instruction in sacred theology and other branches of knowledge, especially those of an historical nature, must also be presented from an ecumenical point of view, so that at every point they may more accurately correspond with the facts of the case" (Abbott 1996, # 10, 353).

This section of the *Decree* was applied to the situation in the United States by the American Bishops in their own guidelines issued by their Commission for Ecumenical Affairs. This Commission proposed some principles as broad guidelines in this matter of educating for ecumenism:

> Ecumenism is fostered by teaching a renewed theology. In elementary and secondary schools, this means a biblical, liturgical, and doctrinal catechesis which forms a Christian who has a deeper understanding of the Gospel and who is responsive to the needs of the world. In universities and seminaries and other institutions of higher learning, it means a realization that this renewed theology has developed through contact with other traditions and their scholars and must continue to develop in the same way.
>
> 1. The success of education for ecumenism rests on an awareness that a poverty exists in the Christian community because of our tragic separations. A basic change of heart (metanoia) is required to become more aware of the scandal of division and the wish to repair it.
>
> 2. Ecumenism is fostered by teaching a renewed theology.
>
> 3. Ecumenism demands a knowledge of and a respect for the beliefs and the practices of other confessions and religions. Where possible, "go to the sources," and "teachers of these other traditions should present this material." This is especially true at the secondary and higher levels of education (Abbott 1996, 353 n40).

If not the first, he was among the first to follow Vatican II's directions that theology must be presented with an ecumenical perspective. He hired a Lutheran, Dr. Kenneth Hagen, a professor of historical theology, to offer Lutheran studies. Likewise, he hired Dr. Gordon Bahr, a Protestant, to teach New Testament studies. He hired Rabbi Dudley Weinberg to offer a course in Jewish thought and practice. He encouraged the Anglican theologian from Christ Church College in Oxford, Professor John Macquarrie, to come to Marquette and assist the new program with his competence and scholarly presence. With these moves, he implemented Vatican II's Decree on Ecumenism and the directions of the United States Bishops to have teachers from the other Christian communions on the Catholic faculty.

Education: He also anticipated, with his administration of the Theology Department, much of what the Vatican II *Declaration on Christian Education* called for in 1965. This document specified:

> In Catholic Colleges and Universities lacking a faculty of sacred theology, an institute or chair of sacred theology should be set up so that lectures designed for lay students too can be given. Since the sciences progress chiefly through special investigations of advanced scientific significance, Catholic colleges and universities and their faculties should give the maximum support to institutes which primarily serve the progress of scientific research (Abbott 1996, #10, 649).

Feminism: Before Feminism was an issue with a capital F and complicated with political correctness, he encouraged lay and religious women to enter both the M.A. and the Ph.D. programs and he encouraged women to prepare themselves in theology both for teaching and research as well as for leadership in the Catholic Church.

None of this was accomplished without opposition. He certainly experienced this opposition in many quarters, but he held to his original vision and showed both tenacity and sagacious political sense in order to accomplish what more timid bureaucracy might have shied from. Barney had already, in 1963, gained approval for the inauguration of the Ph.D. in Religious Studies (Carey 1996, 27-29). This was in addition to his offering an undergraduate major and an M.A. It was such a novelty that, when the permission for the Ph.D. was granted, he was directed not to call it a degree in theology, for that S.T.D. (*Sacrae Theologiae Doctor*) belonged only to Pontifical Seminary Faculties. In granting this approval, the Superior General of the Jesuits was aware of the novelty of the program and did not want to interfere with the rights and privileges of the Pontifical Congregation of Seminaries. Barney, in turn, did not want the new program to come under the jurisdiction of the Sacred Congregation, but wanted only to be responsible to the administration of the University. The program was launched and experienced great success when the following new scene opened.

In 1968-69, Barney had some serious health problems and he began to reflect on the direction of his religious and priestly vocation. It also seems more than probable that he followed personally what he had written in his influential book *Word and Sacrament* about the sacrament of order. He spent a sabbatical leave at Yale University and while there decided to give his talents a wider scope and not return to Marquette University. This was a sad occasion for me personally and a loss for Marquette University. *The Marquette Tribune*, the University's undergraduate newspaper, reported his leaving both Marquette and the priesthood: "Marquette has suffered a great loss, in scholarship and in prestige by the departure of Father Bernard Cooke, S.J." (Carey 1996, 31). Marquette's loss, however, was gain for Barney and for others. He continued to devote his remarkable energies and considerable skills to the Catholic theological enterprise. I have certainly followed his activity from this Marquette distance, but I must leave it to others to document his achievements in Windsor and Calgary, Canada; Boston College University and the College of the Holy Cross in Massachusetts; Saint Mary's in San Antonio, Texas; and in his latest field of endeavor at the University of San Diego, California. Thank you, Barney! *Ad Multos Annos*!

References

Abbott, Walter, S.J., ed. 1966. *Documents of Vatican II: Decree on Education.* New York: Guild Press, America Press, Association Press.

Carey, Patrick. 1987, 1996. *Theology at Marquette University: A History.* Milwaukee: Marquette University Press."Ask the Bookstore If They Have Come In."

3 Bernard Cooke: Creator of the Need for Suitable Theology Texts

Gerard S. Sloyan

In the summer of 1956 some enterprising Belgian Jesuits named Delcuve, Ranwez, and others convened a meeting of catechists in Antwerp under the banner of their bilingual quarterly *Lumen Vitae*. One year later they launched in Brussels a year-long course at their *Centre* in the French-speaking Ixelles neighborhood. Present at the Antwerp gathering were some ten U.S. men and women who were studying at a variety of European faculties. Among them were Thomas Stransky, Paulist; Bernard Cooke, Jesuit, who had just completed his doctoral work at L'Institut Catholique in Paris; an Ursuline nun; and a Sister of Loretto. I was the North American who had gone to Europe specifically for the meeting and at it I made several friendships for life.[1] On day one, I have to record, I could tell that Bernard was a star.

At the time, I was assistant dean of the undergraduate college at The Catholic University of America teaching two sections of freshman religion (Old and New Testament in successive semesters) and a year-long graduate offering in the gospels. One year later I became department head. After the Antwerp meeting Bernard Cooke returned to teach at Marquette University and was named chairman of his department not long after. Along with his colleagues Fathers Kelly and Sheets (no poets they) he initiated graduate studies in theology that offered the

---

[1] Besides the two above named, Drinkwater, Crichton, Hofinger and Jungmann, all contributors to 1959. *Shaping the Christian Message*, ed. Sloyan. New York: Macmillan.

M.A. and Ph.D., while all continued to carry the not inconsiderable burden of undergraduate classes.

It may be worth recalling where things stood at the college level at the time Marquette inaugurated its soon to be distinguished graduate program with the preparation of college teachers as its immediate goal. A starting place might be my freshman year at Seton Hall College (now University) in 1936. The instructor in religion was a priest of Newark whose archdiocese had conducted that institution since 1856 beginning at Madison, New Jersey. At the opening class of a required course he said, "Gentlemen, the textbook will be *The Defense of the Catholic Church* by Francis X. Doyle, S.J. (1927) You can get it at the bookstore. In the meantime, buy a Roman Missal in English translation. You will also receive a nine-month student subscription to the weekly magazine America, for which I will collect at the next class." We never opened Doyle again. I remember, however, that the four gospels were printed at the end of the book, a novum for the Catholic 1930s. The other volumes published by Benziger Brothers in that series were one by Thomas Chetwood and two by Charles G. Herzog, all three members of the then geographically sizeable New York province of Jesuits who had studied under or served on its theological faculty at Woodstock, Maryland. A lively priest instructor brought Chetwood to life for me as a sophomore, while another was somewhat less successful doing Herzog with juniors and seniors. Four subsequent years in the company of Christianus Pesch's four-volume *Compendium*, reduced from the nine of his *Praelectiones Theologiae Dogmaticae* made clear what the U.S. authors were up to: an Englishing of their classroom lectures delivered first in a seminary setting.

What other textbooks were then available? Chiefly three volumes translated from the French with the generic titles *Dogma*, *Moral*, and *Worship* promoted by the Brothers of the Christian Schools (F.S.C.), but each authored, according to the title page, by "A Seminary Professor" (1889, 1919, 1920). In the 'teens of the twentieth century a priest of the archdiocese of Baltimore tried to break the manual mold. He was John Montgomery Cooper, son of James of English Quaker stock and Lillie Toulou, great-granddaughter of French immigrants. In 1909, as an assistant pastor of St. Matthew's Church (later Cathedral), Washington, he began to teach religion to college men on his lunch hour at The Catholic University of America. This was a "first" in that, as a teacher of undergraduate religion only, he succeeded priest teachers in other disciplines, mainly philosophy, who acted as utility outfielders in religion study. Cooper produced in 1913, a series of booklets for student use, there being no realistic textbook in the field. These were the seeds of his four-volume *Religious Outlines for Colleges* (1924, 1926, 1928, 1930). Outlines they surely were. When I began to teach college students in 1950 with the aid of the volume on morality, I immediately realized the truth of the quip reported to me that any bright eighth-grader could grasp the material in large pica, but few with graduate degrees in theology were equal to the material in small. That was because the latter consisted of a series of unanswered queries to students and leads provided to them (and their teachers) in encyclopedias and journals, secular and religious. The textbooks were existential in their address to the problems of men of college age – my first class had two woman students—and in their apologetic tone, in years when Darwinian theory was thought to be a threat to Christian faith and Catholics were a distinct minority in the culture. Alfred E. Smith, governor of New York, made an unsuccessful run for the presidency while the series was being written. At age thirty-five, Cooper had produced from printed sources in 1917, *An Analytical and Critical Biography of Tierra del Fuego*, all the while teaching college religion and serving in parish ministry. When his textbooks finally appeared, they were richer than many in use today with their inclusions of sociological and ethnographic data, while not diluting the Jewish and Christian revelations.

He joined The Catholic University of America faculty full-time in 1920 in the department of philosophy, which continued to be charged with the religion study of lay undergraduates. Ten years later, as a result of a reorganization plan, the Graduate School of Arts and Sciences was inaugurated with eighteen departments, religion being one of them. Cooper succeeded in naming it Religious Education but without catechetics or pedagogy in mind. It was an innocuous-sounding stratagem to provide a theological and biblical education to religious Sisters and Brothers, lay men and lay women, who were ineligible for such study in the country's one graduate faculty in theology. In the mid-1930s he gained M.A. and Ph.D. granting power for the department, at which point there was an attempt of the clerical School of Sacred Sciences to "oversee," that is, take over Religious Education. It happened twice more, unsuccessfully, during the present writer's headship between 1957 and 1967. In the meantime, something of greater importance took place in 1955 with the second meeting of what had become in the previous year the Society of Catholic College Teachers of Sacred Doctrine. Its chief animators were a faculty member of Manhattan College in the Bronx, two from Dunbarton College, and one from Trinity College, both in Washington, D.C. The last named, a Paulist, gave one of the papers at the first professional meeting at the latter institution (1955), while a member of the Order of Preachers and one of the Society of Jesus delivered two others. These were worthy representatives of numerous confreres in college teaching, the Dominicans in their one college and many others conducted by women religious and the Jesuits in their own institutions. The friars had been enthusiastic in conveying Aquinas's *Summary of Theology* via a four-volume work in English by Walter Farrell, O.P. (1947). They called the courses "theology." The sons of Loyola favored courses in "religion," employing the textbooks of John Fernan and others that had come out of Le Moyne College in Syracuse (1952, 1953, 1954, 1955). I was asked to give a paper representing those who had no special stake in the naming or ordering of the discipline. They were the secular and regular clergy, possibly more numerous than the two disputants over nomenclature combined, who taught in the seven diocesan-sponsored colleges of the time and in those conducted by religious congregations (O.S.B., O.F.M., C.M., C.S.C., C.S.B.). The title of the Society was arrived at to break the impasse over the naming of departments and was taken from St. Thomas's designation in Question 1, Article 1 of the *scientia* that he meant to expound, which was dynamic rather than static in meaning, *sacra doctrina,* "teaching" rather than "a body of teachings." The group came into existence for the purpose of gaining professional status for college teachers, most of whom had seminary educations that did not culminate in degrees and were looked on as below the salt, sometimes beneath contempt, by academic peers and administrators. Seminary instructors who had degrees from Rome or Washington were welcomed as members if they were also in college work. A few early members held degrees from the

School of Theology of St. Mary's College, South Bend, diplomas from the Regina Mundi and Jesus Magister Institutes in Rome, and graduate degrees in history, philosophy and classics. From the moment of the second meeting of the S.C.C.T.S.D. the national picture in college theology was changed.

It was into that loose matrix that Bernard Cooke entered when he returned from Paris to Milwaukee to make the huge difference to which some hundreds of Marquette alumni can testify. In 1965 the long awaited "Cooke book" appeared, a summing up of the introductory graduate course he had been offering during his demanding years of administration (Cooke 1965).

This brings us back to textbooks suitable for courses in college theology, before and after that landmark publication. Three such series are worth noting. By the date of the last to appear, titles in English had so begun to proliferate that the idea of one book per year or two briefer ones per semester no longer made sense. The three series originated in the University of Notre Dame, The Catholic University of America, and Boston College/Fairfield College. All were multi-authored. The first appeared in cloth, the second two in paper. Like the works of the predecessors of Cooper, Farrell and Fernan, they are nowadays found in library archives and only occasionally on shelves. The earliest was a set of three appearing over a span of a dozen years (Sheedy 1949, Hesburgh 1950, Schlitzer 1962). Then came eleven volumes in the *Foundations of Catholic Theology Series* dealing with the various mysteries of faith that left their integration to lecturers in their courses (Sloyan 1963-6)[2]. Almost concurrently with this series, another, more ambitious one began to appear (Devine and Rousseau 1966-8)[3]. But the important phenomenon of the times was not the production of textbooks. It was the theological formation of teachers in the three U.S. faculties that offered the Ph.D. in theology. In that venture Bernard Cooke played a central part, the effects of which are

---

[2] Included were 120-page books by D.J. Bowman, P.G. Stevens, M.C.B. Muckenhirn, M.B. Schepers, P.F. Palmer, W.T. Dewan, J.H. Miller, G.S. Sloyan, and W.J. O'Shea. A planned twelfth title, *Eschatology*, did not appear pending the event.

[3] Included are texts in four areas: biblical, historical, ecclesial, and moral theology with three published initially, and another twenty-two projected or published.

everywhere in sight. An immediate outcome of the graduate program at Marquette University that he oversaw was the need for texts in the college classroom that corresponded to the theological education its students had received. In the academic world of fifty years ago, many M.A. graduates were receiving appointments to college faculties, some in secondary education, as were, needless to say, holders of the Ph.D. The Cooke-led program at Marquette was in the vanguard of demand for published works at the level of the graduate traning received.

References

"A Seminary Professor." 1898. *Dogma*. Philadelphia: John Joseph McVey.

————. 1919. *Moral*. Philadelphia: John Joseph McVey.

————. 1920. *Worship*. Philadelphia: John Joseph McVey.

Cooke, Bernard. 1965. *Christian Sacraments and Christian Personality*. New York: Holt, Rinehart and Winston. Notre Dame, IN: University of Notre Dame.

Cooper, John Montgomery. 1924. I. "The Catholic Ideal of Life" Washington: The Catholic Education.

————. 1926. II. "The Motives and Means of Catholic Life" Washington: The Catholic Education.

————. 1930. III. "Christ and His Church" Washington: The Catholic Education.

————. 1928. IV. "Life Problems" Washington: The Catholic Education.

Devine, J. Frank S.J. and Richard Rousseau, S.J., eds. 1966-68. *Contemporary College Theology Series*. Milwaukee: Bruce.

Doyle, Francis X. 1927. *The Defense of the Catholic Church*. New York: Benziger Brothers.

Farrell, Walter O.P. 1947. *A Companion to the Summa*. New York, Sheed and Ward.

Fernan, John J. 1952. *Christ as Prophet and King*. New York: Georgian Press.

————. 1953. *Christ Our High Priest*. New York: Georgian Press.

————. 1954. *The Mystical Christ*. New York: Georgian Press.

————. 1955. *Christ in His Members*. New York: Georgian Press.

Hesburgh, Theodore M. 1950. *God and the World of Man*. Notre Dame, IN: University of Notre Dame.

Schlitzer, Albert L. 1962. *Our Life in Christ*. Volumes I and II. Notre Dame, IN: University of Notre Dame.

Sheedy, Charles. 1949. *Christian Virtues*. Notre Dame, IN: University of Notre Dame.

Sloyan, Gerard S. General Editor. 1963-66. Englewood Cliffs, NJ: Prentice Hall.

II. Speculative Theology

4 The Undistancing of the World: A Theological Anthropology

Bernard J. Lee, S.M.

I propose that *fides quarens mundum agendum propter Deum* [faith seeking to know what kind of a world we should be up to, because of who God is] is as legitimate a rendering of theology as *fides quaerens intellectum* [faith seeking understanding]. The difference between them is the difference between two contrasting theological anthropologies that lie beneath them. The differences are not merely conceptual; they are huge at the level of lived experience.

In *The Distancing of God*, Bernard Cooke's meticulous historical and philosophical acumen demonstrates how Greek thought, which posits a metaphysical divide between supernatural and natural (or between Creator and created) distances God in ways unknown to the Hebrew assumptive world in which Jesus would have come to consciousness. Because Christians introduced Greek presupposition about the world, and God and people in the context of the world, "succinctly put, earliest Christianity faced a task of complete religious remythologizing" (Cooke 1990, 12). In the Hebrew characterization of YHWH, descriptors tend to be historical: God who led us out of Egypt; God who gave us this land; the God of Abraham, Isaac, and Jacob; etc. Increasingly in the Western Christian tradition, categories derived from philosophical presuppositions tend to replace historical categories: omnipotent, omniscient, immutable, impassible, etc.

Given that metaphysical divide between creature and Creator, to say that human beings can naturally participate in God's life is heretical (Pelagianism). Thomas Aquinas saw the problem clearly: if we cannot naturally participate in God's life, then doing so would be unnatural. So he held that the potential for sharing in God's life is in us naturally (a potential), but it cannot function unless we respond obediently towards it (obediential potency). This theory preserves the necessity of God's initiative. Both the Pelagian heresy and the theory of obediential potency protect the metaphysical distance between God and us. In this tradition we learn to feel the distance deeply. The expression "totally other" as a description of God expresses this feeling of distance.

There is another kind of distancing which also has roots in a Greek social construction of reality. In the Greek understanding of the human person, we are made first, foremost, and above all, for the contemplation of truth, beauty, and goodness. We must live in the world, build a life together, and make things that support our life. But building a life together and making things do not give us human fulfillment—the completion, if you will, that comes only from the contemplative act. Traffic with history, some of which is unavoidable, is a distraction from that which satisfies us completely.

This shaping of the Western Christian culture occurred without significant conscious awareness about how a particular anthropology was grounding our religious sense of our relationship with God. "Assumptive world" is just like that—the perceptions of reality that we partly inherit through culture and language, and are partly constructed through our own experience. It doesn't appear to us as assumptions we have made. Rather, it just seems incontrovertibly to be what the really real is like. It is our social construction of reality, in this case, of human reality.

Our experience of God is always mediated by our assumptive world. We receive God's self-gift according to our "receptors": *quodquod recipitur recipitur in modo recipientis.* God comes our way down our road, and God has clearly come our way down this Greek road.

Through some dialogue with Aristotle and then with Philo of Alexandria (a contemporary of Jesus), I will first characterize the Greek influenced anthropology that has shaped the Western Christian tradition so deeply. These and similar convictions about human nature have played a large role in the Western Christian tradition vis-à-vis theology and spirituality, because our normative "texts" came into existence in a Greco-Roman world.

I will then propose an alternative understanding of being human as an underlying anthropology for Christian theology and spirituality, one that emphasizes historical agency as our human destiny. Not surprisingly, this assumptive world is most clearly articulated and lived in those parts of Western culture less deeply rooted in Greco-Roman culture, e.g., in the pragmatic traditions of the United States (William James, John Dewey, Charles Sanders Peirce), in England (Alfred North Whitehead), in Germany (Hannah Arendt), in Scotland (John Macmurray), and others. I will draw especially upon the work of John Macmurray, Hannah Arendt, and briefly, Alfred North Whitehead. The congeniality of this understanding of the human person with ancient Hebrew presuppositions about union with God is no minor recommendation.

The Human Person as Contemplator: Aristotle

Much of what follows is drawn from Aristotle's *Nicomachean Ethics*, book six, unless otherwise noted. The question that interests him is what it means to be a good person, a virtuous human being.

There are three kinds of knowledge and a way of enacting each of them. The highest kind of knowledge is *theoria*, which is not the same as what we mean today in the English word theory. *Theoria* is the knowledge of first principles, the contemplation of beauty, truth, and goodness. Enacting that knowledge in the depth of a person is called *episteme*, and is the highest human fulfillment there is. The knowledge and its enactment create a wise person: a *sophos*.

The next kind of knowledge is *phronesis* and its enactment is *praxis*. *Phronesis* is an understanding of what kind of a world we should be bringing about, an understanding already at work doing—*praxis*—what it knows needs to be done. The knowing and doing go together. Our understanding of what needs to be done is clarified by our already being and doing in the world, which in turn is directed by the knowing. It's circular: action and reflection are derived from each other and direct each other. Since Aristotle is describing virtue, he makes clear that virtue only exists in the *phronesis/praxis* duo. One cannot know what kind of a world we should be bringing into existence and be virtuous without concretely working at that world's realization.

Phronesis/praxis resembles the Hebrew word for "word," *Dabhar.* When God speaks, God is not just communicating a thought. God is speaking a word that needs to be enacted into a full blown, realized Word.

Phronesis/praxis is what people do all the time as they live and work together and bring the human world into existence. This is "action," but action always coordinated with reflection, which in turn is always coordinated with action. Action is the reflective human doing of world, making a life together. Reflection/action, action/reflection is a relentless spiral.

For Aristotle, however, what *truly* fulfills human life is contemplation. The practical life should do all in its power to make as much room as possible for the contemplative life. The contemplation of truth, beauty, and goodness is its own reason for existence and has no practical implementation beyond itself. It doesn't generate common sense for living, it just makes us happy in the doing of it. Aristotle writes:

> . . .the rareness [of contemplation] leads many people to say that people like Thales and Anaxagoras are no doubt wise (*sophoi*), but they lack common sense . . . People grant that their knowledge is 'exceptional,' 'wonderful,' 'deep,' 'superhuman,' but they aver that it is useless because it is not the goodness of humanity that they explore (Aristotle, 1962, 180).

Techne is the third kind of knowing. It is knowing how to make things; applying *techne* to actually making them is *poiesis.* Because we need to make many things to live and sometimes just to enjoy, *techne/poiesis* are obviously essential. But just because I know how to make a table or a chair, I am not lacking in virtue if I do not make one. This is not a knowledge which, by its nature, requires implementation.

As will emerge later, an alternative arrangement, with incredible implications, is to give *phronesis/praxis* the place of honor, and to locate contemplation within it and not above it, and also as a practically fruitful contribution to living in the world, even while deeply fulfilling in itself (but not *finally* fulfilling). This, however, would not be Aristotle's position.

Philo

The life of Philo of Alexandria, also called Philo Judaeus (Philo the Jew), overlapped the life of Jesus. Philo was born about 25 BCE and died about 50 CE, in the great city of Alexandria on the Mediterranean coast of Egypt. Profoundly steeped in Stoic philosophy and Jewish to the core, he found Greek reasons for just about everything Jewish to which he was committed. He is deeply indebted to Platonic thought. While in the final analysis, the Jewish community did not opt to move its traditions in Philo's direction, early Christian writers familiar with Philo moved Christian traditions in Philonic directions.

Philo's anthropology takes shape in response to his understanding of God, who is so totally other as to be utterly inaccessible to human experience. He understands God as mind, *nous*. What a mind does is think, and what it thinks are thoughts. All the thoughts of God, like Plato's idea(l)s, are God's *logos*. *Logos* has the double meaning in English of both pure reason and of words that carry reason.

Now when God chose to create the world, God chose from all the ideas according to which a world might have been created, from all God's thoughts about the world's possibilities, a particular set of possibilities. Philo makes an analogy with an architect: from all the materials that might conceivably be used to make a building, the architect chooses only those that fit the design he or she selects. The set of possibilities according to which God actually created the world constitute a second meaning of *logos*. *Logos* seems to have two inter-related meanings in Philo: all the thought of God, as well as the set of thoughts through which the world is created.

When God created the world, everything that was created was created through the *logos,* without which nothing came into being. The *logos* has a unique double character. What a mind does is think thoughts, so thoughts are as old as the mind that thinks them; thus, the *logos* is eternal like God. But thoughts are derived from the mind that thinks them, and because they have a derived character, they also have something in common with the created world. No small part of Arius' dilemma was grounded in the conceptual framework of *logos*, which is both like God (eternal) and like creatures (derived). He tilted one way; the tradition tilted the other, although the creedal refutation of Arius maintains the derivation reference: God *from* God; Light *from* Light.

Every created thing (and here we get close to Plato) is a created instance of an idea in God's mind, i.e., of the *logos*. Every created instance of an idea, however, is an imperfect embodiment of the perfect idea in God's mind, because perfection never belongs to creatures. We contact things and know them through our sense experience of them. Philo considers sense experience to be the knowledge of the lower mind. But the more we learn to abstract from particular things to know their nature, to know the idea that they imperfectly embody, the nearer we come to God through the *logos,* which is knowledge of the higher mind. Distancing ourselves from the sense world is the condition for experiencing God through (and only through) the *logos* of God. The higher mind puts us in contact with *logos,* and thus with God. There is no approach to God except through the *logos,* and no access to the *logos* except through distancing ourselves from the created world as much as we can, in order to access the perfect original ideas through which the world came into existence.

Reprise on the Greek Anthropology

Although the basics operate differently in Aristotle and Plato, what they share is an anthropology that discounts the value of human activity and the shared action that creates the human world and human culture in which we live. Whatever distances us from the world also distances us from the sacramental potential of the world.

Philo did not know of Jesus. But he used language about *logos* which resonates with how christology developed in the Greco-Roman world: "Beyond the *logos* is God himself, unknowable even to the purest intellect" (Leg. Alleg. 1:36; Post. 15, 168f). For Philo, God can only be known through the *Logos: "Logos* is called God's son . . . people who live patterned after *Logos* are sons of God" (De Con. Ling.145-147) and "*Logos* is that by which God draws a perfect person from things earthly to himself" (Sac. 8). Notice that perfection means being drawn away from the earth. It distances us from the world: "*Logos* is the eldest and most akin to God of all the things that have come into existence" (Leg. Alleg. 3.175) and "Nothing mortal can be made in the likeness of the most high One and Father of the universe, except only in that of the second god who is the *Logos*" (Quest. Gen II 62). Since Platonic thought was so at hand to the early theologians, the emphasis on this sort of conceptuality in theology and doctrine reinforced the implied anthropology, an assumptive world that distanced the Christian from the created world.

Brief Discursus

In the reflections that follow, "action" and "historical agency" should not be thought of in terms of the kind of instrumental activism with which sociologists sometimes characterize U.S. culture. Nor do I intend some of the crasser versions of American pragmatism. It is a caricature of William James, for example, to say that truth refers to whatever works, although empiricism has a legitimate role in many kinds of verification, including religious claims.

When I first reformulated a description of theology that responded to a different anthropology than classical Western theology, the text read: *fides quaerens mundum* **faciendum** *propter Deum.* Several of my helpful conversation partners said that the Latin verb *faciendum* sounded too much like the kind of activism I want to avoid. The Latin verb *facere* is akin to the English sense of *making* things, or of *production* and *productivity.* These are good things, of course, but not those out of which (alone or mostly) one constructs a meaningful life.

The Latin verb *ago, agere, egi, actus,* on the other hand, is more akin to setting things in motion, and the one who sets things in motion is an agent. Action has that sort of meaning. The central human question might be posed: What kind of a world should we set in motion for ourselves and for the children of the world? That is what *mundum agendum* means in the theological descriptor I have suggested. Those of us in the Judeo-Christian tradition (and other traditions as well) believe that God has intentions for history and that our collaboration with God is required for their realization.

The proposals that follow understand the human vocation in terms of action, or historical agency, which has some deep affinities with ancient Hebrew anthropology. Reflection and contemplation are kinds of activity that enrich and empower action (i.e., living in the world with others). Action, in Hannah Arendt's work, is utterly central to *The Human Condition.* In the reflections that follow, "action" has a significantly different meaning than its popular sense (which is close to "activity").

The Human Person as Historical Agent

John Macmurrary writes:

> What is here proposed is that we should substitute the 'I do' for the 'I think' as our starting-point and center of reference; and do our thinking from the standpoint of action . . . We must not underestimate the difficulty of the enterprise to which we are committed . . . To change our standpoint is to transform our habits of thought. It is not to change one theory for another, but to change the basis of all theory (Macmurray 1991, 84-85).

In a Foreword to the *Personal World: John Macmurray on Self and Society*, Tony Blair, England's current Prime Minister, notes Macmurray's importance for keeping spirituality grounded in the world and in history (1991, 9-11). Macmurray's development of this anthropology is most fully developed in his Gifford Lectures in 1953-1954, published in two volumes as *The Self as Agent* and *Persons in Relation*.

Macmurray holds that action "is a full concrete activity of the self in which all our capacities are employed; while thought is constituted by the exclusion of some of our powers and a withdrawal into an activity which is less concrete and less complete" (Macmurray 1991. 86). The distinction between action and activity is important. Action is all that goes into living a life in the world, and this requires a lot of activities, some of which are necessary (like eating or sleeping), and some of which are arbitrary (building a big house or a small house), and others which are capricious (flying a kite). Refraining from an activity is a part of action, and that shows the difference.

Macmurray has understood clearly some of the consequences of this anthropology that give historical agency a central claim:

> If the concept of 'pure thought' is derived from the concept of action by exclusion, then thought, so far as it is actual, falls within action, and depends upon action. Action is primary and concrete, thought is secondary, abstract, and derivative. This must mean that the distinction between 'right' and 'wrong', which is constitutive

for action, is the primary standard of validity; while the distinction between 'true' and 'false' is secondary . . . In other words, a theory of knowledge presupposes and must be derived from, and included within a theory of action (Macmurray 1978, 89).

While this philosophical language is notably un-Hebrew, there are clear resonances with the Hebrew Scriptures: the concern for behavior is far more prevalent than the concern for truth (which appears mostly in Wisdom literature). Right behavior pleases YHWH more than religious ritual, unless ritual provokes justice. In his book *The Prophetic Imagination,* Walter Brueggemann says, "the task of prophecy is to enable people to engage in history" (Brueggemann 1978, 22). This is another way of touching upon selves as agent, although with one major difference, namely, that Bruggemann is often speaking about a communal agent, how a community acts, which is a necessary addition for biblical faith.

Thorlief Boman, in *Hebrew Thought Compared with Greek*, contrasts the stillness of a Greek person at prayer with a Jew at prayer: "When Holy Scripture is read aloud in the synagogue, the Orthodox Jew moves his whole body ceaselessly in deep devotion and adoration . . . the Israelite reaches his zenith in ceaseless movement" (Boman 1960, 208). And there is often, among Jews at prayer, the buzz of whispered articulation.

Even a thinker as classical as T. S. Eliot, in *The Four Quartets,* celebrates "the still point of the turning world," yet confesses that "except for the still point, there would be no dance, and *there is only the dance*" (Eliot 1971, 15/16, emphasis added).

Alfred North Whitehead

In *The Function of Reason,* Alfred North Whitehead comes to similar conclusions. The driving force in organisms is three-fold: first, to survive; then to survive with some satisfaction; and finally, to be in search of ways to survive still better (an habitual openness to transcending the present). Our rational faculties and our imaginative faculties, Whitehead holds, have developed in response to these three intentionalities. Reason is in the service of living [*mundum agendum*], and it develops through this service.

The human desire to make things better tomorrow than they are today is the major driving process in the development of reason. In *The Adventures of Ideas,* Whitehead says that the contrast between what is and what might be is what drives civilization forward. "The function of reason," Whitehead remarks, "is to promote the art of life" (1958, 4). There is some resonance with the *phronesis/praxis* of Aristotle in affirming that "the conduct of human affairs is entirely dominated by our recognition of foresight, determining purpose, and purpose issuing in conduct," except that there is no contemplative function that takes precedence (Whitehead 1958, 13).

For him, again in Aristotelian categories, reason is the interweaving between efficient and final causation which drives the human process: "the practical embodiment of the urge to transform mere existence into the good existence, and to transform the good existence into the better existence" (Whitehead 1958, 28-29). The fact that something else than what is, might be the case, is the function of speculative reason: "Abstract speculation has been the salvation of the world—speculation which has made systems and then transcended them, speculations which ventured to the furthest limit of abstraction" (Whitehead 1958, 76). The inner dynamic that calls to a better existence is derived, for Whitehead, from the efficacy of God within all process. In the Judeo-Christian tradition, this is the efficacious power of the reign of God being enacted.

Hannah Arendt

Macmurray makes the case in a very straightforward, logical way. Action always involves thinking, but thinking can occur without action, as a human activity not directed to building life in the world. Action is more concrete than thinking, a fuller human process. Whitehead makes the case based upon his reading of the emergence and development of reason (or mind) in the evolutionary process.

Hannah Arendt's starting point, in *The Human Condition,* is a political reading of the human condition, based upon what she calls natality, mortality, and plurality. I will focus for the moment on plurality:

> Plurality is the condition of human action because we are all the same, that is, human, in such a way that nobody is ever the same as anyone else who ever lived, lives, or will live . . . Human plurality, the basic condition of both action and speech, has the two-fold character of equality and distinction (Arendt 1959, 8, 175).

For her, *labor* corresponds to the most basic biological needs of human beings, and how we address them. *Work* is the making of all the "artificial" things that come from human ingenuity, which make life simpler or richer. *Action* refers to the huge complex of human behaviors made necessary by plurality: it refers to how we can get along together in the world with all our differences.

The city, the Greek *polis*, is human togetherness required by plurality as the human condition. *Political* names everything that has to do with our being together in the world and trying to make it work for the common good. Action is paired with speech in how people do their political best in the world. Action and speech together serve political life: "Action needs for its full appearance the shining brightness we once called glory, and which is possible only in the public realm" (Arendt 1959, 180).

Arendt names two characteristics of temporality that put human action under requirement: the irreversibility of the past and the unpredictability of the future: "The possible redemption from the predicament of irreversibility—of being unable to undo what one has done though one did not, and could not, have known what he was doing—is the faculty of forgiving. The remedy for unpredictability for the chaotic uncertainty of the future, is contained in the faculty to make and keep promises (1959, 237)." Religion is frequently an important place where the human condition structures support for forgiveness and fidelity to promises.

The point here is not to restate the rich development of human action in *The Human Condition*, but to name one more principal advocate of the primacy of action over thinking (action always includes thinking) in interpreting human destiny. Macmurray and Arendt both articulate their awareness that this turn is a fundamental upending of Greek interpretation, which has structured the Western social construction of reality for twenty-five hundred years and more.

So what?

None of the approaches I have surveyed denies the importance of contemplative moments, or those powerful moments of ecstasy in a love relationship, whether with God or with another human being. Equally, the importance of reflection and of speculative thought is everywhere affirmed. Moments of ecstasy are fleeting, not constant. But they have the power constantly to transform all that comes after them. In the anthropology I have been sketching, contemplation is for the action called living, rather than living for the sake of contemplation, as in Aristotle.

Union between two people occurs when their action (not activity!) overlaps and coincides: lives pitched together in marriage, in friendship, in community. Union with God, no less, occurs whenever human action coincides with divine action—the closer all that we are (up to) coincides with all that God is (up to), the deeper the union.

We human beings are in the world in and through our bodies. Whatever we can come to know will be mediated by our bodily presence in the world. If God can be experienced by us, then God must be in the world and in time with us. The immanence of God, of course, does not ever exhaust God; however, there is nothing we could ever know about God's transcendence except in so far as there are signals of transcendence in God's immanence. Withness and otherness are coordinate notions. The worldly appearances of God are the proper matter for theology. We can speculate beyond them but only on the basis of them. One indication that this underlying anthropology is being taken seriously is a major shift in many strands of contemporary theological partnership from metaphysics to the human sciences, which are disposed to interpret human experience.

The sort of anthropology presented here through Macmurray, Whitehead, and Arendt thoroughly temporalizes, localizes, and historicizes our experience of God. In his recent book on Christian sacraments, Kenan Osborne says, "human thinking is *constitutively* drenched in temporality" (Osborne 1999, 26, italics added). I would not minimize the complexities and ambiguities of temporal, local, historical existence. But there is nothing in this approach that recommends distancing ourselves from the world, especially a world that, as Hopkins would have it, "is charged with the grandeur of God."

I am not supposing that an anthropology that centers its attention on action is a superior interpretation to one that centers attention on contemplation. Both have supported rich cultures and genuine religious experience. But I want to hold that it is a viable alternative that fits some significant traditions in Western life, and also that it has resonances with the underlying anthropology of classical Hebrew.

The anthropology of action has more kindship with the Synoptics than with the Fourth Gospel. The contrast is visible in the differences of spirit in the synoptics from that of the Fourth Gospel. There are 18 references to the reign of God in Mark, 37 in Luke, and 47 in Matthew but only 5 in the Fourth Gospel (Dunn 1985, 34). The reign (kingdom) of God regularly specifies God's intentions for the world and the ways in which discipleship of Jesus commits to collaboration with God in realizing God's intentions in history and in the world. But the number of times in which Jesus focuses upon himself in his message is 118 in the Fourth Gospel, but only 9 in Mark, 10 in Luke, and 17 in Matthew. To gaze upon Jesus in the Fourth Gospel is phenomenologically to gaze upon God. While the Fourth Gospel patently is concerned about how we live, in the early centuries there were some perceived Gnostic tendencies in this Gospel (e.g., know the truth for the truth will set you free), which contrast markedly with the last judgment scene and its criteria in Matthew 25.

Texts from the Fourth Gospel are far more prevalent in the patristic materials than synoptic texts (although the wisdom Christology in Matthew 11 often appears). Neo-platonism and Philonic stoic philosophy underpin much of the doctrinal development of the Western Christian tradition. It is not difficult to understand that the emphasis on "action" in U.S. Catholic experience sounded to Rome like the heresy of Americanism (which it would be whenever action simply meant activity).

Practical Theology and the
Anthropology of Historical Agency

Practical theology has multiple meanings. One is that it is the application of systematic theology; another is that it names the institutional practices of religion, like preaching or church administration. In theology in this country another understanding is developing, especially in ministry education, but also more broadly. It tends to be deeply dialogic and inductive. Practical theology has much in common with liberation (Latin America) and political (Germany) theology. The following characterization of practical theology is indebted to David Tracy and also to the emancipatory tradition. It can be rendered as follows:

> Practical theology is a mutually critical conversation between interpretations of faith and its resources and interpretations of the social world(s) in which we live,

> Practical theology intends to be generative of transformative pastoral strategies.

> It takes place ideally in a community, in a relentlessly circular rhythm of action-reflection, reflection action.

This is grounded in the Aristotelian development of the virtue of *phronesis/praxis,* when *phroneis/praxis* is not in second place to contemplation but holds pride of place in describing the human condition: the action of people in the world. Rather, contemplation has a vital role within the panorama of action. Action, of course, names the totality of intentionally lived experience.

The Undistancing of the World

Paul's Christians in Corinth asked him what life was like on the other side of this life. He finally had to say that this is a useless question, since nobody knows. But in the meanwhile we have only this world to deal with, and "historical agency" is as good a turn of phrase as any to catch the sense of human destiny. This also happens to be a world which is the theatre of God's action. The analogical imagination, as David Tracy describes it, situates us always between the already and the not-yet, but with firm conviction that grace outruns evil, that the world is more like God than unlike God—a conviction upon which a rich sacramentality depends.

Catholic thought has taken to the image of *sacramentum mundi,* the sacrament of the world. Kenan Osborne offers a healthy reminder not to make the sacramentality of the world automatic, as it were: "there is, therefore, no such 'thing,' as such, that is a sacrament" (Osborne 1999, 70). What makes the world be *potential* sacrament is that it is the locus of God's action; but, the world's actual, functional sacramentality requires a human response to God's action. Only in the coincidence of divine and human action can the *sacramentum mundi* mediate redemption. A theological anthropology which accepts that action is the human condition on earth and is a basis here for human kind's fullest union with God is a theological anthropology that undistances from the world.

References

Arendt, Hannah. 1971. *The Human Condition.* Chicago: University of Chicago.

Aristotle. 1962. *Ethics*, ed. E.V. Rieu. London: Penguin.

Boman, Thorlief. 1960. *Hebrew Thought Compared with Greek.* Philadelphia: Westminster.

Brueggemann, Walter. 1978. *The Prophetic Imagination.* Philadelphia: Fortress.

Cooke, Bernard. 1990. *The Distancing of God: The Ambiguity of Symbol in History and Theology.* Minneapolis: Fortress.

Macmurray, John. 1996. *Persons in Relation.* Atlantic Highlands, NJ: Humanities Press International.

Macmuray, John. 1996. *The Self as Agent.* Atlantic Highlands, NJ: Humanities Press International.

Osborne, Kenan. 1999. *Christian Sacraments in a Postmodern World: A Theology for the Third Millennium.* New York: Paulist.

Tracy, David. 1981. *The Analogical Imagination: Christian Theology and the Culture of Pluralism.* NY: Crossroad.

Whitehead, Alfred North. 1962. *The Function of Reason.* Boston: Beacon Press.

5 Intersubjectivity and a Theology of Presence

Joseph A. Bracken, S.J.

In *The Distancing of God*, Bernard Cooke sets forth what he calls a "theology of presence with focus on the function of symbol in enabling and blocking divine presence"(1990, 1). To that end, he first sketches an overview of the history of Christian theology, indicating how the reality of God has been "distanced" from the minds and hearts of individual Christians through a combination of three interrelated factors: an overemphasis on cult and priesthood stemming from classical Judaism, an ontology of human participation in divinity or deification coming from Neo-Platonism, and a patriarchal ecclesiastical structure coming from Roman law and custom (1990, 56, 108). Then in the second part of the book he reviews some of the advances made in anthropology, psychology and literary criticism with respect to the role of symbols and symbol making in contemporary human life. Finally, in the concluding pages of the book, he notes how a new understanding of divine providence or God's saving activity in this world is gradually taking shape under the influence of two interrelated factors:

> On the more philosophical level there is the insight into a creative role of "ground of being," that is, the sustaining of things in existence and operative potential by an uncreated transcendent "other." On the theological level there are the beginnings of a sophisticated "theology of presence," growing out of traditions of divine revelation

and divine granting of "grace" but transformed by modern insights into the development and transformation of persons through communication (1990, 357).

While I basically agree with Cooke in his analysis of the historical reasons for the "distancing" of God in the Christian tradition and while I share with him the conviction that a new "theology of presence" is indeed in the making within the academy at the present time, I still feel somewhat uneasy about specific details of his own solution to the problem of distancing God from the faithful.

In the above-cited quotation, for example, how is one to reconcile the notion of a creative ground of being with the affirmation of a transcendent personal God as the necessary dialogue-partner for human beings in a theology of presence? Is God therefore simultaneously both personal and impersonal and, if so, how is this to be understood? Secondly, is an ontology of participation necessarily alienating or is perhaps only the classical understanding of such ontological participation derived from the philosophy of Plato and Aristotle ultimately alienating? A different understanding of creaturely participation in the divine life could possibly make clear, for example, how ordinary human experience is truly sacramental, one of Cooke's key points. Along the same lines, how is one to understand the passion, death and resurrection of Jesus Christ as paradigmatic for what it means to be human (1990, 364)? Does not the doctrine of the resurrection, for example, also demand a type of deification or participation in the divine life for human beings, perhaps even for the material universe as a whole? These are, to be sure, primarily metaphysical questions that Cooke for his own reasons may have chosen not to address. Yet, as Etienne Gilson sagely commented many years ago, metaphysics tends to bury its undertakers (Gilson 1982, 306). Sooner or later, metaphysical implications have to be acknowledged and addressed.

Hence, as my own modest contribution to this volume honoring the life and work of Bernard Cooke, above all in the area of sacramental theology, I will first offer some reflections on possible metaphysical presuppositions of the theology of presence set forth by Cooke in *The Distancing of God* and then indicate how, in my judgment, a revised form of the metaphysics of Alfred North Whitehead such as I have proposed in a recent book might provide a systematic framework for organizing and further developing the vast amount of historical and empirical data that Cooke has assembled in defense of his thesis in that same book. Admittedly, as Cooke points out with reference to the classical Platonic metaphysics of participation, there is always a danger in metaphysical speculation of gradually becoming distant from one's own immediate experience (what Whitehead calls "the fallacy of misplaced concreteness" [*Science and the Modern World* 1967, 51]). But, provided that one keeps in mind the provisional and purely symbolic character of the theoretical scheme in question, one has in hand a mental tool of considerable value for giving further order and coherence to one's investigation of a highly complex subject matter. As Cooke comments, "people shape their personal awareness [of what is happening to them] according to certain models, though for the most part they are not aware of the interpreting role of the most basic of these models precisely because they are so basic" (1990, 354). My intention here then will be first to raise questions about what is meant by (human) subjectivity and, above all, by intersubjectivity and then to set forth one philosophical model by way of further explanation.

We may begin our analysis of a theology of presence by asking what is involved in the presence of human beings to one another. People are physically present to one another when they can see, hear, or touch one another. But this does not always mean that they are at the same time psychically present to one another. As Martin Buber pointed out many years ago in his classic work *I and Thou*, there is a natural tendency for human beings to objectify their relations to one another, implicitly to treat one another as mere objects of thought or aspiration within their separate mental worlds (Buber 1958, 3-34). As a result, they effectively treat themselves as objects also. That is, they live in a world implicitly governed by custom or logic in which reflective awareness of their own subjectivity is normally at a minimum. It is therefore likewise an awakening of their own subjectivity when they periodically recognize the deeper subjectivity of another human being or, even more emphatically, the subjectivity of the God to whom they conventionally pray and offer worship. One is jolted into the recognition of the freedom of the other vis-à-vis oneself, an experience that can arouse love, fear, or both love and fear at the same time. In any event, one unexpectedly sees the other in a new way. The psychological estrangement between oneself and the other has been temporarily eliminated and one is consciously in the personal presence of another subjectivity.

In my judgment, some such experience of intersubjectivity is what Cooke finds lacking in his analysis of the ways in which God has been historically distanced from the consciousness of the faithful through excessive preoccupation with the details of a liturgical celebration, through abstract philosophical speculation and through a notion of grace as dispensed to individuals through human mediators. In all three cases, one has lost a sense of direct interpersonal contact with the God one seeks to worship and has settled for a mediated experience of God that in the end fails to satisfy. Cooke comments:

> Discovery of and personal relatedness to the divine does not involve a God at a distance. While conceptual and imaginative formulations of this divine presence is intrinsic to human knowing, and therefore a certain "distancing" is unavoidable at the level of understanding, the consciousness of presence – like the knower's consciousness of self – continues to enjoy a logical priority that is capable of challenging the idolatry of mental structures. . . . Evangelization and catechesis, consequently, must deal with this primary level of human awareness if they are to effect the transformation of the human person that constitutes the reality called "sanctifying grace" (1990, 359).

As Buber realized and as Cooke confirms with this quotation, however, a human being cannot remain indefinitely in an intensive I-Thou relationship. One inevitably slips back into a more conventional I-It relationship if only to reflect upon what one has experienced. At the same time, the strictly intersubjective character of the I-Thou relationship remains the goal of human beings in their relations with one another and, above all, of human beings in their relationship with God.

Still another feature of Buber's understanding of the I-Thou relationship is his affirmation of the reality of "the Between," that which comes into being in virtue of the dynamic exchange between two subjectivities and which serves as a common objective ground for their ongoing exchange (Buber 1958, 37-72). Cooke seems to make reference to this co-constituted reality as follows: "The process of intertwined symbolization and communication involves a constantly evolving dialectic between the conscious self and 'the other'; people identify themselves as they construct their world. Through this creative self-world experience people establish the 'space' within which they can act with benefit to themselves and others" (1990, 349). What needs emphasis in Cooke's statement is that this is not a private "world" or a private "space" but a common world and a common space that binds the two subjectivities to one another even as they each remain ontologically independent of one another. In principle, neither is subordinate to the other. Yet they together construct a common world of meaning and value by their dynamic interrelation. As I see it, this is a key point in the understanding of intersubjectivity as opposed to transcendental subjectivity that was originally proposed by Immanuel Kant and then carried forward by many others, including such notable contemporary Roman Catholic theologians as Bernard Lonergan and Karl Rahner. Transcendental subjectivity, however carefully elaborated, logically involves an ontological subordination of the other to the self; the other becomes part of my world, no matter how hard I try to respect the "otherness" of the other. Recognizing this logical impossibility, Emmanuel Levinas in *Totality and Infinity* sought to remedy the situation by postulating the ontological priority of the other to the self (Levinas 1969, 39-40). But in my judgment this otherwise brilliant countermove on the part of Levinas only deepened the mystery associated with the issue of intersubjectivity. What is needed for genuine intersubjectivity is not the ontological priority of the self to the other or of the other to the self, but the conjoint creation of an objective common ground or "Between" within which both parties can be themselves and yet contribute to something bigger than themselves as individuals.

For, as Levinas also made clear, subjectivity is of itself unobjectifiable (Levinas 1969, 49-51; also *The One in the Many* 2001, 27). As the principle of potentiality for the existence and activity of a given subject of experience, it cannot be objectified, become fully actual, without ceasing to be a principle of potentiality. As such, not simply the subjectivity of God but likewise every created subjectivity is in a qualified sense infinite; that is, it remains in principle capable of still further self-expression or self-revelation as long as it exists. On the other hand, if subjectivities are by nature incommunicable, how can there be communication and exchange between them? Solipsism would seem to be the natural consequence of focusing on human subjectivity unless one with Buber postulates an objective common ground or Between, something, which in my judgment, gradually takes shape through the ongoing interplay of different subjectivities. That is, all the various features of life in community, namely, language, customs and (eventually) formal laws, institutions of various kinds, come into being thorough interpersonal exchange and perdure as conditioning features of that same interpersonal exchange as time goes on and as the number of participants continues to grow. Cooke, for example, takes note of the fact that all experience is interpreted experience: "People's life-style and housing and dietary patterns, their family and civic and religious celebrations, their occupational and recreational use of time, their technology and art, their processes of education–in short, all the things we lump under the notion of a people's *culture*–constantly speak symbolically about the meaning people attach to human life and incarnate the values that govern the conduct of life" (1990, 353). But how does all this "culture" arise except as the by-product of the dynamic interaction of different human subjectivities over extended periods of time? The culture of a group or community is the objective manifestation of its Between, that which endures as individual members of the group come and go.

Does this notion of the Between likewise apply to the God-world relationship? Does there exist a common ground between God and creation, something which is shaped and structured by the conjoint activity of both God and creatures? Given the logical implications of the notion of subjectivity and intersubjectivity that I have sketched above, the answer would seem to be yes. Shortly I will make clear how this answer can be explained in terms of the modified form of Whiteheadian metaphysics that I have developed in recent years. But for now it is only important to note how such an understanding of intersubjectivity with its concomitant notion of the Between protects the ontological independence of God vis-à-vis the world and the world of creatures vis-à-vis God. God can be in ongoing communication with creatures and creatures can be in ongoing communication with God without danger of either dualism or pantheism. That is, because God and creatures co-constitute a common world, dualism is eliminated. Yet, because this common ground is generated by ontologically independent subjects of experience in dynamic interrelation, pantheism is avoided. As I shall explain more clearly below, what results is a form of panentheism, namely, the belief that creatures somehow exist in God but as themselves and not simply as parts of the divine being.

Given the theoretical advantages of this notion of the Between for the God-world relationship, how is it to be further explained? Here Buber's own work is not very helpful since he described it in phenomenological rather than strictly metaphysical terms. But, as I have tried to make clear elsewhere, a modest revision of the key category of "society" in the metaphysical scheme of Alfred North Whitehead might provide the theoretical underpinning needed to support the notion of the Between (*The One in the Many* 2001, 109-30). For in a curious way Whitehead, whose own background was in mathematics and theoretical physics before turning to philosophy late in life, may inadvertently have been one of the first major Western philosophers to give serious attention to the notion of intersubjectivity. His basic presupposition, after all, was "[t]hat the actual world is a process, and that the process is the becoming of actual entities" (*Process and Reality* 1978, 22). But what are actual entities but momentary self-constituting subjects of experience? Hence, the cosmic process is made up of dynamically interrelated subjects of experience; the world is constituted by intersubjectivity. Here one might object that Whitehead overreached himself in stating that actual entities (or actual occasions) "are the final real things of which the world is made up" (*Process and Reality* 1978, 18). Thus in the end there are no material things except as the by-product of the interplay of momentary subjects of experience. But logically this is what is required for a *metaphysics* based on intersubjectivity. Literally everything must be a derivative of subjects of experience in dynamic interplay. Furthermore, as I shall indicate below, there are distinct theoretical advantages for explaining both the Christian doctrine of the resurrection and the recapitulation of all things in Christ, if one antecedently assumes that "matter" is not opposed to "spirit" but somehow derivative from it.

My focus here, however, is not on Whitehead's notion of an actual entity as such but on two corollaries of that presupposition. The first is that actual entities are constituted by *internal* rather than *external* relations to one another. That is, as interrelated *subjects of experience* they are internally present to one another and affect one another's self-constitution in a way that would be impossible for material things in purely external relation to one another in space and time. The second corollary is that actual entities as strictly *momentary* subjects of experience inevitably aggregate into "societies" which are extended in space and time and thus bear some resemblance to Aristotelian substances. Both of these corollaries need further elaboration if they are to be seen as integral to a metaphysics of intersubjectivity. Whitehead himself was fully aware of the implications of the first corollary, but, it seems, not fully aware of the implications of the second. He himself, for example, called attention to "the fallacy of simple location": "To say that a bit of matter has *simple location* means that, in expressing its spatio-temporal relations, it is adequate to state that it is where it is, in a definite finite region of space, and throughout a definite duration of time, apart from any essential reference of the relations of that bit of matter to other regions of space and to other durations of time" (*Science and the Modern World* 1967, 58). While "simple location" conceivably could apply to material things from a common sense point of view, it emphatically does not apply to interrelated immaterial subjects of experience. Subjects of experience are present to one another psychically. That is, through the medium of some objective symbol or sign they enter into one another's internal self-constitution at any given moment. As such, they need not be physically present to one another in the same way that, in terms of common sense experience, material things stand in spatial or temporal contiguity to one another. In characterizing this conventional way of looking at physical reality as a "fallacy," Whitehead evidently recognized what he was doing in stipulating that immaterial subjects of experience rather than inert "bits of matter" are the building blocks of physical reality. As he notes elsewhere in *Science and the Modern World,* "everything is everywhere at all times. For every location involves an aspect of itself in every other location. Thus every spatio-temporal standpoint mirrors the world" (1967, 91).

With reference to the second corollary, however, in my judgment Whitehead was not so fully aware of the implications of his own thought. In *Adventures of Ideas*, written some years after *Process and Reality*, for example, he first notes that "[t]he real actual things that endure are all societies. They are not actual occasions" (1967, 204). But he then adds: "A society has an essential character, whereby it is the society that it is, and it has also accidental qualities which vary as circumstances alter. Thus a society, as a complete existence and as retaining the same metaphysical status, enjoys a history expressing its changing reactions to changing circumstances. But an actual occasion has no such history. It never changes. It only becomes and perishes" (1967, 204). Thus by his own admission a society somehow resembles an Aristotelian substance. But Whitehead could not reintroduce the notion of substance into his philosophy without undercutting his even more fundamental presupposition that actual occasions or actual entities "are the final real things of which the world is made up" (*Process and Reality* 1978, 18). In the end, he seems to have contented himself with the generic description of societies as aggregates of actual entities with an enduring "common element of form" (ibid. 34). But he did offer in *Process and Reality* the hint of still another explanation of the reality of societies, which I will explore now.

In the chapter entitled "The Order of Nature," Whitehead has the following comments on the way in which societies are "layered" or nested within one another:

> Every society must be considered with its background of a wider environment of actual entities, which also contribute their objectifications to which the members of the society must conform. . . . But this means that the environment, together with the society in question, must form a larger society in respect to some more general characters than those defining the society from which we started. Thus we arrive at the principle that every society requires a social background, of which it is itself a part. In reference to any given society the world of actual entities is to be conceived as forming a background in layers of social order, the defining characteristics becoming wider and more general as we widen the background (1978, 90).

If one substitutes "field" for "environment" in the above-cited quotation, then a new image for the Whiteheadian category of society emerges.

A society is no longer an aggregate of actual entities with each entity exhibiting roughly the same form or pattern of self-organization. Rather a society is a place of context for the ongoing interaction of actual entities; it is an antecedently structured field of activity for each new set of actual entities. That is, the field presumably comes into existence in virtue of the dynamic interplay of an initial set of actual entities. But, unlike its constituent actual entities, the field does not go out of existence in the next moment, but rather remains in place with a given structure so as to provide a pattern of self-organization to the next set of actual entities. It serves therefore as the ontological principle of continuity between successive sets of actual occasions. Moreover, as Whitehead indicates in the above-cited quotation, these environments or structured fields of activity can be "layered" within one another, with the broader fields of activity providing the more general characteristics for a given set of actual occasions and the more immediate field (or fields) of activity providing the more specific characteristics of that same set of actual occasions. Thus, as Whitehead also notes in that same chapter, "in a society, the members can only exist by reason of the laws which dominate the society [read, field], and the laws only come into being by reason of the analogous characters of the members of the society" (1978, 91). There is an ongoing reciprocal relation between societies and their constituent actual entities.

What is important for our present discussion, however, is that a Whiteheadian society thus understood serves as a metaphysical explanation for the reality of the Between in Buber's philosophy. That is, just as the Between for Buber is not an I or a Thou but the objective reality constituted by the relationship between an I and a Thou, so a Whiteheadian society is not itself a subject of experience but the law-like or structured context within which subjects of experience exist over time in dynamic interrelation. Whereas in Buber's philosophy, to be sure, the reality of the Between is tenuous because it seems to depend on an equally fragile I-Thou relationship, in Whitehead's philosophy the society by definition must endure while individual sets of constituent actual entities come and go. As already noted, a Whiteheadian society "has an essential character, whereby it is the society that it is, and it has also accidental qualities which vary as circumstances alter" (*Adventures of Ideas* 1967, 204). But the key point of comparison nevertheless remains. Like Buber's Between, a Whiteheadian society is something objective in a world governed by intersubjectivity. That is, in a world where subjectivities are in themselves incommunicable, something objective, a common ground, must exist as the basis for their ongoing interaction. Inevitably, this common ground will be shaped by the dynamic interplay of those same subjectivities, but it in turn will shape the self-expression of subsequent subjectivities in their efforts at mutual communication. One need only think of the way in which a common language shapes the thought-patterns and behavior of the human beings who use it in order to see the logical necessity of Buber's Between and Whiteheadian societies within an intersubjective context.

But how does all this metaphysical speculation impact upon Bernard Cooke's theology of presence? I will begin by referring to the questions about Cooke's work that I raised at the beginning of this essay. There I asked, for example, about the relation between what Cooke called the creative "ground of being" and the understanding of God as dialogue-partner with human beings in a theology of presence. Certainly one way to answer that question would be to point to the ontological reality of the Between as the common ground between God and created subjectivities. That is, both God and creatures, albeit in different ways, have contributed to the ongoing existence of the cosmic process. Everything that exists is thus symbolic of the presence and activity of both God and creatures because everything is the self-expression both of God as a transcendent subjectivity and of all the different kinds of created subjectivities (both human and non-human). So stated, however, key details are still missing. How do God and creatures thus cooperate to produce a common world? In what sense does God as Creator necessarily take the initiative in this joint effort? Once again, I revert to my neo-Whiteheadian scheme for the understanding of "societies" by way of further explanation.

Both in *The One in the Many* and in an earlier book *The Divine Matrix*, I proposed that my understanding of Whiteheadian societies as structured fields of activity for their constituent actual occasions allows for a specifically trinitarian understanding of God within the framework of Whitehead's metaphysical scheme (*The One in the Many* 2001, 120-30; *The Divine Matrix* 1995, 62-69). That is, if one presupposes that the three divine persons of the classical Christian doctrine of the Trinity can be construed as three dynamically interrelated subjectivities (or, in Whiteheadian terms, three interrelated personally ordered societies of actual occasions), then by that same token they co-constitute the communal reality of a divine community (in Whiteheadian terms, a structured society of actual occasions with a single totally unlimited field of activity). This divine matrix or ground of being for the divine persons in their internal self-relatedness likewise serves in my theory as the creative ground of being for the cosmic process once the three divine persons have made the decision to create. That is, the same principle of creativity that empowers the divine persons to exist in dynamic interrelation is graciously extended by the triune God to all created subjectivities so that they can exist in dynamic interrelation with one another and with the divine persons. Thus the three divine persons and all their creatures co-constitute a common world, albeit in different ways. The three divine persons communicate to created subjectivities the power to be together with a "lure" (what Whitehead calls a divine initial aim: *Process and Reality* 1978, 244) for the exercise of that divinely given power of existence and activity in a productive rather than in a harmful way. Thus empowered and directed, the created subjectivities have over billions of years brought into existence the universe as we know it today. The results, to be sure, have not always been satisfactory; but this is because the divine persons "lure" or persuade rather than coerce their creatures to the transcendent goals of creation (truth, beauty, goodness, adventure, and finally peace: Whitehead, *Adventures of Ideas* 1967, 241-96). But, in any case, creation as it exists today is the self-expression of both the divine persons and all their creatures and as such has symbolic and revelatory power for those who properly understand and respond to it. In a word, creation is through and through sacramental. As Cooke maintains, sacred rites and places are only necessary to draw our attention to what is universally present and active in human experience (1990, 365-68).

Turning now to the second question that I posed at the beginning of this essay, namely, whether an ontology of participation is necessarily alienating to the human spirit, I would argue that this is the case only within a basically dualistic understanding of the God-world relationship rather than in the panentheistic understanding which I have sketched above. For example, within the philosophy of Plato there is a clear division between reality and appearance. Reality is the realm of the eternal ideas; appearance is the empirical world of common sense experience (Plato, *The Republic*, nn. 509-18). When this ontological divide is transferred uncritically to the exposition of Christian sacramental theology, then, as Cooke properly notes, only sacred rites as administered by sacred ministers allow the faithful to escape from the world of appearances and make contact with the eternal unchanging reality of God and the saints in heaven (1990, 28-46). Furthermore, when the workings of the individual sacraments are analyzed in terms of the four causes propounded by Aristotle (material, formal, efficient and final), then any sense of the sacraments as symbols mediating interpersonal communication between God and human beings is lost as one ends up in logical disputes about the matter and the form of each sacrament, the *ex opere operato* vs. *ex opere operantis* effect of the sacrament, etc (cf., e.g., Chauvet 1995, 9-45). On the other hand, if one has at hand a panentheistic understanding of the God-world relationship whereby, as noted above, both the three divine persons and all created subjectivities are at work in different ways to bring about the reality of the cosmic process from moment to moment, then for the perceiving eye "everything is grace." Everything has sacramental value in virtue of this governing paradigm for the God-world relationship. So, rather than serving as an impediment to interpersonal communication between God and human beings, the right metaphysical understanding of the notion of human participation in the divine life would seem to enhance it. As Cooke himself notes in his chapter on the symbolic value of ordinary human experience, "neither experience nor interpretation can exist independently of the other" (1990, 355). But foundational to interpretation is an at least implicit set of metaphysical principles that give order and coherence to an individual's and a community's world view. Everything depends upon the right choice of metaphysical principles.

Finally, with respect to the third question about the paradigmatic character of Jesus' passion, death and resurrection, I would state even more emphatically that everything depends upon one's antecedent metaphysical principles. The tendency in contemporary theology to downplay the Scriptural accounts of Jesus' appearances to Mary Magdalene, the other holy women and the apostles reflect a basic uneasiness with the notion of a bodily resurrection in the light of contemporary natural science. A metaphysical issue is at stake here, namely, the apparent dichotomy between matter and spirit such that neither one can be seen as emergent from or otherwise dependent on the other. Methodological naturalism is an important operational principle in natural science: namely, that a scientist should not appeal to God's providential activity in the universe to explain unexpected occurrences in the natural world (Barbour 1997, 78-82). But many scientists have consciously or unconsciously likewise endorsed ontological naturalism which is a philosophical position claiming that either God does not exist (atheism) or that in any case God is not active in this world (deism). Thus put on the defensive by the *philosophical* claims of prominent natural scientists, some theologians have tended to recast the traditional understanding of Jesus' resurrection in moralistic or strictly psychological terms: e.g., Jesus "rose" into the minds and hearts of his followers as the enduring symbol of what it means to be a full human being. What is really needed by way of reply to philosophical atheists or deists, in my judgment, is a credible counter position, a metaphysical scheme that makes clear how material reality is derivative from the spiritual reality of a Creator God and is destined to be reintegrated into the divine life upon completion of its earthly existence. Every metaphysical scheme, to be sure, is only a symbolic representation of features of reality not directly accessible to human observation and experiment (Barbour 1997, 115-24). But at least one is dealing with exponents of ontological naturalism on the same footing, that is, by setting in contrast rival metaphysical systems.

I have over the years favored the metaphysics of Whitehead for this purpose because it presupposes that matter is ultimately derivative from spirit. That is, better than Teilhard de Chardin with his proposal of "radial" or spiritual energy as well as "tangential" or conventional physical energy as driving forces within the evolutionary process (Teilhard de Chardin 1959, 53-66). Whitehead, following the lead of Leibniz in his *Monadology*, boldly proposes that matter in all its configurations is the necessary by-product of subjects of experience in dynamic interaction. This may seem an outrageous claim until one asks oneself how a purely immaterial God can create a material universe. Why not instead propose that three divine persons as themselves subjects of experience in dynamic interrelation create finite subjects of experience which by their dynamic interplay produce the objective reality of a material world? Subjectivity, in other words, seems to require objectification in something other than another subjectivity. In the case of the divine persons, this would be the divine community, their objective unity as one God; in the case of created subjects of experience, this would be the material world in all its ramifications. Thus the universe as a unified interconnected reality constituted by subjects of experience in dynamic interrelation would be the true *imago Dei*, the symbol of the triune God. The deeper justification for this line of thought, of course, is that one can then contest the claim of ontological materialists that in the end only matter exists, that the reality of spirit is an illusion. Rather, with equal right one can assert that the reality of matter is in a qualified sense an illusion since it exists only as the by-product of immaterial subjects of experience in dynamic interaction. Neither metaphysics can be proven to be true in a factual sense. It is simply a question of which one makes more sense, all things considered.

Whitehead's metaphysics, to be sure, does not provide a rational explanation of classical Christian belief in the resurrection of the body and the "recapitulation" or transformation of all things in Christ at the end of the world. Since he composed *Process and Reality* as a philosophical cosmology rather than as a systematic theology, Whitehead contented himself with the proposal that all created actual entities are "prehended" by God and thus enjoy objective immortality within the divine "consequent nature" (*Process and Reality* 1978, 344-46). In *The End of Evil*, Marjorie Suchocki sought to remedy this defect in Whitehead's scheme by proposing that God prehends created actual entities at the precise moment when they have completed their process of self-constitution and yet are still subjects of experience, "enjoying" what they have just become (Suchocki 1988, 81-96). In this way, God can prehend created actual entities in their subjective immediacy and confer on them subjective as well as objective immortality within the divine consequent nature (Suchocki 1988, 97-114). What Suchocki failed to see, in my judgment, was that she was thereby converting Whitehead's notion of prehension into a subject-subject relationship and introducing intersubjectivity into a metaphysical scheme thus far dominated by the classical subject-object relationship. Furthermore, given the preconditions for the exercise of intersubjectivity that I have sketched above, place must be made for the Between as the necessary common ground for the interaction of subjectivities (whether divine or created). Not Whitehead's divine consequent nature, therefore, but what I have called the divine matrix (understood as the ontological ground of being both for the divine persons and for all created actual entities in their dynamic interrelation) is the necessary philosophical precondition for belief in bodily resurrection and the transformation of all things in Christ.

In the language of Sacred Scripture, the divine matrix thus understood would be called "the kingdom of God" or "the kingdom of heaven." That is, it is an ontological reality that is primarily constituted by the three divine persons in their ongoing interrelation, but which, in a significant way, is likewise co-constituted by creatures (created actual entities) in their dynamic interaction both with one another and with the divine persons. As such, it is a reality that spans heaven and earth. What happens on this earth is simultaneously part of the life of the three divine persons insofar as they are involved with their creatures. In more technical Whiteheadian language, the individual actual occasion goes through its process of self-constitution and contributes its form or pattern of existence to the field out of which it emerged. That field, however, is invariably part of a hierarchically structured set of fields, which ultimately terminates in the divine matrix as the common ground of interaction between the three divine persons and all their creatures. Thus understood, the self-constituting decision of every actual entity has contributed in some small way to the ongoing history of the God-world relationship. It has sacramental value in that it belongs to two worlds simultaneously: the world of creation and the life of the three divine persons.

Furthermore, in terms of this scheme, bodily resurrection and the transformation of all things in Christ can be seen as an ongoing reality. One does not have to wait until the end of the world for these events to take place, since at every moment (without our realizing it) the world of creation is passing into the divine life and sharing the immortality of the divine persons. Here, of course, is where the postulate that matter is the by-product of subjects of experience in dynamic relation is so important. What is incorporated into the life of the three divine persons at every moment is not material reality as such since it exists only in terms of our limited human powers of perception. What really exists are created immaterial subjects of experience in dynamic interrelation which create the effect of material reality. These immaterial subjects of experience can be readily incorporated into the intersubjective life of the three divine persons, thereby broadening the scope of the divine community from one moment to the next. Naturally, we human beings are not here and now aware of this progressive incorporation of created reality into the divine life. Our subjective focus is invariably on the present and the future, but the past has in the meantime slipped away and can never be completely recovered. To be sure, we think of the past as still present because we feel its effects in the present moment of self-constitution. But de facto our retention of the past is quite selective. Otherwise, the present moment would not be something new but a simple repetition of the immediate past moment.

In terms of my own understanding of Whiteheadian societies as enduring structured fields of activity for their constituent actual entities, one may make the same point as follows. The enduring reality of human self-consciousness and indeed of all other "societies" of created actual entities is a field which exists in the present moment as the necessary environment for the current set of concrescing actual entities. But in the next moment when a new and slightly different environment for the next set of actual entities is required, the previous environment recedes into the divine matrix as part of the ongoing history of the God-world relationship. Even so, how is one to understand the special case of bodily resurrection for human beings? How do human beings consciously begin to live a new life within the divine matrix? My presupposition here is that the actual occasion which coincides with the moment of death for a human being is elevated or transformed by divine grace so as to take full possession of the structured field of activity which it has inherited from its predecessors. That is, whereas its predecessors selectively inherited characteristics from that same field so as to form a new identity just for that moment, the actual occasion coinciding with the moment of death is enabled by divine grace to prehend the field in its entirety, both spatially and temporally. In this way, a human being sees his/her life in its entirety and likewise his/her life within the context of the ongoing divine life or salvation history. This is the moment of resurrection for a human being, but it is also a moment of judgment. Individuals must decide whether they accept the full truth about themselves in the light of salvation history or whether they find this to be, for the moment at least, psychologically impossible. In that case, a purgatorial period (presumably an interval of sustained self-reflection) might be necessary before they accept incorporation into the Mystical Body of Christ and full membership in the "Kingdom of God." Furthermore, given the unconditional character of human free will, still another possibility exists: namely, that some individuals would choose permanently to deny the full truth of their lives on earth and thus place themselves in a "hell" of their own choosing, a state of psychic alienation from God, other creatures, and themselves even as they physically remain within the divine matrix and thus never cease to be.

The key point, however, in this rethinking of Whitehead's and Suchocki's eschatological vision is to note the shift of emphasis from the individual actual occasion to the society of which it is a member. It is not individual actual entities that are incorporated into the divine life (as Suchocki presumed with her theory of subjective immortality within a Whiteheadian context), but societies as enduring fields of activity structured by the ongoing succession of actual entities. Only the final actual entity coinciding with the end of life on this earth will presumably survive to take full possession of its field of activity within the divine life. This is the moment of resurrection to eternal life and of judgment, however, not just for that individual actual occasion but for the society as a whole with the individual actual occasion as its subjective focus for all eternity. In this way, one avoids the unwanted implication of Suchocki's theory that billions of actual entities or moments of consciousness within the life of a human being would be separately resurrected into the divine life and thus be in implicit or even explicit competition with one another as the subjective focus for the society as a whole.

One final question remains before bringing to a close this reflection on resurrection and the recapitulation of all things in Christ.

What is to be said about the doctrine of the Last Judgment? How is it compatible with the notion of a continuous transformation of the material world into the divine life and the immediate resurrection of human beings at the moment of death? Here I would argue that the Scriptural passages dealing with the Last Judgment have to do with the end of our human world but not necessarily with the destiny of the universe as a whole or the end of the cosmic process. Given the enormous size of the known physical universe, it seems presumptuous to claim that the demise of our solar system and, even before that, the expiration of human life on this earth will mean the end of the cosmic process as a whole. Somehow the "Kingdom of God" will perdure in an altered form. As I see it, all that is required for validation of the Scriptural understanding of the Last Judgment is that every human being at the moment of his/her death will be confronted with the full truth of the meaning and value of his/her life on earth and be asked to accept or reject his/her small but still significant role in salvation history. Whether that ultimate decision for an individual be made almost at the beginning of salvation history, somewhere in the middle of the process or close to the end is relatively unimportant. The key point, as Scripture reminds us (e.g., Deut. 30:15-20), is that in the end one must choose between life and death, friendship with God and one's fellow creatures or self-imposed alienation from them.

To sum up, in this essay I initially posed three questions about the metaphysical presuppositions of Bernard Cooke's thesis of a new "theology of presence" as the remedy for the "distancing" of God within the Christian tradition over the centuries. As I subsequently made clear, an adequate response to these metaphysical issues would seem to require that one eventually work out a metaphysics of intersubjectivity at least somewhat akin to what I have presented in a series of books and articles over the years and then summarized in these pages. What is far more important than the adequacy or inadequacy of my own scheme for this task, however, is the issue of a metaphysical foundation for Cooke's theology of presence. If this essay persuades him (or others currently involved in sacramental theology) to give serious attention to the development of a metaphysics of intersubjectivity as the theoretical basis for their further reading and research, I will consider my efforts in this essay amply rewarded.

References

Barbour, Ian. *Religion and Science: Historical and Contemporary Issues.* San Francisco: Harper, 1997.

Bracken, Joseph A. *The Divine Matrix: Creativity as Link between East and West.* Maryknoll, NY: Orbis, 1995.

———. *The One in the Many: A Contemporary Reconstruction of the God-World Relationship.* Grand Rapids: Eerdmans, 2001.

Buber, Martin. *I and Thou.* 2nd edition. Translated by Ronald Gregor Smith. New York: Scribner's:1958.

Chauvet, Louis-Marie. *Symbol and Sacrament: A Sacramental Reinterpretation of Christian Existence.* Translated by Patrick Madigan, S.J., and Madeline Beaumont. Collegeville, MN: Liturgical Press, 1995.

Cooke, Bernard J. *The Distancing of God: The Ambiguity of Symbol in History and Theology.* Minneapolis: Fortress, 1990.

Gilson, Etienne. *The Unity of Philosophical Experience.* Westminster, MD: Four Courts Press, 1982.

Levinas, Emmanuel. *Totality and Infinity: An Essay on Exteriority.* Translated by Alphonso Lingis. Pittsburgh: Duquesne University Press, 1969.

Plato. *The Republic.* Translated by Paul Shorey. *The Collected Dialogues of Plato.* Edith Hamilton and Huntington Cairns, eds. Princeton, NJ: Princeton University Press, 1961.

Suchocki, Marjorie Hewitt. *The End of Evil: Process Eschatology in Historical Context.* Albany: State University of New York Press, 1988.

Teilhard de Chardin, Pierre. *The Phenomenon of Man.* Translated by Bernard Wall. New York: Harper & Row, 1959.

Whitehead, Alfred North. *Science and the Modern World.* New York: The Free Press, 1967.

———. *Adventures of Ideas.* New York: The Free Press, 1967.

———. *Process and Reality: An Essay in Cosmology.* Corrected Edition. David Ray Griffin and Donald W. Sherburne, eds. New York: The Free Press, 1978.

6 On Finding God in All Things

Michael Horace Barnes

There is a division among Christian theologians and philosophers on their approach to the world. Much of the time this division is not one of stark opposition but of different emphases. Mild or strong, however, the differences imply somewhat different ways of living the Christian life, even though both perspectives contribute to that overall life. One way to characterize the difference is through the use of the word "sacramental." Some are more likely to define sacraments as symbolic forms that mainly take us out of ordinary or profane life to discover the drama or beauty of the divine. Others are more likely to think of sacramental presence as a general truth about all of reality, dramatic or ordinary, beautiful or flawed.

Bernard Cooke is able to appreciate both perspectives, I am sure. But what I learned from him long ago and what I have continued to see in his life and activities, is a powerful sense of the pervading sacramental presence of God in all things. This article is one more attempt to describe that sense, to make the perspective available in one more form. It is best thought of, perhaps, as a small coda to Cooke's great historical-theological analysis in *The Distancing of God*.

Two Theological Cultures

Among Christian theologians there are two fairly distinct ways of relating to the world.. Before getting to specific cases, we can summarize the general differences: On the one hand is a positive openness to the world, as it were, including both the human social world in all its many forms and the cosmic world, and in spite of all the evils in both society and nature. On the other hand is a distinctly less worldly attitude. This attitude is manifest in various forms. One form is just an insistence that ordinary secular reality is indeed secular, profane, and ordinarily at least not the locale for discovering the power of God's grace. Another form is a deep pessimism about modern society. A third form, sometimes derived from the first two, is the search for a highly particularist interpretation of Christianity which segregates Christianity from the world. The division among theologians manifest itself on a variety of topics. In ecclesiology, as John Coleman once indicated, some look inward and seek community, others look outward promoting mission to the world. In terms of society, some take up the role of prophetic opponent of society, others seek to cooperate with it in pursuit of a public common good. In terms of salvation, some concentrate on following a path to another world, while others focus on hopes for humane worldly developments. In cosmological terms, some seek to escape the limits of matter, others see the entire physical universe as God's activity. In terms of history, some tend to ignore it or see it as at best merely profane, others celebrate it all as part of the divine purpose.

Karl Rahner provides useful language to label the two approaches. He speaks of a vertical dimension and a horizontal dimension to human experience (Rahner 1976, 295-313). The vertical dimension is a sense of the presence and activity of God. The horizontal dimension is nature and history. A radical horizontalism claims that there is *only* nature and history, that there is no vertical dimension at all. Rahner condemns this. But he nonetheless insists that the vertical can be found only mediated by the horizontal. It is at this point that the division between the two attitudes appears again. For some Christians it is difficult to find God or grace in the horizontal course of everyday history and nature; these Christians look upward, as it were, towards the extra grace that needs to be added to this fallen world, for the extra dimension of divine presence and power that profane or secular life seems to lack. Other Christians tend to see God already present in *all* things. They more readily agree with Rahner that the vertical can be found only mediated by the horizontal. They find God in all of nature and history as the empowering presence which enables the world in spite of itself to become more than itself.

Each side is likely to object to the other approach. Those who emphasize the vertical will perceive the horizontalists to have reduced the supernatural to the merely natural and worldly and historical. The horizontalists appear all too willing to skirt the edges of the radical horizontalism which Rahner condemns, thereby living a life which in practice is all too secular or worldly, regardless of the supposed theoretical legitimacy given that life by analyses like that of Rahner. If everything is sacred, if everything is graced, then nothing *in particular* is truly sacred.

On the other hand, those who emphasize the horizontal will see the verticalists as much too other-worldly and pessimistic about history, too antagonistic to the major processes of history, too critical of involvement in liberal or secular society to engage in the cooperation needed to improve this world, too exclusivist in their ecclesiology.

I would like first to discuss major differences between these two groups, to clarify what I mean by some of the language I have just used and explore some implications. This will consist of two sections. The first section will illustrate some vertical approaches. The second will describe a more world-oriented theology in terms that show a stronger potential for a deep Christian spirituality in this approach than might otherwise be evident. It will provide a theology of openness, if you will, based on the notion of the presence of God in all things. By temperament and theology I am enthusiastic about the world, both social and cosmic, so I may not represent the more particularist views adequately. In the end, however, the more important truth is that both those turned more towards the world and those turned more away from the world can work together in many practical ways. (Those devoted to Catholic Worker communities, for example, could in principle represent either group) (Doyle 2000).

Looking up and away from the World

The mildest of the ways of finding the secular world inadequate lies in a sense that the world is by itself profane and ungraced, or that the grace in it does not at least speak clearly and strongly enough to have an effect in our lives. In this case special religious symbols are needed to take us into the vertical dimension of life. Hans Urs von Balthasar insists on something like this approach to the world. Near the end of the first volume of von Balthasar's *The Glory of the Lord*, for example, he turns to a kind of mythical language which he says is necessary to appreciate what God and Christ are doing (Balthasar 1982, 661-65). He rather dramatically describes the conflict between Christ and the "powers" of the world. Von Balthasar summarizes scriptural statements about the spirit-like beings who represent a kind of demonic beauty from below, beings who struggle against subjection to the divine beauty from above. At the center of these powers is the Prince of this world. He is revealed and disarmed only by the power of the Cross, says von Balthasar.

This mythic imagery personifies powers and principalities that have a dire dominion over the course of events in the world. Our current secular and rationalistic culture leads even theologians to demythologize such language. Balthasar argues, however, that these images must not be demythologized. To do so "would mean transforming the rich depth of the Biblical understanding of the world and of salvation into a flat and moralising enlightenment." Similarly he argues that the many stories of Jesus's miracles should also not be demythologized. Each miracle is a sign of the fullness of power that will come at the end of time, and that will overcome the "powers and dominations." The miracles are important, not as "'disruptions' of the natural order but rather as signs of its restoration, which fundamentally occurs when Christ appears" (Balthasar 1982, 661, 1982, 661). Balthasar's overall message is that the drama of salvation described in these biblical stories, including the stark contrast between the unholy and the holy, must not be flattened out into theological generalities for the sake of rational or secular sensibilities.

Balthasar is not ultimately pessimistic about the world. In the section on dark powers, he speaks of the eventual subjection of the entire cosmos to Christ and its fulfillment in him at the end of time. And Balthasar hopes for a universal salvation. So in the end Balthasar expects a unifying fulfillment. But in the meantime, one must look to very particular events and places to find there the specially revealing presence of God. God's presence in *all* things is not always dramatic enough to be revelatory. To appreciate the divine drama one must hold to the stories that show the contrast between the worldly and the Godly, between the powers here below and the power of Christ.

In his well-received book, *After Virtue*, Alasdair MacIntyre approaches the world with much greater suspicion, illustrating those who severely criticize modern society and find little reason for hope in it. By the end of this book MacIntyre arrives at a rather striking conclusion. After a lengthy tour through theories of morality in the last century or so, he looks about him and sees a new dark ages enveloping society. In reaction he recommends the construction of "local forms of community within which civility and the intellectual and moral life can be sustained through the new dark ages which are already upon us" (MacIntyre 1981, 245). Clearly MacIntyre is not optimistic about social processes today. His response is to hunker down in the equivalent of monasteries while culture grows chaotic and the light fades. His approach has found favor with others who warn of the inability of modern secular society to listen to the Christian moral message and change their ways.

Less than ten years later, John Milbank published his *Theology and Social Theory*, an "onslaught" as he sums up his book, "against secular reason" (Milbank 1990, 432).[4] Where MacIntyre recommends a retreat from society, Milbank proposes to overcome the current social order, by replacing its dreary violence-based 'metanarrative' with a Christian metanarrative based on belief in an "original harmony." Milbank describes a conflict between two frameworks for understanding social reality. One, he says, has a "MacIntyrean voice," promoting the ancient Aristotelian idea of virtues. This voice speaks out against the second framework, a Nietzschean nihilism which finds no basis for social order other than power. Milbank clearly favors virtue over power, but says he distinguishes his own position from McIntyre's by uncovering a secular dimension in MacIntyre's Aristotelian virtues. The ancient notion of virtues, says Milbank, supposed that there is an "original violence" which must be overcome by reason and virtue. A truly Christian vision, Milbank argues, would begin not with belief in an original violence but with belief in a divine harmony more

---

[4] In Milbank's article "Out of the Greenhouse," 257-67 in *The Word Made Strange: Theology, Language, Culture* (Cambridge, MA: Blackwell, 1997), he rejects Teilhard's approach as too scientific and too humanistic. He has similar things to say about Reinhold Niebuhr's "Christian realism" in "The Poverty of Niebuhrism," 233-56.

fundamental than all else. In that case MacIntyre's appeal to classical virtues will not be enough. Nietzschean nihilism is able to deconstruct this vision, to show there is a belief in violence at its roots and thus to argue that this is but one more power-based perspective among many perspectives, none of them able to prevail in the end except through the application of power.

Only a Christian theological position, says Milbank, can overcome this nihilism. We must "reassert theology as a master discourse," because Christian theology is the discourse which "alone is the discourse of non-mastery," of peace and harmony (Milbank 1990, 5-6). Von Balthasar, MacIntyre, and Milbank, in spite of their differences, all find the secular world at best deficient in grace, seriously lacking in true virtue or vision. They are not alone in this (Barnes 1990, 27-52).[5]

Loving the World by Finding God in All Things

More familiar with and at home with the horizontalist position, the job I have assigned myself is to try to make more clear how this world and its history, including human history, is worthy of affection as God's work, as the ongoing sacrament of God's self-gift. Better yet, I would like to describe secular reality, that seemingly flat and rationalized secular order, in terms that are deeply theistic and Christian. To do this I will begin with ideas borrowed from de Caussade and from Teilhard de Chardin, borrowed and made more secular, I must confess. De Caussade's thought reflects a traditional notion of the presence of God in all things. Teilhard's links this to the history of the cosmos. These ideas will make it possible, I hope, to return to Rahner's notion of finding the vertical in the horizontal, and to see his position then not just as a rather abstract theological analysis but as a significant spiritual path for Christian life.

The name Pierre de Caussade, S.J., is familiar to generations of members of Roman Catholic religious orders. De Caussade's treatise *Abandonment to Divine Providence,* first written in the early eighteenth century, continues in use still today as a source of spiritual guidance (de Caussade 1921). The attitude therein is perhaps too passive, even

---

[5] I omit here a discussion of others who seek somewhat similarly to distance themselves from the secular world, including Hauerwas, Baxter, Lindbeck, and to a lesser degree McClendon.

quietist. Written for religious seeking the path of perfection apart from the world, it is also rather unworldly. Finally, it is rather individualistic; while the path of perfection may be found within religious community, in the end de Caussade speaks as though one has to walk this path by oneself. Behind these flaws, however, if I may judge them as such, is the tradition of finding God in *all* things. Here are words from de Caussade:

> All creatures that exist are in the hands of God. The action of the creature can only be perceived by the senses, but faith sees in all things the action of the Creator. It believes that in Jesus Christ all things live, and that His divine operation continues to the end of time, embracing the passing moment and the smallest created atom in its hidden life and mysterious action. . . . . If we could lift the veil, and if we were attentive and watchful God would continually reveal Himself to us, and we should see His divine action in everything that happened to us and rejoice in it. At each successive occurrence we should exclaim: 'It is the Lord,' and we should accept every fresh circumstance as a gift of God (1921: 15) (de Caussade 1921, 15).

We can translate this sacramental awareness of the presence of God in all things into a more worldly, more activist, and less individualistic form. Begin with a sense that human life is social, formed within communities and their traditions, developed through social interaction. A theological perspective more cautious about the world will emphasize life in the Church. It will perceive the presence of God in the Church, the work of God in the inner workings of the Church. A theological perspective more open to the world will emphasize the presence and activity of God not just in the Church but in all of human sociality. Every community, every tradition, every history, in fact the entire history of humankind, is a response, consciously or not, to the single all-embracing and powerful presence of God (Himes and Pope 1996).[6]

---

[6] The festschrift for Michael Buckley, S.J. is entitled *Finding God in All Things*, an appropriate title for, it is an appropriate title to honor one whose writings often focus on God's presence. There is a small irony, however, in that even where some of the articles point to Buckley's insistence on the presence of God in everything,

A full theology of the Church would be required to develop the distinction between the presence of God in the Church and the presence of God in the entire history of humankind. I will not attempt that, however important it may be. A theology of revelation would have a great deal to elaborate also. Nor will I attempt that. The goal here is to discuss the *attitude* of worldliness, and to show that it need not be assimilated exclusively to a flat, secular, enlightenment approach.

One way to do this is to take fully seriously what de Caussade says about the presence of God. This implies that everything in social reality is always already overflowing with the presence and power of God. In de Caussade's spirituality one should be ready to recognize that a note posted on a bulletin board represents the will of God; a meeting of a school organization is the presence of God. The grand flow of history, the course of national development, the pattern of the spread of a religion or an ideology—all these are within the scope of God's intent and all in some way are also responses to the active presence of God. When a few people decide to devise a liberation theology to change the direction of a society, they are not moving into a secular realm bereft of God. They are moving to where God has always already been, with the poor and deprived certainly but also with the rich, in the midst of all the social interactions that have ever taken place.

Teilhard takes us to a similar kind of awareness, perhaps once again a deeply Jesuit awareness of the presence of God in all things. Though his overall perspective on the universe may be flawed in many ways, there is an unavoidable basic truth for a Christian in his claim that the entire universe is what God is doing. This activity of God stretches back well over ten billion years and encompasses billions of galaxies. It includes the gradual evolution of matter-energy, then of life, then of conscious life, and at least on this tiny planet of self-reflective consciousness—spirit—from simpler forms of consciousness. All of human history is incredibly insignificant on this cosmic scale. At the

---

they select those things that a von Balthasar might point to rather than emphasize God's presence everywhere. William C. Spohn, for example, follows Jonathan Edwards in perceiving the beauty of God in certain things (251) and mentions God in nature only in passing (257-58) near the end of his article. It is difficult to find direct discussions in this volume about finding God in truly *all* things.

same time this long history of the cosmos is Creation. It is what God is doing and has been doing from the beginning of the universe. What God is doing on this scale overwhelms the mind and imagination both. The brief little history of Judaism and Jesus and the Church are less than a flicker of a spark amid the glow of billions of galaxies. All the same, from the Christian perspective of Teilhard de Chardin, and even more so from that of Karl Rahner, the Incarnation of God in Jesus on this speck of a planet in a flyby historical moment contains the basic truth and meaning of the whole of Creation. God who created a universe other than Herself, from the first and constantly calls it back into unity with Herself.

On such a scale the failings of our society and of every society take on a different perspective. These failings, along with whatever accomplishments, are somehow also part of the larger story of what God is doing. The distinction between this worldly and evolutionary presence of God and the presence of God in the Church is still a significant one. But the distinction need not be a distinction between ordinary places where God's presence is only flat and secular, and the ecclesial places where God is specially dramatic and effective. Such a distinction *can* be made; it is legitimate. Balthasar's theology is not mistaken. Rahner also declares that the special historical moment of Jesus and the historical reality of the Church have in fact proved to be the way that the ultimate cosmic truth, including the human place in that cosmos, has been revealed.[7] Yet what it has revealed is that "to the eyes of faith," as de Caussade has it, God is effectively and dramatically present in *everything*, from the tiniest atom to ordinary daily events to the cosmic whole.

---

[7] For a general discussion see Karl Rahner, *Foundations of Christian Faith: An Introduction to the Idea of Christianity*, trans. William V. Dych (NY: Crossroad, 1982), chapter, especially section 4, "On the Relationship between the History of Universal, Transcendental revelation and Special, Categorical Revelation," 153-161. Or see a specific application in Rahner's *Theological Investigations*, Vol. XIII, tran. David Bourke (NY: Crossroad, 1983), "Remarks on the Importance of the History of Jesus for Catholic Dogmatics," 201-12,

Horizontalism without Illusion

Those critical of a worldly horizontalism may add another complaint to those cited earlier, that only a Polyanna or romantic would look at the social and natural order and fail to see that something is seriously wrong. In this century in particular the Holocausts in Germany and Poland and, later, Cambodia, as well as the horrendous death toll in Stalinist Russia and Maoist China, should severely restrict any optimism about the power of human beings to bring about secular good, or about the power of cultural development to lead us beyond great evil. Clearly a religious vision and the power of God are needed to heal the secular scabs and prevent new cancers. As for nature itself, it does provide a glorious general revelation of the grandeur and creativity of God. But nature, as John Stuart Mill once remarked, does such things to us all as only the greatest human monster would do (Mill 1969, 27-31). Yet there are examples of a horizontalism that are neither polyannish nor romantic. Two quick examples can illustrate this openness to and appreciation of the world.

The first is an openness to the social reality in spite of its serious flaws, in spite of what Baum called "social sin." In a recent issue of *Jesuit Journeys*, an article on John Staudenmaier, S.J., tells of his anger at American culture (Nero 1999, 12-15). He lived for a few years on the Pine Ridge Reservation in South Dakota. The Lakota Sioux culture there was fragmented and crippled. Unemployment, alcoholism, and spousal abuse were common. Staudenmaier attributed this sad cultural state to the impact of Western European expansion over the many decades. Then later, during the Vietnam war as it happened, he moved near St. Louis. There he saw neighboring farm lands being torn up to make houses for workers at a nearby aerospace plant building planes to help kill Vietnamese. "The culture I had returned to made me want to vomit," said Staudenmaier.

But Staudenmaier changed his mind. "I heard Jesus in my prayers and his message was clear: 'I do not hate this culture. I am devoted to this culture every bit as much as the Lakota culture you've just been immersed in for a time.'" (13). Staudenmaier continued: "Theologically, any part of reality is worthy of affection. So Staudenmaier experienced the two responses to culture, both rejection and acceptance. (Whether we judge his conversion to a new openness to society to be correct depends on which of the two types of sacramental conscious-ness predominates in us.)

Staudenmaier's later judgment is certainly not the only legitimate response to modern culture. Ongoing prophetic challenges to social failings are needed constantly. But the challenges can be made with different degrees of openness to even the seriously sinful social order. Such challenges may be more effective if they are accompanied by an optimism that cultures can develop, that any society can learn eventu-ally to respond positively to a moral challenge. Western culture has done some good things, such as abolishing slavery and working still to diminish racism and sexism. A Christian who approaches culture critically but with openness to the possibility that compassion and justice can be found and developed there will, I think, be more pro-ductive of the good and a better witness to the good than one who sees mainly the unholy in the world, though prophetic challenges to culture remain necessary also.

An illustration of openness to the cosmos appears in Teilhard de Chardin's thought. He is well known, of course, for his rather romantic celebration of cosmic evolution as a God-driven Christ-centered process. But less well known, perhaps, is his response to the many natural evils that are part of the cosmos. In the Divine Milieu he faces directly the human loss, pain, and death that occur as part of the natural order. His response to this evil is twofold. On the one hand the Christian is always to oppose evil. On the other when evil comes nonetheless, the hand of God is there also. He applies this to himself.

> Grant that when my hour has come that I may recognize you under the appearance of each alien or hostile force that seems bent on destroying or uprooting me. When the signs of age begin to mark my body (and still more my mind); when the illness that is to diminish me or carry me off strikes from without or is born within me; when the painful moment comes at which I suddenly awaken to the fact that I am ill or growing old; and above all at that last moment when I feel I am losing hold of myself and am absolutely passive within the hands of the great unknown forces that have formed me: in all those dark moments, O God, grant that I may understand that it is you (provided only my faith is strong enough) who are painfully parting the fibres of my being in order

to penetrate to the very marrow of my substance and bear me away within yourself (Chardin 1965, 89-90).

Perhaps this still deserves the label of "romantic." But this openness to the world of nature is not based on the sort of romanticism which sees only loveliness in nature. Teilhard deliberately faced its harsh consequences, and yet insisted that this too is somehow what God is doing.

The prayer of Teilhard reminds us that an awareness of the presence of God does not provide a comfortingly pious fog to blur all pain. It is certainly legitimate to find great comfort and serenity from a sense that God is in even the harshest moments. Yet the gospels do not describe God's presence at Gethsemane and Golgotha as a source of sweet relief. Likewise God was at Dachau and Treblinka, in the murderous Great Leap Forward of Mao, in the killing fields of Cambodia, in the ethnic cleansing in the Balkans. For that matter, even in the explicitly religious places in life, where one might go to find the divine when ordinary history and nature do not seem to provide this, there can be evil. The Church in history is not without sin. But God is there also. All things fall within the sustaining and empowering presence of God, and somehow within God's ultimate intent.

To say quite seriously that great evils in nature and history also fall within the scope of God's presence and intent raises two problems. The first is a kind of fatalism or determinism. If God is doing *all* things, what is left of human freedom and responsibility? The second problem is the traditional issue of theodicy. How can we say that great evils are within the scope of God's intent?[8] An answer to these questions that is relevant to the context here can be found in traditional theology of God, so familiar as not to require repeating, yet worth repeating nonetheless at least as a reminder.

In Christian theology God is Creator, Sustainer, Providential Orderer of all things without exception, encompassing even truly free human

---

[8] An important response to this is Terry Tilley, *The Evils of Theodicy* (Washington, D.C.: Georgetown University Press, 1991), in which Tilley argues that we ought not to do theodicy. There are no reliable answers, and the attempt to create some intellectual solution diverts us from the consciousness and activities that do count: seeking justice, caring for the sick and the poor, etc. My response here takes a different tack but is not at odds with his.

decisions somehow within the scope of the divine intention. Teilhard and Rahner remind us that God is always somehow empowering the universe to become more than itself over the billions of years of cosmic evolution. Were God an extraordinarily powerful finite agent, a being among other beings, contending with them for authority and power over specific events, God could readily be thought of as a threat to human freedom. But Christian theology can assert that God is overwhelmingly and intimately present in all things precisely because that theology says that God is absolutely Infinite. The real theological problem this presents to a theist considering the question of God's power is how creation is possible at all. If we assert that the universe is real, that it does indeed have its own real order of secondary causality and is not just a shadow-show, then the old theological conundrum appears: there is something that God is not, which is the universe; therefore it seems that God cannot be infinite. The genuine existence and causal efficacy of the created universe can be reconciled with God's absolute infinity only by an admission we cannot comprehend the infinite. How God acts to create out of nothing except divine power a real universe that is not God is not comprehensible; how God maintains a universe which is a process of development is not comprehensible; how God empowers that creation to continuously become more than it had so far been is not comprehensible.[9]

A theodicy tries to explain how or why God would allow evil to be part of creation. Perhaps such attempts at intellectual solutions to the problem of evil may be of comfort to some people or have some apologetic value, yet these are also attempts to comprehend the incomprehensible. Christian theology can only say it does know that God is Creator of all out of nothing, and that the universe and its development are what God has been doing all along. If we can affirm

---

[9] It is perhaps redundant to refer to works which confirm the place of God's incomprehensibility in Christian tradition. But as philosophy has lost its hold as prerequisite for theology, this tradition has dimmed for many. Karl Rahner's three lectures on the concept of mystery have been influential, as in his *Theological Investigations*, Vol. IV (Baltimore: Helicon, 1966), 36-73. He reaffirmed these ideas more succinctly in "Thomas Aquinas on the Incomprehensibility of God" in David Tracy, ed., *Celebrating the Medieval Heritage*, Journal of Religion, Vol. 58 Supplement, 1978, S107-S125. For a whole book devoted mostly to this topic see David Burrell, *Analogy and Philosophical Language* (New Haven: Yale University Press, 1973).

that this universe which God is doing is a true set of secondary causal patterns, even if we cannot explain how this is possible, then we can affirm human freedom also. In fact we could go further and with Rahner argue that we are most dependent on God precisely when we exercise the genuine conscious freedom that God is now and always empowering us to have (Rahner 1966, 12).[10] Every place where humans are deciding things, God is there sustaining and empowering. Everyplace where people are acting, whether for good or for evil, God is there sustaining and empowering. In every event of nature, whether it heals or nourishes or whether it devastates and kills, God is there sustaining and empowering.

This attempt at a theological answer may seem to imply all the more strongly, however, that there is something sadly deficient about the whole worldly or horizontal theology. Analyses of the absolute infinity and incomprehensibility of God surely vindicate Balthasar's claim that revelatory power lies in drama and in beauty rather than through abstract rationality, in special and particular moments in history rather than in the general presence of God in the world. To respond to this I would like to go back to the word I used much earlier to distinguish between a horizontal and a vertical approach. The word is "experience." It is a question of whether it is possible to *experience* the presence of God in all things. If it is not, then Balthasar is alone correct. If it is, however, then Balthasar's approach is only part of the truth, a valid alternative to a more worldly approach. Where von Balthasar and Rahner would agree, for example, is that the specific historic moments of Jewish history and scripture, of Jesus' life and death, of the formation of the Church, have revealed what God is doing not just in human history but in the entire cosmic story of which human history is a part. In spite of Milbank's mistaken claims to the contrary, Rahner places great emphasis on the necessity of history, of concrete categorical mediations, in particular the event of the Incarnation in Jesus (Milbank 1990, 222-223).[11] But from this

[10] "For a really Christian doctrine of the relationship of the world to God, the autonomy of the creature does not grow in inverse but in direct proportion to the degree of the creature's dependence on, and belonging to, God." See also Vol. I, 1961, p. 162 for a similar statement.

[11] "Karl Rahner fears to entrust the supernatural to the merely historical, to the succession of human actions and human images." (223). The context is a discussion

starting point of faith, the entire cosmos along with all the seemingly secular moments of human history can then be experienced vividly in all its aspects as God's close and dramatic presence.

There is no need to desecularize the cosmos and history in order to find God there. A horizontalist attitude should not have to ecclesialize or liturgicize the world to reveal its sacramentality. The world's form of God-presence is none of these, though Church and liturgy may provide contexts for learning to recognize God in the secular. Every secular act can be God-filled without ceasing to be secular or worldly.

Habitual awareness of this all-pervasive God-presence does not come easily. Like all habits, awareness of the presence of God must be cultivated. Perhaps the reality of God's presence will ordinarily be forgotten in daily moments, and be there only as a presence which *can* be remembered and experienced again. Even then the presence of God in the ordinary things of life may not strike the person with anything like the vividness of a religious experience evoked by explicitly deliberate religious rituals or readings or reflections. Church, sacraments, prayer will remain the fonts of religious awareness. But the awareness can flow into every corner of life.

Ironically, it is the contemplative tradition developed in monastic contexts, highly unworldly contexts, that is helpful to explore this. De Caussade's book represents many books about finding the presence of God in all things. The mystical awareness of God that lies beyond the dark night of the senses and soul, beyond all images and ideas whatsoever, points to a God that can nonetheless be *experienced* as intimate and all-embracing presence. This experience of God finds nothing devoid of God's intense presence, no tiniest place, no simplest time, no most prosaic or even most horrendous event. The world *is* charged with the grandeur of God, all of it. Guided, enlightened, and inspired by the power of those special and dramatic events or things or places that in the actual history of the world have revealed the cosmic truth, it is then possible to perceive God also in those events and things and places that otherwise would have appeared only as a fully horizontal flatness. The daily world of work and politics, of social negotiations

---

of human nature and the gratuity of grace rather than on historicity as such, but Milbank consistently overlooks Rahner's emphasis on the necessity of the categorical, i.e., the concrete natural and historical.

over values, of buying and selling and building and tearing down, are also full of God's presence. This daily world does not so readily invite one, perhaps, to experience it precisely as an experience of God's presence. But this world is God's presence also. To turn away from it as from a merely flat and secular reality is at least partly mistaken. It overlooks the sacramentality of all creation and history.

References

Balthasar, Hans Urs von. 1982. *The Glory of the Lord: A Theological Aesthetics*, Vol. I Seeing the Form. San Francisco: Ignatius Press, 1982. 661-65.

Barnes, Michael. 1996. "Community, Clannishness, and the Common Good," James Donahue and M. Theresa Moser, eds., *Religion, Ethics, and the Common Good.* Mystic, CT: Twenty-Third Publications.

Burrell, David. 1973. *Analogy and Philosophical Language.* New Haven: Yale University Press.

Himes, Michael J. and Stephen J. Pope. 1996. *Finding God in All Things.* New York: Crossroad.

MacIntyre, Alasdair. 1981. *After Virtue: A Study in Moral Theory.* Notre Dame, IN: University of Notre Dame Press.

Milbank, John. 1990. *Theology and Social Theory: Beyond Secular Reason.* Cambridge, MA: Blackwell.

————. 1997. "Out of the Greenhouse," 257-67 in *The Word Made Strange: Theology, Language, Culture.* Cambridge, MA: Blackwell. He rejects Teilhard's approach as too scientific and too humanistic. He has similar things to say about Reinhold Niebuhr's "Christian realism" in "The Poverty of Niebuhrism," 233-56.

Mill, John Stuart. 1969. *Three Essays on Religion.* New York: Greenwood Press.

Nero, Phil. 1999. "In Search of the Holy Dark," *Jesuit Journeys.* (The Wisconsin province magazine). Summer, 12-15.

Rahner, Karl. 1966 three lectures on the concept of mystery have been influential, as in his *Theological Investigations.* Vol. IV. Baltimore: Helicon, 36-73.

————. 1976. *Theological Investigations*, Vo. 14, Ch. 18, "The Church's Commission to Bring Salvation and the Humanization of the World," 295-313. New York: Seabury Press.

————. 1978 "Thomas Aquinas on the Incomprehensibility of God" in David Tracy, ed., *Celebrating the Medieval Heritage*, Journal of Religion, Vol. 58 Supplement, S107-S125.

————. 1982. *Foundations of Christian Faith: An Introduction to the Idea of Christianity*, trans. William V. Dych. New York: Crossroad. "On the Relationship between the History of Universal, Transcendental revelation and Special, Categorical Revelation," 153-161.

————. 1983. *Theological Investigations.* Vol. XIII, tran. David Bourke. New York: Crossroad. "Remarks on the Importance of the History of Jesus for Catholic Dogmatics," 201-12,

Teilhard de Chardin, Pierre, S.J. 1965. *The Divine Milieu.* NY: Harper Torchbooks.

Tilley, Terry. 1991. *The Evils of Theodicy.* Washington, D.C.: Georgetown University Press.

7 Two Revisionist Christologies of Presence Roger Haight and Piet Schoonenberg

William P. Loewe

The past half century has witnessed a paradigm shift in Roman Catholic Christology. In 1951, the fifteen hundredth anniversary of the Council of Chalcedon sparked a flurry of scholarly activity which brought to light the docetic tendencies of the then-current neoscholastic manuals and set Christology the task of recovering the full humanity of Jesus (Bacht and Grillmeier 1951-1954; Rahner 1961). Pursuit of this task began as a corrective movement within the neo-scholastic paradigm in which the dogmas of Nicaea, Chalcedon, and III Constantinople set the framework, terms, and questions for Christology. Exegetes began retrieving those features of Jesus' humanity, particularly his human ignorance, clearly portrayed in the New Testament but minimized in subsequent theology (Brown 1967), while theologians turned to contemporary philosophical developments to reconcile those newly highlighted features both with classical dogma and with such scholastic theses regarding the perfection of Christ's humanity as the perichoresis of his two natures, his human impeccability, and his this-worldly enjoyment of the beatific vision (Gutwenger 1960; Rahner 1966; Lonergan 1967).

When in the mid-seventies, however, Catholic theologians began drawing upon the results of historical-Jesus research (Kasper 1976; Küng 1967; Schillebeeckx 1974), the wineskin of the neo-scholastic treatises burst, and since then subsequent christologies have taken on a new shape (Galvin 1994). Whereas the Christology of the manuals was basically commentary on Chalcedon, the new Christologies offer a genetic and evaluative account of the entire Christological tradition from Jesus' ministry, death, and resurrection onward, with a view toward mediating the revelatory and redemptive import of Jesus Christ into the contemporary situation. Within this new paradigm the classical dogmas of Nicea and Chalcedon find themselves relocated as particular moments within the ongoing tradition, normative moments to be sure, but no longer paradigmatically defining the entire Christological enterprise. Thus relocated, classical Christological dogma requires interpretation, while that interpretation in turn comprises only one task within a more broadly conceived christological project.

In some instances the interpretations of classical dogma at which the newer christologies arrive are markedly revisionist, so much so that they prompt one to ask whether they are not in fact proposing a unitarian conception of God and a fully, if merely, human Jesus. One recent work that prompts this question is Roger Haight's *Jesus Symbol of God* (Haight 1999). In his book, Haight elaborates a Christology of presence strikingly similar to that proposed three and a half decades earlier by Piet Schoonenberg (1911-1999). Although Schoonenberg seems to have exerted little direct influence on Haight,[12] the similarity is such that *Jesus Symbol of God* may be fairly read as a recontextualization and updating of the early phase of a project Schoonenberg initiated in a paper delivered to a group of Dutch theologians in 1964 and which he carried forward in numerous articles thereafter.

As a substantive example of the new Christological paradigm that recapitulates several of the major currents through which the paradigm has emerged, Haight's book especially commends itself by a thoroughgoing methodological explicitness. Not only does Haight devote his first two chapters to a clear and ample exposition of the method he will follow, a method he had previously worked out at length in a

[12] In a discussion of his book at the 1999 Annual Meeting of the Catholic Theological Society of America, upon hearing a summary of Schoonenberg' early Christological moves, Haight remarked that "Schoonenberg sounds pretty good." A lack of direct influence is also suggested by the absence of Schoonenberg's works, particularly his article entitled "Spirit Christology and Logos Christology" (*Bijdragen* 38; 1977, 350-375) from the sources cited in Haight's "The Case for Spirit Christology" (*TS* 53: 1992, 257-287).

work devoted to fundamental theology entitled *Dynamics of Theology* (Haight 1990), but at each crucial stage of his argument he lays out fully the methodological principles informing the particular move he is making. There is no obfuscation, no sleight of hand, no ducking of issues in this work. This methodological responsibility in turn renders the work tightly coherent. Haight's opening proposal concerning the method and structure of Christology (Part I) finds both exemplar and warrant in an analysis of New Testament sources (Part II), thoroughly controls his review of the classical tradition (Part III), and comes to full fruition in the several chapters of his constructive synthesis (Part IV) .

Haight's book is also acutely responsive to the contemporary context in and for which he practices theology. Construing this context as postmodern (24-25) he exhibits a deep concern to serve a world church aware in an entirely new way of the challenge of global religious pluralism. In his view "perhaps the most catalytic of the Christological questions being asked today concerns the relation of Jesus Christ to other religions and mediations of ultimate reality" (26). Equally important to his project is a concern for social justice as ingredient to the church's redemptive mission. He notes that "although human suffering cannot be reduced to social suffering …. [t]he negativity of human existence reaches its most mysterious, widespread, and scandalous form in social suffering and oppression imposed by human beings on other human beings" (25). Hence "Jesus cannot be Christ and salvation cannot be real without having some bearing on this situation" (26).

These strengths suggest *Jesus, Symbol of God* as a good candidate for conversation about the interpretation of classical dogma within the new Christological paradigm. In what follows, after an overview of Haight's work, the present essay will lay out the lineaments of Schoonenberg's Christology in order to establish the continuity of Haight's project with it; the essay will then attend to some critical issues, material and methodological, raised by both authors.

Jesus, Symbol of God—An Overview

Like E. Schillebeeckx, Haight identifies Jesus as the bearer of God's salvation for Christians and locates the genesis of Christology in the Christian experience of salvation (Haight 1999, 14; for the reference to Schillebeeckx, see Haight 1992, 264), especially as that experience was celebrated ritually (180-181). The Christian experience of salvation in Jesus shares a common structure with all religious experience. The infinite God is both utterly transcendent and yet, as creator, immanent throughout created reality. As infinite, God cannot be the immediate object of human knowing; human knowledge of God is always mediated through something other than God. Media of this knowledge function as symbols: they participate in and render present to human consciousness that which they symbolize. In so doing symbols exhibit a dialectical quality according to which they both are and are not the reality they symbolize. As finite creatures, they are not God, pointing away from themselves to God, and yet they are the locus of encounter with the reality of God, drawing human consciousness into depths of reality otherwise inaccessible.

In constructing this experiential and universalistic notion of revelation, Haight insists that it constitutes a symbolic realism in that symbolically mediated religious experience has a cognitive dimension whereby it establishes a "real contact" (5) with transcendent reality. This structure of religious experience is, as John Hick suggests (13), common to the world's religions, and within Christianity it operates with Jesus of Nazareth as its central concrete symbol to provide the element of historical continuity as well as the standard of orthodoxy for Christian belief and theology.

Beliefs, as the human interpretive response to the divine self-communication, are integral to religious experience and they partake of its symbolic quality. As a human interpretive response, however, they always reflect the historical and cultural context in which they arise and function, and hence the beliefs of a historical tradition are necessarily pluralistic and subject to change. Faith, the existential response to revelation, remains a constant, and while faith never exists apart from its expression in beliefs, those beliefs have no independent cognitive status. They are not to be confused with objective knowledge, a term Haight generally reserves for verifiable knowledge of this-worldly reality, and their validity consists in their ability to mediate the revelatory encounter which evokes faith. Revelation is therefore never a source of objective information that might serve as the basis for further deductive reasoning about the transcendent. Haight insists on this point: while faith and revelation are inseparable from belief, one must beware of "belief masquerading as faith" (Haight 1990, 76).

Thus Haight explicates how Jesus bears God's salvation by proposing a theory of religious experience, revelation, and faith centered on the category of symbol, a category which he construes eclectically by drawing together elements from Karl Rahner, Paul Tillich, Mircea Eliade, and Paul Ricoeur. The notion of symbol in turn serves to define the status and limits of religious and theological discourse as always symbolic and never "objective."

With these foundations secured, Haight turns to the biblical sources of Christology. Since it is Jesus who is the central symbol of Christianity, a Christology "from below" has an interest in the results of historical Jesus research. While historical research is not the ground of faith, it can offer "critical leverage over the multiplicity of interpretations of Jesus" (87) and, hermeneutically appropriated, its results can disclose possibilities for Christian living. Hence Haight scans the major contemporary historical images of Jesus—prophet, teacher, healer, savior/liberator—and offers a summary centering around the prophet who proclaims and enacts the reign of God.[13] A separate chapter sketches the character of God as it emerges from Jesus' teaching and actions; systematically, it is this image/perception of God which will inform the rest of the book. Turning to the symbol of resurrection as the bridge between Jesus' ministry and early Christologies, Haight builds on the work of E. Schillebeeckx and P. Carnley to propose an account of the genesis of belief in Jesus' resurrection in which faith,

---

[13] While Haight writes that "I do not mean to recommend harmonization," (78), he does seem to give short shrift to the conflictual state of contemporary historical Jesus research with regard to sources, method, and results and indeed to choose one image, that of prophet, as central. This impression is reinforced when he later writes "the historical person of Jesus as he is depicted by the consensus of historians must enter into the imagination in any portrayal of Jesus Christ" (428). At the present stage of what is called the "Third Quest" for the historical Jesus, one may well ask where such a consensus lies.

hope, and Eucharistic celebration play a role in engendering the experience of Jesus as raised and exalted, alive with God. Concluding his section on biblical sources, Haight offers a rapid survey of New Testament Christologies as warrants for his argument for the necessity and appropriateness of Christological pluralism.

When he takes up the classical patristic tradition, Haight's foundational and methodological positions come to the fore. With regard to the dogmas of Nicaea and Chalcedon, their formulation is so historically conditioned as to require extensive revision in the present context. While their enduring point remains valid, their actual content is hopelessly compromised by their context. Thus, they rest on a pre-critical reading of the scriptures. They disregard the symbolic character of revelation and render it a source of objective information. They derive from a culture that was extensively populated by superterrestrial beings. They violate the pluralism of the New Testament which forbids making any single theology (John) normative. They exhibit a grievous error in hypostasizing the figurative metaphors whereby the attributes and activity of God are literarily personified—particularly, of course, the figure of God's Logos. Thus, in their formulation the classic dogmas step beyond the bounds of the kind of knowing and discourse generated and validated by religious experience. Furthermore, it is apodictic for Haight that modern historical consciousness and the historical imagination to which it gives rise simply preclude any notion of Jesus' personal preexistence, a notion that he also deems incompatible with Chalcedon's affirmation of Jesus' consubstantiality with us (175 n.79, 459 n. 67).

What remains of the classic conciliar dogmas is their point. What we are to retain of the dogmas of the full divinity of Christ, the Trinity, and the hypostatic union is the point that in the human being, Jesus, Christians really encounter nothing less than God's saving presence. The man Jesus is for Christians the symbol of God.

In his final section Haight works out what it means for Jesus to bear God's salvation today, appealing heavily to liberation theologies. With regard to other religions, he argues that, formally, the symbolic character of religious experience, and, materially, the benevolent character of the God of Israel whose saving presence Christians encounter in Jesus, combine to render it antecedently probable from a Christian viewpoint that adherents of other religious traditions encounter God in other saviors who symbolize God's saving presence for those traditions and who like Jesus are also universally relevant. His penultimate chapter on "The Divinity of Christ" offers a re-reading of both Logos and Spirit Christologies to make the point he derived from his critique of the classical tradition, and a concluding chapter recommends a trinitarian theology from below in which, critiquing Rahner's "jump" from an economic to an immanent Trinity (487), Haight forswears speculation about distinct differentiations within the Godhead as a matter for the affirmation or denial of which insufficient data are available, in order to return the doctrine to its experiential roots: "God symbolized as Father, Son, and Spirit is one God who is loving creator, and who was present and active for the salvation of humankind in Jesus, and who is consistently present in the Christian community, in individuals within it, and, indeed, in all human beings" (485).

Piet Schoonenberg: Initial Position

Piet Schoonenberg's project took its impetus from a pastoral problem. Many Christians, he observes, no longer find their faith conviction consonant with the image of Jesus as both God and man, one Christ in two natures, on which they have been raised (Schoonenberg "God and Man," 50). Tracing the root of the problem to what he called the Chalcedonian two-nature pattern or model (51-53), he discovers that pattern to be conditioned by a gradual post-biblical process in which the title "Son of God" absorbed the variety of New Testament titles for Christ. One aspect of that title, union with the Father, received emphasis and further elaboration through a hypostatization of the Logos of John's prologue. This step was greatly facilitated by Origen and his middle-Platonic speculations regarding the preexistence of souls (55), and once taken, it led directly to Nicaea's oneness of being with the Father. Once the preexistence of the Word as person was thus established, the premise was in place that ruled the Alexandrian-Antiochene debate heading into the Chalcedonian settlement. Schoonenberg notes that although the dogmatic formula of Chalcedon does not explicitly qualify the person of Christ as divine (74), Alexandrian dominance of the post-Chalcedonian interpretation of the council completed the pattern in which Jesus was identified as divine person, eternal

Son, Second Person of the Trinity. The logical outcome of this neo-Chalcedonian pattern of interpretation was Leontius of Byzantium's notion of the enhypostasis of Christ's human nature in the divine hypostasis of the Word (57).

Moving back to the New Testament, Schoonenberg proposes that it evidently presents Jesus as one person and human, and on that basis he lays down the principle that no New Testament text may be interpreted in such a manner as to compromise Jesus' full humanity. Having employed that principle to reinterpret the classic pre-existence texts as referring to Jesus' central place in the divine plan as the one predestined from before creation, to whom all is ordered, and in whom God is present with redemptive fullness (80), Schoonenberg proceeds to reverse the traditional notion of enhypostasis: in the human person Jesus, God's previously impersonal Logos achieved personal existence (87). In order to reconcile this position with the doctrine of the Trinity Schoonenberg appeals to the logic of revelation. Since revelation occurs concretely in the human being Jesus, it is only in him that God is known as the one who is for us Father, Son and Spirit, so that we can neither affirm nor deny that God exists as triune apart from Jesus' appearance (82). At the same time we must be prepared to entertain the possibility of becoming in God. By the logic of revelation we know the Word only in the pre-history of Christ and we know it as person only in Christ; hence, revelation suggests that the Word achieves a special relation as person vis à vis the Father through becoming the human person Jesus (86-87). Finally, to capture Jesus' difference-in-identity with us, Schoonenberg proffers the category of Jesus as the "eschatological man," the human being in whom God dwelt with unique revelatory and salvific fullness (96-97). Hence Schoonenberg's title: rather than continuing to speak of Jesus as "God and man," he concluded that it is theologically and pastorally preferable to speak of "God in man," to replace a "two natures Christology" with a "Christology of presence."

In a lecture entitled "From a Two-Nature Christology to a Christology of Presence" (Schoonenberg "From a Two-Nature ...") delivered at Villanova University in the year between the appearance of the Dutch and English versions of *The Christ*, Schoonenberg refines and expands the position advanced in that book in several ways. First, he places greater emphasis on a dilemma which he claims issued from the "Chalcedonian pattern." If one begins from a divine person with two natures, then either one reduces the human nature to merely instrumental status which, in Apollinarian fashion, lacks a subject for human consciousness and thus denies Jesus' full consubstantiality with us, or, recognizing that that consubstantiality requires that one posit a human psychological and ontological subject in Christ, one divides Christ into two persons (222, 224-225). In more popular terms, one arrives at either a disguised Christ or a divided Christ (226).

Second, Schoonenberg revises and nuances his account of the emergence of the two- nature model, which he now lays to the account of two factors. First, while the entire New Testament is at one in attributing all that is divine and all that is human to Jesus, it is only with the transition from Semitic to Hellenistic thinking evident in the latest layer of the New Testament tradition, when Jesus begins to be acclaimed as God, that a note of duality is struck between the two sets of attributes. Second, this note of duality still falls short of two-nature language, and the latter only becomes necessary when, after the Wisdom hymns of the Hellenistic mission and John's Prologue have developed the theme of prophetic sending through poetic personifications of the figures of Wisdom and the Logos, these personifications are conceived ontologically in the Hellenistic tradition from Justin on, yielding the problematic notion of a preexistent divine person which generates the dilemma discussed above (229-231).

Even thereafter, however, the developing tradition retained grounds for acknowledging Jesus as a human person. Leo's *Tome* on the eve of Chalcedon attributes Christ's human actions to his human nature. Chalcedon's text does not explicitly deny that Christ was a human person, and III Constantinople attributes to him human operations of intellect and will (228). Nonetheless, this possibility is foreclosed and Hellenism triumphs with the dominance of the Alexandrian line of interpretation culminating with Leontius' anhypostatic human nature of Christ.

Third, although only of incidental interest to the present inquiry, it should be noted that in the Villanova lecture, after again proposing a reversal of Leontius and a Christology of God's eschatological fullness in the human person Jesus, Schoonenberg shifts from the biblical-theological categories with which he had filled in his portrait of Jesus in *The Christ* (Schoonenberg "God and Man") to a fuller appropriation of the concrete historical lineaments of Jesus' ministry yielded by the "New Quest" (Schoonenberg "From a Two-Nature Christology," 238-241).

Magisterial Response

Without naming individual theologians or works, the Congregation for the Doctrine of the Faith issued in 1972 a brief declaration entitled "Safeguarding Basic Christian Beliefs" concerning the Incarnation and the Trinity. Among "recent errors concerning the Son of God," it lists three: 1) opinions which hold that it has not been revealed and made known to us that the Son of God subsists from all eternity in the mystery of the Godhead, distinct from the Father and the Holy Spirit. 2) opinions which would abandon the notion of the one person of Jesus Christ begotten in his divinity of the Father before all ages, and born in His humanity of the Virgin Mary in time. 3) the assertion that the humanity of Christ existed not as being assumed into the eternal person of the Son of God, but existed rather of itself as a person, and therefore that the mystery of Jesus Christ consists only in the fact that God, in revealing Himself, was present in the highest degree in the human person Jesus 29 (64). In addition, with regard to the Trinity, the document cautions against "[t]he opinion that Revelation has left us uncertain about the eternity of the Trinity, and in particular about the eternal existence of the Holy Spirit as a person in God distinct from the Father and the Son …" (67).

Further Development

In response to this challenge Schoonenberg sought to hold fast to his rejection of the anhypostatic character of Christ's humanity while giving a fuller account of his divinity.[14] To this end his thought moved in two related directions. In the first of these (esp. Schoonenberg 1972, 1980), instead of simply reversing Leontius' position, he proposes that

---

[14] For his own retrospective account of this further development, see P. Schoonenberg, "Der Christus 'von oben' und die Christologie 'von unten,'" *Trierer Theologische Zeitschrift* 99 (1990): 95-124.

Jesus' identity as divine and human person is constituted by a fully mutual perichoresis of the divine and the human from which results an again fully mutual enhypostasia of Jesus and the Logos. That is, in an intensification of the creative relation between God and all created reality, God's Logos, eternally the Verbum incarnandum, so thoroughly forms and penetrates Jesus' human reality in the process of incarnation beginning at Jesus' conception and completed at the resurrection as to render Jesus uniquely one with itself. In classical language, the Word thus totally underlies Jesus' humanity as its hypostasis.

This enhypostasia, however, is mutual. In order to establish this point, Schoonenberg aligns himself with a current in modern trinitarian theology represented by Rahner, Barth, and others, who sharply distinguish between the classical and modern senses of the term "person." Whereas the former is metaphysical, designating a distinct manner of subsistence, the latter denotes the psychological subject characterized by self-presence and free activity. For these authors this modern sense of the term is unsuitable to trinitarian discourse, because to speak of three subjects in God evokes tritheism.[15]

Hence Schoonenberg can maintain his earlier position that, apart from the incarnation, God's Logos is impersonal in the modern sense of person. Scripture nowhere portrays a relation of personal mutuality between God and the Logos, nor between Jesus and the Logos. Apart from the incarnation, the Logos exists in a relation of pure receptivity of God's self-outpouring as oriented toward creation and the incarnation. Thus, in the event and process of the incarnation, in forming the human person Jesus, God's Logos achieves personhood in the modern sense. Only as incarnate in Jesus does the Logos turn back to the Father in the mutuality of an I to a Thou. In the incarnation God's eternal Logos becomes Son of the Father, and thus the enhypostasia between Jesus and the Logos is fully mutual.

---

[15] P. Schoonenberg, "Trinity–The Consummated Covenant," *Studies in Religion/ Sciences Religieuses* 5 (1975): 111-116, at 114: "God in himself cannot be designated three persons according to the current meaning of this word, for three subjects of divine consciousness and divine freedom mean three gods. Nor is this conclusion avoided by conceiving the divine persons in an I-thou relationship which emphasizes their mutual surrender to each other, for the subjects of this relationship and this surrender precisely as such are distinct from one another and opposed to one another."

As we saw, when Schoonenberg proposes his reversal of the enhypostasia in *The Christ*, he reconciles his position with the doctrine of the Trinity through recourse to a principle of revelation. What we know of the Trinity, we only know on the basis of our experience of Jesus. Hence we do not know whether God exists as a Trinity of persons prior to Jesus, and this opens the way to Schoonenberg's advocacy of divine becoming.

For Schoonenberg, God really experiences change and becoming in the incarnation (Schoonenberg 1985). God's Logos becomes Son, rendering God Father, and—to complete his position—with the Son's exaltation their Spirit becomes Paraclete. All this flies in the face of the conventional understanding of divine immutability and the coequality of the divine hypostases. With regard to the latter, Schoonenberg proposes that not only is the term hypostasis applied analogously to human beings and to God, but that a further analogy governs its application to the Trinity, each member of which is hypostasis, but in different fashion. As for the divine immutability, the classical doctrine rightly denies any lack or imperfection in God, but it cannot gainsay the biblical witness to the fullness of life which God is and possesses, and which God freely determines to pour out in extending the divine processions in the divine missions.

In this first line of development Schoonenberg responds to the "Statement" issued by the CDF by modifying his original proposal, in which he simply reverses the traditional doctrine of the anhypostasia of Christ's human nature, with an effort to think through a mutual enhypostasia between Jesus and the Logos. In a related development, he sets about retrieving and developing a Spirit Christology (Schoonenberg 1977). His interest, he asserts, is fidelity to the biblical witness. While historically Logos theology has so developed as to overshadow and absorb the plurality of New Testament Christologies, he seeks to redress the imbalance and to recover a theme important in Paul, Luke, and indeed in the Fourth Gospel as well.[16]

---

[16] "My reason is simply that here, as in all my theological efforts, I want to introduce more of the Bible's own theology into dogmatics. I find it intolerable that a main theme of Paul's, Luke's, and even John's Christology remains either banished from our Christological treatises or confined to some *scholion*." Schoonenberg, "Spirit Christology" 360.

Within the New Testament Schoonenberg traces the development of Spirit Christology as a movement from an ascending to a descending Christology. For Paul, Jesus is raised in the power of the Spirit and, exalted, becomes life-giving Spirit and sends forth the Spirit. In the Synoptics, God anoints Jesus with the Spirit at his baptism, establishing him as beloved Son and Messiah. Luke adds that Jesus is conceived by the power of the Spirit, conducts his entire ministry in the power of the Spirit, and at the Last Supper promises to send the Spirit upon the disciples, a promise fulfilled in Acts at Pentecost. In John, the Baptist declares that Jesus baptizes with the Spirit, while at the Last Supper Jesus promises to send the Spirit as Paracelete, and when expiring on the cross, which is itself Jesus' "raising" up for John, Jesus gives up/hands over the Spirit. Furthermore, the Johannine Spirit Christology is not unrelated to the Logos of John's Prologue, especially if Reginald Fuller is correct in reading the Prologue as commentary not so much on Jesus' conception and birth as on his baptism (Schoonenberg 1986).

If the New Testament presents Spirit Christology as an alternative way to express Jesus' uniqueness and divine sonship, rendering him no less divine than does Jn 1:14, further developments nonetheless relegate it to the periphery. Schoonenberg traces a process whereby interest focuses on the incarnation, the language of anointing is extended to the Logos' role in the incarnation, the incarnation of the Logos is conceived as the substantial sanctification of Jesus' humanity, leaving only an accidental role to the Spirit, and the Spirit's distinct role in sanctifying both Jesus and believers is further reduced in the West by the theory of appropriation, which posits an indistinct operation of the Godhead *ad extra* (Schoonenberg 1977, 356-8).

After reviewing modern and contemporary efforts to revive pneumatology either alongside Logos Christology (M. Scheeben, H. Mühlen) or in place of it (E. Irving, G. Lampe), Schoonenberg turns back to the biblical data with a startling question: are Logos and Spirit perhaps identical? An exegetical survey allows him to state that "in some ways Wisdom/Word and Spirit coincide: both are God's outpouring which brings about insight, wisdom, prophecy, and even life." Yet there remains a distinction. In the Old Testament "[W]isdom is God's presence as founding, as protological, the Spirit is God as eschatological." The

New Testament continues to maintain this distinction between the Logos and the Spirit, and so Schoonenberg proposes that "[t]he Spirit does not influence Jesus' human reality alongside the Logos, but as the overflowing fullness of the Logos' self-communication, overflowing *in* Jesus during his earthly life, overflowing *from* Jesus since his glorification" (374). With this line of thought Schoonenberg returns to his notions of the divine-human perichoresis and divine becoming: "So the Logos goes out of the Father and becomes Son at the incarnation. And the Spirit, filling the Son together with the Logos, goes out from the Son at his glorification and becomes the Water flowing into eternal life and the Paraclete guiding to the full truth" (375). Schoonenberg's excursion into Spirit Christology thus returns to the main lines of his thought as it developed after the 1972 CDF "Statement."

Haight and Schoonenberg

On at least three counts Haight's work bears similarity to Schoonenberg's. First, like Schoonenberg, Haight has sought to retrieve and develop New Testament Spirit Christology to account for the relation between God and Jesus. Second, and here the similarity is most direct, Haight proposes what he terms an Antiochene Logos Christology, which seems identical to Schoonenberg's original proposal for the reversal of the enhypostasia of Jesus' humanity in the Logos. Third, both authors embrace a methodology from below that issues in a professed agnosticism regarding the immanent Trinity.

Haight's Spirit Christology

Like Schoonenberg, Haight also delves into Spirit Christology, initially proposing it as "more relatively adequate to Christological data in our time than is a Logos Christology" (Haight 1992, 286-7). He finds it relatively more adequate on several counts. First, in contrast to Logos Christology, which tends to relegate other scriptural Christologies to the periphery, Spirit Christology can include and integrate them. Thus, "God as Spirit working in the life of Jesus can form the basis for the multiple interpretations of him by explaining why he was the Wisdom of God who spoke and even represented God's Word." Second, the symbol of God as Spirit is less apt to suffer the person-alization and hypostatization which befell the symbols of Wisdom and Word whereby they came to connote something distinct from and less than God, thus leading, in Haight's opinion, to the Arian crisis. Hence, Spirit Christology more clearly expresses what Haight takes to be the point of Nicaea, that "nothing less than God was at work in Jesus" (272). Third, it avoids creating the notion that Jesus was preexistent, a notion stemming from an undialectical reading of Chalcedon reinforced by the unhistorical and abstract practice of the communication of properties, a practice which, in Haight's view, contradicts Chalcedon's affirmation that Jesus is consubstantial with us (274-6).[17] Fourth, Logos Christology tends to become exclusivist with regard to other religions, and Haight finds attempts to remedy this tendency, either in Rahner's direction of positing a salvation constituted by Jesus Christ but universally available, or in Panikkar's conception of multiple incarnations of the Logos, "highly speculative, gratuitous, and redundant within the context of historical consciousness. Quite simply, they do not appear credible" (281). Spirit Christology, on the other hand, can account for the Christian experience of salvation in and through Jesus without denying that God as Spirit is at work in other mediations as well.

Haight very soon received a response to his "case" from John H. Wright (1992). Wright summarizes Haight's proposal in terms similar to those condemned in the 1972 CDF "Statement."[18] Then, using as criteria the six Haight himself put forward—an apologetic style, fidelity to the New Testament, and to the Councils, intelligibility and coherence, responsiveness to contemporary issues, and the ability to

---

[17] Already in his work on fundamental theology Haight had found "one inherent difficulty" in Rahner's Logos Christology. Despite Rahner's intent "to establish the continuity between Jesus and other human beings," his "Christology makes this conceptually impossible, since God communicates God's self uniquely to Jesus as Logos and to other human beings analogously as Spirit. . . .It is difficult to see how one can hold the qualitative uniqueness of Jesus and still affirm the doctrine of Chalcedon that Jesus is consubstantial with us." Haight, *Dynamics of Theology*, 257-258 n. 9.

[18] "In brief: Haight sees Jesus simply as a human person filled from the first moment of his existence with God as Spirit. There is in him no preexistent divine subject who has become an actor in human history through the human nature he has made his own. There is no eternal Son of God who has become a human being, but simply a man preeminently filled with God as Spirit." (730)

inspire Christian living—Wright judged Haight's position coherent in itself, but faulted it for otherwise falling short on each of the other criteria.

Whereas Schoonenberg significantly changed his position after 1972, seeking to satisfy the CDF's concerns by working out his notions of the mutual perichoresis of divinity and humanity in Jesus and the ensuing mutual enhypostasia of the Logos and Jesus, Haight proceeded to develop his christological project with no significant concession to Wright's critique.

An Antiochene Logos Christology

What one does find in the penultimate chapter of *Jesus Symbol of God* devoted to "The Divinity of Jesus Christ," however, is a section preceding Haight's presentation of Spirit Christology in which he elaborates a Logos Christology as well. Haight's earlier article had not entirely precluded this possibility, "as long as it remains conscious of the metaphorical and symbolic character of Logos language" (Haight 1992, 287). In *Jesus Symbol of God*, however, he mutes his argument for the greater relative adequacy of Spirit Christology. Both Spirit Christology and Logos Christology are viable options, and if he gives a more ample exposition to Spirit Christology, this is because the case for it still needs to be made for the church at large (Haight 1999, 424).

Citing Karl Rahner as the most successful proponent of a modern Logos Christology, Haight proposes a retrieval of Rahner's thought which will take account of five post-modern critiques it has evoked (432-435). First, Rahner works in many ways "from above," structuring his Christology within the context of a metaphysically conceived doctrine of the immanent Trinity. Second, by positing Jesus' humanity as enhypostatic in the Logos, Rahner threatens the integrity of Chalcedon's affirmation of Jesus' consubstantiality with us. Third, Rahner's view that the incarnation can occur but once is tied to a speculative view of Jesus' constitutive role in effecting salvation which coheres but poorly with historical consciousness. Fourth, such a constitutive Christology stands in tension with Rahner's view of the unity of creation and redemption, appearing gratuitous within that context. Fifth, and lastly, the final causality Rahner attributes to the hypostatic union is but one way of expressing Jesus' centrality to Christianity and universal significance and need not exclude other religious and theological visions, which articulate those points differently.

In light of these critiques, Haight sets about recasting Rahner's Logos Christology, retaining Rahner's theology of symbol but insisting on the metaphoric quality of the terms Logos and incarnation. Like Spirit or Wisdom, Logos is a metaphor for the experience of God as immanent in the world. Each metaphor possesses distinct imaginative virtualities which capture different aspects of the experience of God, but all are basically the same in pointing to that one core experience. To hypostatize them violates this metaphorical quality and vitiates their symbolic power, creating intermediaries between God and world and thus transgressing Nicaea's point that nothing less than God is present to be encountered in and through Jesus.

In order to obviate the difficulties posed by the metaphor of incarnation, which can generate a three-stage narrative of the descent and ascent of a divine being, Haight takes a cue from the framework of Antiochene Christology, starting "from below" with the historically-informed figure of Jesus as a human being, entirely consubstantial with us. God as revealing presence and Word dwells in this human being from the first moment of his existence, and through Jesus' free response to this presence he becomes its concrete symbol, embodying God as Word in himself and revealing its presence to others. This concrete symbol must, of course, be understood dialectically. Jesus remains a human being, and yet he renders God as Word present to humanity. Thus, for Haight, the incarnation designates "the union of no less than God as Word with the human person Jesus," and this union is an "enhypostatic union" (Haight 1999, 442). With this latter statement the similarity between Haight's construal of the incarnation and Schoonenberg's early reversal of the conventional doctrine of enhypostasia finds direct expression.

Theology From Below and
Trinitarian Agnosticism

Both Schoonenberg and Haight construct a Christology "from below," and both assign the category "presence" the place of honor in their respective Christologies. Identifying as their common starting point the Christian experience of the fullness of God's saving presence in and through the man Jesus, they also both impose strict limits on theological discourse on the basis of this experiential starting point. We have seen that Schoonenberg, having laid out his original proposal that the traditional enhypostasia be reversed, appeals to a principle of revelation to secure the compatibility of this proposal with the dogma of the Trinity: since we only know God as Father, Son, and Spirit for us through Jesus, we can neither affirm nor deny that God so exists "prior" to Jesus. This restriction in turn creates the opening for Schoonenberg's further proposal that God becomes a Trinity of persons through Jesus' incarnation and exaltation. He reiterates his epistemological and methodological point in a series of trinitarian theses, of which the first states that "[a]ll our thinking moves from the world to God, and can never move in the other direction." On this basis the eighth thesis asserts "[t]he question of whether God is trinitarian apart from his self-communication in salvation history. . . is thereby eliminated from theology as a meaningless question," so that, according to the next thesis, "trinitarian theology can describe the immanent Trinity fruitfully only in so far as it restricts itself to the limits established by the history of salvation." Hence, for Schoonenberg, religious knowing and theological reasoning must always proceed from below, by the *via inventionis*. No *via doctrinae*, in which the term of the latter serves as starting point for an analogical, quasi-explanatory understanding of the original revelatory experience (a "high, descending" approach), is legitimate. Schoonenberg's third thesis provides an example: "There is no way that we can draw conclusions from the Trinity to Christ and to the Spirit given to us; only the opposite direction is possible" (Schoonenberg 1975, 111, 112).

In a unique instance of direct influence, Haight cites Schoonenberg's first thesis as he begins developing the section entitled "Trinity From Below" in the final chapter of *Jesus Symbol of God*, introducing the quotation with a statement that "Piet Schoonenberg proposes principles for trinitarian theology that run parallel to principles from the early chapters of this book" (Haight 1999, 471). This similarity in principles leads Haight to an outcome much like Schoonenberg's. As we have seen, Haight finds Rahner's move from the economic to the immanent Trinity an unwarranted leap, while he himself eschews the question of distinct differentiations within the Godhead as a speculative matter for which insufficient data is available. For Haight the divine names of Father, Son, and Holy Spirit are symbolic, evoking the presence of the one God in creation, in Jesus, and in all humankind.

Haight's agnosticism on the question of the immanent Trinity seems inconsistent with the manner in which he previously applied his methodological principles to the interpretation of classical dogma. In that context he criticized as outmoded and mistaken conditioning factors a precritical reading of the sciptures, a reification of revelation as information, a hypostatization of poetic figures, etc. On Haight's own terms, he would be more consistent if he simply denied the objective status of differentiations within the Godhead, having removed any basis for affirming them. His foundational position on religious experience, faith, belief, and symbol is even more restrictive than Schoonenberg's insistence on the one-way direction of religious knowing, and it positively excludes the possibility of affirming God's existence as eternally triune.

Fault Lines

Several fault lines run through Haight's position. First, Haight properly distinguishes between the realm of finite reality to which human mind is proportionate and the mysterious, inexhaustible, incomprehensible, transcendent reality of God which exceeds the grasp of the human mind. At the same time, however, he appeals to ordinary usage to construe proportionate knowing as "the process of understanding objects of this world which are finite and able to be comprehended on the basis of public and verifiable evidence" (Haight 1990, 23) and reserves the term "objective" for such knowledge (57, 70, 74, and passim). This restrictive notion of objectivity, however, common though it may have become in ordinary usage, derives from Enlightenment rationalism and empiricism and burdens contemporary culture with the distinctively modern fact/value dichotomy which has relegated religion to a matter of subjective experience and personal preference.

Second, Haight's construal of religious faith as commitment to the transcendent and his sharp distinction between faith and belief bear a heavily existentialist coloration. Faith arises in a symbolically mediated encounter with the transcendent, which for Haight even in this encounter remains unobjectifiable. And if Haight acknowledges that "[t]he affirmation of belief statements as true requires faith," and that "faith cannot exist without some belief," nonetheless "the same faith need not be wedded to any particular belief" (27, 29). The truth of beliefs resides in their reference to the symbolically mediated experience of the transcendent and their ability as themselves symbolic discourse to evoke that experience. It is the experience, and not any symbolic belief, which constitutes the continuity of tradition. Haight writes that "[s]ameness consists in the mediation of transcendence, and interpretation is faithful to past symbols when it is faithful to the salvific point of encounter with transcendence that the symbols of the tradition mediate." From this he concludes that "[t]he criterion of 'orthodoxy', therefore, lies in the experience of transcendence mediated by the symbols of the past, and any constructive theological interpretation that succeeds in coherently expressing that experience is 'orthodox'" (210-11). To put the point negatively, no particular doctrine or theology can replace the experience of transcendence as the criterion of orthodoxy.

Haight can also write, however, that what Christian interpretations of reality must be "faithful to ultimately is the inner and consistent experience that they objectify, express, and communicate, that is, the encounter with a personal and self-communicating God" (84). This raises a question about the cognitive dimension of religious experience: beyond "contact" with transcendent reality, does religious experience also give rise to insights into the character of transcendent reality? Is it true that God is personal and self-communicating? By the end of *Jesus Symbol of God,* Haight answers positively. Whereas early in the book he finds it a "paradoxical tension" that "[f]aith is not knowledge; but faith is cognitive" (Haight 1999, 8), in the final chapter he abandons the convention of restricting the use of "objective" upon which he insisted in his work on fundamental theology and endorses a principle which "opposes the theological view that one cannot make any objective statements about God" (486).

This development points to a fault line in Haight's fundamental theology. On the one hand, he espouses an existentialist conception of faith, which insists on the non-objectifiability of God and minimizes the role of beliefs. Yet at some point, he recognizes that religious experience generates insight, not simply into itself, but into the character of the transcendent, and that insight finds expression in statements about the transcendent that are objectively true: God is personal and self-communicating.

A similar fault line runs though Haight's concept of symbol. With Rahner he wants to attribute to it an ontological density, according to which the other in which a being expresses itself can belong to and participate in the reality of that being, and thus the human being, Jesus, is also divine. But with Tillich, heir to Schelling's version of modern idealism, Haight insists on the dialectical character of symbol. The symbol both is and is not the reality symbolized. Jesus is both human, and thus not divine, and he is divine. But there is a major difference in the meaning of "is" in each arm of the couplet. Jesus is human, simply and directly, while he is divine only in a secondary, derivative sense, in so far as he mediates the divine. The eclectic manner in which Haight borrows from both Rahner and Tillich to define descriptively his category of symbol militates against the theological potential of the category.

In the final chapter of *Jesus Symbol of God*, having recognized the possibility of making objective statements of God, Haight retreats to a Schleiermachean interpretation of the doctrine of the Trinity, reducing it to a statement about the three-fold structure of Christian experience as constituted by the outer self-expression of God through Jesus and the inner self-communication of God as Spirit. Yet Schleiermacher's reduction of the truth of doctrine to the expression of experience,[19] while an important response to the rationalism of Protestant Orthodoxy, fails to take into account the dynamic Haight recognized whereby experience gives rise to insights that transcend it and lead to judgments of objective truth. If Schleiermacher, and in his trinitarian theology Haight with him, remained captive to Kant's restriction of human knowing to the realm of the phenomenal, of reality as it appears to me, Haight had nonetheless already written that "the inner

---

[19] In *Dynamics of Theology* Haight engages George Lindbeck, recognizing the validity of the latter's cultural-linguistic model but arguing that in order to account for the origin of a tradition, it needs to be complemented by an experiential-expressionist model (24 n.32). Haight does not, however, offer any critique of this latter model and seems instead to embrace it.

imperative and logic of truth in important matters transcends any idea of 'truth for me'" (Haight 1999, 6).

All knowing may begin from experience, but it is nonetheless possible to arrive at an objectively true grasp of the intelligibility of what we experience. Haight grants this statement regarding the character of God as personal and self-communicating, but not for the character of God as triune. In this he is inconsistent. On the one hand, if religious knowing is simply reducible to experience of the ineffable transcendent, then the grounds for maintaining the objectivity of the affirmation of God's personal and self-communicating character are undercut. Other forms of religious experience are carried by other traditions that do not make these affirmations, and given the relation Haight claims between religious experience and belief, belief in the personal and self-communicating character of God would precisely not transcend "any idea of 'truth for me.'" Indeed, within the development of his argument, these affirmations may derive from a dogmatic *a priori* that Haight imported in the course of appropriating Rahner's theology of grace.

On the other hand, however, even if Haight's account of religious knowing as reducible to its experiential origin fails to account for his claim to objectivity in characterizing God as personal and self-communicating, Haight also recognizes the dynamic orientation toward the true and the real, which would burst the limits of his restrictive account of religious knowing. If that dynamic validates the affirmation of God as personal, Haight foreshortens it arbitrarily with his reductive interpretation of classical Christological and trinitarian dogma. Religious experience is the necessary condition for religious knowing, but that knowing is not reducible to experience. This idea both Haight and Schoonenberg would seem to contest.

If this reading of Haight has detected tensions, ambivalences, and fault lines in Haight's foundational position, I would suggest that it is on their account that in *Jesus Symbol of God,* despite his express intentions, Haight ultimately puts forth a unitarian conception of God and a fully, and merely human Jesus.

References

Brown, Raymond E. 1967. "How Much Did Jesus Know?" In *Jesus God and Man,* 39-102. New York: Macmillan.

Congregation for the Doctrine of the Faith. 1972. "Safeguarding Basic Christian Beliefs." Declaration given 8 March 1972. In *The Pope Speaks* 17:64-68.

Galvin, J. P. 1994. "From the Humanity of Christ to the Jesus of History: a Paradigm Shift in Catholic Christology." *TS* 55:252-273.

Grillmeier, A. and H. Bacht, eds. 1951-1954. *Das Konzil von Chalkedon,* 3 vols. Würzburg: Echter-Verlag.

Gutwenger, E. 1960. *Bewusstsein und Wissen Christi.* Innsbruck: Rauch.

Haight, R. 1990. *Dynamics of Theology.* New York/Mahwah: Paulist.

———. 1992. "The Case for Spirit Christology." *TS* 53:257-287.

———. 1999. *Jesus, Symbol of God.* Maryknoll, NY: Orbis.

Kasper. W. 1976. *Jesus the Christ.* Translated by V. Green. New York: Paulist.

Küng, H. 1976. *On Being a Christian.* Translated by E. Quinn. Garden City, NY: Doubleday.

Lonergan, B. 1967. "Christ As Subject: A Reply." In *Collection: Papers by Bernard J. F. Lonergan, S.J.,* ed. F. E. Crowe, 164-197. New York: Herder and Herder.

Rahner, K. 1961. "Current Problems in Christology." In *Theological Investigations,* vol. 1, trans. Cornelius Ernst, 149-200. Baltimore: Helicon.

———. 1966. "Dogmatic Reflections on the Knowledge and Self-consciousness of Christ." In *Theological Reflections,* vol. 5, trans. K.-H. Kruger, 193-215. Baltimore, Helicon.

Schillebeeckx, E. 1974. *Jesus: An Experiment in Christology.* Translated by H. Hoskins. New York: Seabury.

Schoonenberg, P. 1970. "From a Two-nature Christology to a Christology of Presence." In Joseph Papin, ed., *Christian Action and Openness to the World,* vols. 2-3 of The Villanova University Theological Symposium, 219-243. Villanova PA: Villanova University Press.

———. 1971. "God and Man." In *The Christ: A study of the God-man relationship in the whole of creation and in Jesus Christ,* trans. Della Couling, 105-175. New York: Herder and Herder.

———. 1972. "Ich Glaube an Gott." *Trierer Theologische Zeitschrift* 81:65-83.

———. 1975. "Trinity—the Consummated Covenant." *Studies in Religion/Sciences Religieuses* 5:111-116.

———. 1977. "Spirit Christology and Logos Christology." *Bijdragen* 38:350-375.

———. 1980. "Denken über Chalkedon." *Theologische Quartalschrift* 160:294-305.

———. 1985. "Gott Ändert Sich am Andern." *Theologische-praktische Quartalschrift* 135:323-332.

———. 1986. "A Sapiential Reading of John's Prologue: Some Reflections of Views of Reginald Fuller and James Dunn." *Theology Digest* 33:403-421.

———. 1990. "Der Christus 'Von Oben' und die Christologie 'Von Unten'." *Trierer Theologische Zeitschrift* 99:95-124.

Wright, John H. 1992. "Roger Haight's Spirit Christology." *TS* 53:729-735.

8 The "Invention" of Clergy and Laity in the Twelfth Century

Gary Macy

Dr. Bernard Cooke, in his masterful study *The Distancing of God: The Ambiguity of Symbol in History and Theology,* suggests that in three important ways Christians were "distanced" from God in a manner never intended in the earliest years of Christianity. Liturgy gradually became a separate and sacred realm distanced from the everyday world of real life. Hellenistic thought further distanced people by replacing experience as the medium for understanding the divine and by substituting abstract thought as a more reliable way of accessing God. Finally, church structures artificially separated the Christian community into clergy and laity, a process that installed the former as the mediators of the divine for the latter.

Basing itself on these important insights, this study hopes to help clarify one important moment in the third process identified by Dr. Cooke. The gradual separation of the clergy from the laity, indeed what might better be described as the invention of both classes, took place, as Dr. Cooke demonstrates, over centuries. Three important moments in this development were the new legal standing of the clergy attained in the fourth century under Constantine and his successors, the Carolingian renaissance of the eighth century, and the Gregorian reform movement of the eleventh and twelfth century. At each stage of this process, the laity became more and more passive in the liturgy and the clergy came to be seen more and more as the indispensable and, indeed, the only mediators of the divine.

Dr. Cooke followed the best scholarship of the time in identifying the Carolingian period as the point when the clergy were clearly understood as the mediators of the divine in the eucharistic action. The passage is worth quoting in full:

> Logically, too, the understanding of the liturgical celebrant's role changed; he was now thought of as the one who "administered" the sacrament, as the only essential agent of the eucharistic action. This attribution to the celebrant alone of the active role in liturgy was reinforced by the spreading practice of private masses. Such isolation of the laity from liturgical participation created a new need for sacramental catechesis. Now eucharistic liturgy became something apart from people's immediate religious experience; it became a "word" addressed to their faith, a word that needed interpretation as it became more and more foreign (135).

Recent research has demonstrated that Dr. Cooke, once again, is more prophetic than his cautious scholarship here would indicate. First, it seems that the separation of clergy and laity was a more gradual process than earlier studies had indicated and that as late as the twelfth century, theologians would still define clerical roles as more inclusive than scholars had first thought. Secondly, there is evidence that as late as the twelfth century some theologians would still not ascribe to the priesthood alone the power to consecrate the eucharistic elements. This is important since it affirms and reinforces one of Dr. Cooke's basic insights: the lay/clerical split in Christianity is not only not inevitable, but is in fact inimical to the original insights of Christianity. The evidence from contemporary sources would indicate that for over half of Christian history, the priesthood and diaconate were not understood to be a separate caste over and against the laity. Nor was the power to consecrate the bread and wine in the Eucharist universally understood to be reserved to the priesthood alone. The "invention" of a sacred priesthood metaphysically apart and above the laity was, then, a later invention than scholarly research would have indicated at the time that Dr. Cooke was writing *The Distancing of God*.[20] The

---

[20] Although Dr. Cooke had indicated the centrality of the twelfth and thirteenth centuries in the gradual separation of the clergy from the laity in his *Ministry to Word and Sacrament: History and Theology*. 574-590.

deep insights of that book, and the "freedom from the tyranny of the present" that it offers, would make possible studies such as this. Dr. Cooke's research challenges historians (especially this one) to question the history of the Church and the theology behind that history. If things were not always as they are now, then things in the future need not be as they presently are. We, the community of the Risen Lord, are free to embody the teachings of the Lord as best we can in our historical, economic, and social location, just as our predecessors did. This brief historical study is offered as small token of appreciation for the inspiration, encouragement, and challenge presented by Dr. Cooke in *The Distancing of God*, and indeed in all his works.

Studies on the understanding within the Christian community of what it meant to be ordained have been immensely helpful in tracking the history of the split between clergy and laity. Thanks particularly to the research of Cardinal Yves Congar, it is now clear that for the greater part of Christian history, to quote Congar, "instead of signifying, as happened from the beginning of the twelfth century, the ceremony in which an individual received a *power* henceforth possessed in such a way that it could never be lost, the words *ordinare, ordinari, ordinatio* signified the fact of being designated and consecrated to take up a certain place or better a certain function, *ordo*, in the community and at its service" (1977, 180, author's emphasis). In short, ordination (*ordinatio*) was the ceremony by which an individual moved into a new rank or profession (*ordo*) in both ecclesial and lay society. Within the church, anyone who moved into a new ministry or vocation in the community was "ordained" to that new ministry. Thus all the minor orders, abbots, abbesses, deacons, deaconesses, priests, nuns, monks, emperors, empresses, kings, and queens were all considered ordained up until the end of the twelfth century. Up until that time, there was no distinction made between the ordinations of priests, for instance, and abbesses. All were equally sacramentally ordained, even if their functions and roles were separate and distinct. This understanding of ordination minimizes to a large extent the difference between laity and clergy. There was no one ordained vocation or role in the Christian community that was less "ordained" than any other one was. Further, this understanding of ordination appears not only in theological writing, but also in the letters of popes and bishops, as well as in surviving rituals for ordinations themselves (Macy 2000, 481-507). Even the word for clergy in Latin, *clericus*, would retain its original meaning of one who could read and write, well into the twelfth century. The twelfth-century Premonstratensian abbot, Philip of Harvengt, certainly includes nuns among the clerics in his *De institutione clericorum*.[21] Philip even wondered why the term *"clerica"* does not appear in the writings of the Fathers since they clearly knew of learned religious women.[22] Extensive evidence exists, then, that would indicate that in the

[21] Philip of Harvengt, *De institutione clericorum tractatus sex*, e.g. 21, "In multis quoque monasteriis videmus feminas religionis gratia congregari, quas loquendi consuetudine, sanctimoniales vel monachas novimus appellari, ad usus quarum cum certum sit oblationes et decimas delegari, satis liquido declaratur non omnes esse clericos qui vivunt de altari. Denique Apostolus (1 Tim 5: 9) vult ut vidua sexaginta annorum eligatur, quae de templi aerario temporalem alimoniam consequatur; et fidelem quemque ut ministret suis viduis diligentius adhortatur, ne gravata Ecclesia his quae vere sunt viduae minus sufficiens habeatur. Ex quo patet quia, etsi proprium est clericorum vivere de altari, jam tamen non omnes clerici sunt qui vivunt de altari. Sicut autem non omnes qui vivunt de altari clerici sunt, sic e regione non omnes vivunt de altari qui tamen clerici sunt." *Patrologiae cursus completus…Series latina*, Jacques Paul Migne, ed.. 1878-90. 217 vols. and indexes. Paris: Garnier Fratres and J.P. Migne (hereafter *PL*) 203: 811C.

[22] "Inter eas quoque sanctimoniales, vel monachos a quibus Deo in Ecclesia labore litterario deservitur, si qua perfectius imbuta litteris invenitur, non proprio sed improprio sermone bonus clericus appellatur, in quo nihil aliud quam ejus scientia praedicatur. Cum aliquando, me praesente, vir quidam moribus et habitu religiosus in quamdam ecclesiam deveniret, et sanctimonialem, tam aetate quam scientia praematuram, coram altario tenentem libellum in manibus inveniret, inter caetera quae ad invicem mature contulerunt, sciscitatus est ab ea quid teneret, quid videlicet libellus quem tenebat in manibus contineret. At illa: 'Vitam, inquit, cujusdam virginis quam dictavi, quam scripto cum essem juvencula commendavi.' Et adjunxit: 'Fui enim bonus clericus.' In quo dicto nihil aliud intelligendum adnotavi quam quod bene litterata fuisset, cum junior vitam virginis descripsisset. Sic et de quibusdam aliis quas scio admodum litteratas, vel esse, vel fuisse, recolo frequentius me audisse, ut cum de cujuslibet earum scientia sermo in medium versaretur, ipsa bonus clericus diceretur. Et miror cum in muliere clericalis scientia praedicetur, cur non bona clerica, sed bonus clericus nominetur, cum satis convenientius videretur, ut sicut a monacho monacha, sic a clerico clerica diceretur. Eas quidem quas sub religionis habitu constat in monasterio conversari, vel sanctimoniales, vel nonnas, vel monachas in Patrum opusculis invenio nominari; clericas vero utrum uspiam scriptum invenerim, non possum recordari, et a nullo sermonem Latinum proferente, aliquas audio sic vocari." Phillip of Harvengt, *De institutione clericorum tractus sex*. 110, ed. *PL* 203: 816D-817B).

twelfth century, the older understanding of *ordinatio* as the ceremony marking any change in function or role within the community was still widely accepted. A momentous change in the understanding of ordination occurred in the middle of the twelfth century, as the above quote from Congar indicates. Again, recent scholarship has been able to track more precisely the timing of the change. Over twenty-five years ago, Dr. Ida Raming researched the canonical debate over the ordination of women in the twelfth century.[23] Dr. Raming identified a definite shift in the understanding of ordination when the great collator of canon law, Gratian of Bologna, asserts in one of the very few places where he offers his own opinion, that "women cannot be admitted to the priesthood nor even to the diaconate."[24] The *Decretum*, as Gratian's work is commonly known, quickly became the standard work of canon law for the Western church and would remain so until canon law was completely revised in 1917. Gratian's comment was a real problem, since there was substantial evidence, even within the *Decretum* itself, that women had certainly been ordained deaconesses. Writing soon after Gratian had finished his work, the canon lawyer Rufinus of Bologna suggests a solution that would soon become the standard understanding of medieval scholars. The ordination of deaconesses is not a true sacramental ordination, Rufinus explains, but rather a simple blessing. True ordination is limited only to those who served at the altar, that is, priests, deacons, and subdeacons. Dr. Ram-

---

[23] Dr. Raming's work first appeared in German in 1973 under the title *Der Ausschluß der Frau von priesterlichen Amt: Gottgewollte Tradition oder Diskriminierung?*. Cologne: Boehlau Verlag. An English translation appeared in 1975, *The Exclusion of Women from the Priesthood: Divine Law or Sex Discrimination*. Metuchen, N.J.: Scarecrow Press. Dr. Raming has recently published a revised German edition of the work under the title *Priesteramt der Frau: Geschenk Gottes für eine eneuerte Kirche*. 2002. Muenster: Lit Verlag. An English translation of this work, including a translation of the Latin references, is being prepared by Bernard Cooke and Gary Macy, to appear 2003. *A History of Women and Ordination: Volume 2: The Priesthood of Women: God's Gift to a Renewed Church*. New York: Scarecrow Press. References in this article will be to the 1975 English translation.

[24] "Mulieres autem non solum ad sacerdotium, sed nec etiam ad diaconatum provehi possunt" C. 15, q. 3, *princ.*, 1959. *Corpus Iuris Canonici, Decretum*, d. 60, c. 4, E. Friedberg, ed., 2 vols. Graz: Akademische Druck- u. Verlagsanstalt 1: 750. For an analysis of Gratian's thought on this issue, see Raming, *The Exclusion*: 26-27.

ing notes that Rufinus had based his position on an alleged teaching of St. Ambrose, which he found in the standard commentary on the bible (in Latin, *Glossa ordinaria*) that had been compiled in the early twelfth century at the School of Laon. The teaching, actually from the anonymous fourth century writer now known to scholars as the "Ambrosiaster," asserts that only heretics ever held that women could be ordained deacons (Raming 1975, 50-54).[25]

An investigation of theological sources from the twelfth century supports Dr. Raming's conclusions. The teaching that ordination is limited to the priesthood and diaconate alone first appears in the Council of Benevento of 1091. The decree proclaims, "we say, however, that sacred orders are the diaconate and the presbyterate. It is read of the primitive church that it had these alone, concerning this only do we have a precept from the apostles."[26] The canon would later be included by Gratian in his *Decretum*. This law would also be copied into a *sententia* (short teaching) preserved from the same School of Laon that produced the *Glossa ordinaria*.[27]

The teaching of the School of Laon was copied by several twelfth century writers, the most influential being Peter the Lombard, who

---

[25] For a further discussion of the influence of the Ambrosiaster gloss, see John Hilary Martin. 1986. "The Ordination of Women and the Theologians in the Middle Ages." *Escritos del Vedat*, 36: 133-4. This article and a second by Gary Macy on the same topic have been edited and published with the Latin notes translated into English by Bernard Cooke and Gary Macy, *Women and Ordination*, vol. 1.

[26] "Nullus deinceps in episcopum eligatur, nisi qui in sacris ordinibus religiose inventus est. Sacros autem ordines dicimus diaconatum ac presbyteratum. Hos siquidem solos primitiva legitur Ecclesia habuisse; super his solum praeceptum habemus Apostoli." Canon 1. *Echiridion symbolorum*, Heinrich Denziger and Adolf Schönmetzer, eds. 1963. Freiburg: Herder, no. 703: 231. "Nullus in episcopatum eligatur, nisi in sacris ordinibus religiose uiuens inuentus fuerit. Sacros autem ordines dicimus diaconatum et presbiteratum. Hos siquidem solos primitiua legitur habuisse ecclesia, subdiacones uero, quia et ipsi altaribus ministrant, oportunitate exigente concedimus, si tamen spectatae sint religionis et scientiae. Quod ipsum non sine Romani Pontificis uel metropolitani scientia fieri permittimus." *Decretum*, d. 60, c. 4, E. Friedberg,, 1:227.

[27] "Sacri ordines tantum dicuntur sacerdotium et diaconatus, quia in illis tamen [*lire*: tantum] datur Spiritus, et ideo nulla necessitate possunt ab inferioribus tractari; sed alia possunt, ut Apostolus potest legi." *Sententia* n. 390 "L'école d'Anselme de Laon et de Guillaume de Champeaux," chapter 3 of Odon Lottin. 1959. *Psychologie et morale aux XIIe et XIIIe siècles*. Gembloux: Duculot : 283.

himself wrote a commentary on the Letters of Paul that would become a standard source for later theologians. The Lombard, however, adds a new twist to the argument, adding that references to deaconesses must refer only to the wives of deacons. Using this assumption, then, historical references to the ordination of women could be conveniently explained away.[28]

For the first time in Christian history, ordination was redefined to exclude all but the priesthood and the diaconate. As one can well imagine, this innovation was not at first widely accepted. Several theologians continued to use the older definition of ordination, and a few, most notably, Abelard of Paris, wrote movingly against the new teaching.[29] Unfortunately, the popularity of the *Glossa ordinaria,* of Gratian's *Decretum,* and of Peter the Lombard, as well as the support of the papacy carried the day. In time, the definition of ordination first put forward by the School of Laon and by Rufinus of Bologna would not only be the standard understanding of Western Christianity, but would be read back into all of Christian history. The more ancient understanding of ordination, an understanding that had shaped Christianity for over half its history would slowly fade from memory.

This important twelfth century debate, then, constitutes a crucial turning point in the relationship of clergy and laity. Only the priesthood and the diaconate were true sacramental orders (*ordines*) in the Church. All other vocations or ministries in the Church were henceforth merely jobs done by laity. Women were definitely excluded from that exclusive group and even the ancient order of deaconesses was relegated to lay status. Despite all the evidence to the contrary, the

---

[28] Ideoque etiam mulieres quae in infimo gradu sunt, vult esse sine crimine ut munda sit Ecclesia. Sed Cataphrygae occasione horum verborum, quia, scilicet ubi de diaconis agit, de mulieribus loquitur, dicunt diaconas debere ordinari: quod contra auctoritatem est. Diacones, post interpositionem de mulieribus, iterum de diaconis dicit: *Diacones sint viri unius uxoris,* quam Deus decrevit homini, cum qua benedicitur, non cum secunda." *Collectanea in epistolas Pauli, In_epistolam I ad Timothaeum, PL* 192:346A. "Modus talis: Primo salutat eum, deinde monet, ut pseudoapostolis resistat, postea instruit de episcopali officio docens quales debeat ordinare presbyteros et diacones, et quales debeant esse mulieres eorum; deinde quales viduas recipere debeat; postea de modo correctionis instruit eum." Ibid., ed. *PL* 192:326D.

[29] The history of this theological debate has been traced in Gary Macy "Heloise, Abelard and the Ordination of Abbesses" (to appear).

theological argument could be made that women had, in fact, never been (truly) ordained, and, of course, neither had abbots or canons or kings or emperors. More than ever, the priesthood (and to a lesser extent the diaconate) became the only mediators between the merely baptized and the divine. It is important to note, however, that this change was relatively late in the history of Christianity. For over half of Christian history, *ordinatio* meant something quite different from ordination as understood by later theologians and councils, particularly the Council of Trent. One cannot assume, therefore, that the word *ordinatio* as used in these earlier centuries refers to that later understanding; indeed, the contrary is true. One cannot argue, then, that since the term *ordinatio* was used in the fourth, sixth, eighth, or eleventh century, there existed a continuous practice of ordination, as it would be understood in the sixteenth, nineteenth, or twentieth centuries. The word had shifted meaning so radically as to create an entirely new caste among the Christian community.

The new exclusionary definition of "ordination" was dependent on the function of the priest (and to a lesser extent that of the deacon and subdeacon) to preside at the Eucharist. The role of the priest as special mediator of God's grace, moreover, rested to a large extent on the power of the priest to lead the liturgy and, most importantly, to confect the presence of the Risen Lord in the Eucharist.[30]

Just as important, therefore, as the redefinition of ordination in accomplishing a definitive split between clergy and laity, would be the theological assumption that only a properly "ordained" priest could make the Risen Lord present in the Eucharist. At the beginning of the twelfth century, though, scholars were not at all in agreement that a priest alone could effect the transformation of the bread and wine into the body and blood of Christ. At least three twelfth century

---

[30] "Contrary to the opinion of earlier periods and to the patristic overshadowing of presbyterate by episcopacy, the medieval theologians see the essence and loftiest powers of priesthood being conferred in presbyteral ordination. ... In a sense, this is a logical conclusion from the emphasis placed on the Eucharist as the changing of bread into Christ and on the priestly power of transubstantiation. Not that pastoral concerns have vanished, but priesthood as a cultic reality has gradually gained center stage in preference to apostolic proclamation of the gospel." Cooke, Bernard. *Ministry to Word and Sacrament*: 580.

scholars are known to have put forward the theory that the words of consecration themselves confect, regardless of who says the words.

Abelard, writing in his *Theologia christiana*, describes their position: "I know of two brothers who are numbered among the highest masters, the other of whom imputed such power to the divine words in the confecting of the sacrament that by whomever they are pronounced they have the same efficacy, so that even a woman or someone of whatever order or condition through the words of the Lord is able to confect the sacrament of the altar." The great medieval scholar Marie Dominique Chenu has identified these two brothers as the famous brothers Bernard and Thierry of Chartres (Macy 1984, 159-160, n.110).[31]

The Chartrians, however, were not the only theologians to teach that the words of consecration alone confect the sacrament. Teaching in Paris in the early 1160s, the liturgist John Beleth describes the secret of the Mass in the following terms:

> The secret is so-called because it is recited secretly, although in the past it was said aloud so that it was known by lay people. It happened, therefore, that one day shepherds placed bread on a rock which, at the recitation of those words, was changed into flesh, perhaps the bread was transubstantiated into the body of Christ since vengeance was most rapidly taken against them by divine agency. For they were struck down by a divine judgment sent from heaven. Hence it was decreed that in the future it be said silently.[32]

---

[31] "Novimus et duos fratres qui se inter summos connumerant magistros, quorum alter tantum uim diuinis uerbis in conficiendis sacramentis tribuit, ut a quibuscumque ipsa proferantur aeque suam habeant efficaciam, ut etiam muler et quislibet cuius- cumque sit ordinis uel conditions per uerba dominica sacramentum altaris conficere queat." l. 4, c. 80, *Petri Abaelardi opera theologica*, E. Buytaert, ed., 1969. Corpus christianorum, continuatio mediaeualis, 12. Turnhout: Brepols: 302.

[32] "Secreta dicitur, quia secreto pronuntiatur, cum olim tamen alta uoce diceretur, unde et ab hominibus laicis sciebatur. Contingit ergo, ut quadam die pastores super lapidem quendam ponerent panem, qui ad horum uerborum prolationem in carnem conuersus est, forsan transsubstantiatus est panis in corpus Christi, in quos diuinitus factus est acerrima uindicta. Nam percussi sunt diuino iuditio celitus misso. Vnde statutum fuit, ut de cetero sub silentio diceretur," *De ecclesiasticis officiis*, c. 44, Heribert Douteil, ed., Iohannes Beleth. 1976. *Summa de ecclesiasticis officiis*, Corpus christianorum, Continuatio medievalis, 41A. Turnhout: Brepols : 78.

The story originally appears as a cautionary tale in the sixth century *Pratum spirituale* of John Moschius[33] The story is repeated by the anonymous *Speculum ecclesiae*, written ca. 1160-1175.[34] In this version, there is no mention of transubstantiation, however the shepherds are punished by divine vengeance for their lack of reverence for such a great mystery.[35] This version of the story was copied into the *De missarum mysteriis* of Cardinal Lother of Segni c. 1195.[36] He was soon to be elevated to the papacy as Pope Innocent III. Although neither author speaks of the words of institution as consecrating of themselves, as did the brothers from Chartres and John Beleth, they ascribe to the words great power apart from their enunciation by an ordained priest.

The position of the brothers from Chartres and that of Beleth may have formed the basis of the teaching of some of the heretical Waldensians, who argued in the late twelfth century that if no worthy priest could be found, a lay person, even a woman, could lead the liturgy and consecrate the bread and wine (Cameron 2000, 33, 45-46, 129-129; Macy 1984, 57). Their position is reflected in the creed written for those Waldensians returning to the church in 1208 by Innocent III: "Therefore we firmly believe and confess that however honest, pious, holy or prudent someone may be, he [the adjectives are masculine; only a male is intended here] is not able to nor ought to consecrate the Eucharist nor perform the ritual of the altar, unless he is a priest regularly ordained by a bishop in a visible and tangible way."[37] The

---

[33] C. 196, *PL* 74: 225C-226D.

[34] On the dating of this work, see Macy, Gary. 1999. *Treasures from the Storeroom: Medieval Religion and the Eucharist*. Collegeville, MN: Liturgical Press: 171.

[35] "In primitiva autem Ecclesia alta voce proferebatur, donec pastores memoriter ex quotidiano usu verba retinentes, in camnis eadem cantabant. Sed ipsi divina vindicta ibidem percussi sunt. Unde Ecclesia consuevit propter reverentiam tantum mysterium secreto agere." *Speculum ecclesiae*, c. 7, *PL* 177: 368C-D.

[36] "Caeterum ne sacrosancta verba vilescerent, dum omnes pene per usum ipsa scientes, in plateis et vicis, aliisque locis incongruis decantarent, decrevit Ecclesia, ut haec obsecratio quae secreta censetur, a sacerdote secrete dicatur, unde fertur, quod cum ante consuetudinem quae postmodum inolevit, quidam pastores ea decantarent in agro, divinitus sunt percussi." Lothar of Segni, *De missarum mysteriis*, l. 1, c. 1, *PL* 217: 840C-D On the dating of this work, see Macy, *Treasures*: 171.

[37] "Unde firmiter credimus et confitemur, quod quantumcumque quilibet honestus, religiosus, sanctus et prudens sit, non potest nec debet Eucharistiam consecrare nec altaris Sacrificium conficere, nisi sit presbyter, a visibili et tangibili episcopos regulariter ordinatus." *Enchiridion symbolorum*, Henricus Denziger, op. cit., n. 794: 257.

words are quite similar to those used to describe the position of Bernard and Thierry, and so suggest that this was not just an isolated academic opinion, but one that found resonance with at least one Christian community.

Along with the discussion of the power of the words of consecration, a further discussion occurred in the twelfth century over which words could be used for consecration. Gregory the Great, writing in the sixth century, explains in a letter to John, the bishop of Syracuse, the liturgical customs of the Roman church: "We say the Lord's Prayer immediately after the intercession (the Kyrie) for this reason because the custom of the apostles was that they consecrated the sacrifice of offering by this prayer alone. It seemed exceedingly unsuitable to me that we would say an intercession over the offering which a scholar had composed and that we would not say the very tradition that our Redeemer had composed over his body and blood."[38]

In the late eleventh century, Bernold of Constance produced a lengthy commentary on the papal liturgy. While explaining the history of the canon, he referred to the letter of Gregory, adding that Gregory inserted the Lord's Prayer into the liturgy since this was the prayer that "the apostles themselves were believed to have used in the confection of these sacraments by the institution of the Lord."[39] By the twelfth century, Gregory's teaching had been slightly changed. While scholars continued to teach that the Lord's Prayer was the original prayer over the gifts, they added that the blessings of Jesus over the bread and

---

[38] "Orationem vero Dominicam idcirco mox post precem dicimus, quia mos apostolorum fuit ut ad ipsam solummodo orationem oblationis hostiam consecrarent. Et valde mihi inconveniens visum est ut precem quam scholasticus composuerat super oblationem diceremus, et ipsam traditionem quam Redemptor noster composuit super ejus corpus et sanguinem non diceremus." Gregory the Great, *liber* 11, *epistola* 12, *PL* 77: 956D-A. For an excellent summary of the tradition of using the Lord's Prayer in the Canon, see Joseph A. Jungmann, Joseph A. 1955. *The Mass of the Roman Rite: Its Origin and Development (Missa Sollemnia)*, transl. Francis Brunner, 2 vols. New York: Benziger Brothers, Inc. 2: 278-281.

[39] "Item [idem] quoque Gregorius Dominicam orationem se Canoni adjecisse in Registro suo asserit, ubi quibusdam inde murmurantibus, humili responsione satisfecit, inconveniens esse asserens ut oratio quam scholasticus composuit super oblationem diceretur, et illa praetermitteretur quam ipsi apostoli ex institutione Dominica in confectione eorumdem sacramentorum usitasse crederentur [creduntur]." Micrologus de ecclesiasticis observationibus, *PL* 151:985A. On Bernold and the *Micrologus*, see Macy, *Treasures*: 169.

wine were also part of the original prayer of consecration. One of the most fascinating of these accounts comes from an anonymous work found in a thirteenth century manuscript in the British Library. The author gave a history of the prayers used in the Mass, which begins, "Saint Peter the first celebrated Mass in Antioch in which only the words of the Lord and the Lord's Prayer were said."[40] Less colorful explanations of Gregory's teaching appeared in the *Gemma anima* of Honorius Augustodunensis, written ca. 1102-1133: "The Lord Jesus, priest according to the order of Melchisedech, at first instituted the Mass when he made his body and blood from bread and wine, and ordered this to be celebrated in his memory. The apostles added to this when they said the words which the Lord said and the Lord's Prayer over the bread and wine."[41]

Rupert of Deutz, writing in 1111 explains that the elaborated liturgy is not holier than earlier times "when it was consecrated by the words of the Lord alone and by the Lord's Prayer alone."[42] Robert Paululus, writing ca. 1175-1180, copied this teaching of Honorius.[43] John Beleth taught that the apostles originally simply recited the words of institution, but then added the Lord's Prayer.[44] Sicard of Cremona, writing ca. 1185-1195, taught that the words of institution transubstantiated the bread and wine, but added that the apostles added

---

[40] "Sanctus petrus primus in antiochem missam celebravit in qua tantum verba domini et oratio dominica dicebantur." London, British Museum, Royal MS. 5 F.xv, fol. 120r.

[41] "Missam in primis Dominus Jesus, sacerdos secundum ordinem Melchisedech, instituit, quando ex pane et vino corpus et sanguinem suum fecit, et in memoriam sui, suis celebrare haec praecepit; hanc apostoli auxerunt, dum super panem et vinum verba quae Dominus dixit, et Dominicam orationem dixerunt." *Gemma anima*, PL 172:572B. On Honorius and the *Gemma anima*, see Macy, *Treasures*: 170.

[42] *De divinis officiis*, l. 2, c. 21, Rhaban Haacke, ed. 1967. *Ruperti Tjuitiensis Liber de divinis officiis*, Corpus christianorum, Continuatio medievalis, 7. Turnhout: Brepols: 52. On Rupert and the *De divinis officiis*, see Macy, *Treasures*: 169.

[43] "Apostoli missam auxerunt, dum super panem et vinum verba quae Dominus dixerat, et Orationem Dominicam dixerunt." *De officiis ecclesiasticis*, l.2, c. 11, *PL* 177: 416C. On Paululus and the *De officiis ecclesiasticis*, see Macy, *Treasures*: 171.

[44] "Prius enim apostoli dicebant hec uerba tantum, que Dominus dixit: *Hoc est corpus meum* et cetera, et *Hic est sanguis novi testamenti* et cetera. Sed apostoli postea addiderunt dominicam orationem, et hec consuetudo apostolorum hic representatur." *Summa de ecclesiasticis officiis*, c. 98, Douteil : 181.

the Lord's Prayer to the words said over the bread and wine.[45] Once again, the Waldensians appear to have used this teaching in their liturgies. According to Alexander of Alexandria, the Dominican friar who recorded early practices of the Waldensians, the heart of their liturgy was a seven-fold repetition of the Lord's Prayer (Macy 1984, 160, n. 111; Audisio 1999, 105, 122-123, 134).

The Lord's Prayer is not the only element in the liturgy, however, that twelfth century theologians consider as candidates for the power to consecrate. The *Speculum ecclesiae* is quite explicit concerning the role of the sign of cross in the consecration: "And by this everything is given in those words of the Lord given in the supper which the priest adds. But this about to be said, thus first he begins, 'Who on the day before he suffered.' With these words, he raises the still common bread from the altar and having raised it, he blesses and imprints the sign of the cross, and before he sets it down he reproduces the words of the Lord when he says, 'He blessed and broke,' and that which follows. Then he takes up the chalice and signs it and reproduces the words of the Lords saying, 'And he gave it to his disciples saying, 'Take and drink from this, all of you.' Here that extraordinary miracle is done. With these words food for the flesh becomes food for the soul. Through these words and through the sign of the cross nature is renewed, and bread becomes flesh and wine blood."[46] Richard the

---

[45] "Missam instituit Dominus Jesus, sacerdos secundum ordinem Melchisedech, quando panem et vinum in corpus et sanguinem transmutavit, dicens: Hoc est corpus meum, hic est sanguis meus ; ecce quod Dominus missam instituit, id est haec verba constituit, eisque vitam substantivam dedit; quibus panis in corpus, et vinum mittitur, id est transsubstantiatur in sanguinem. Item missam instituit et causam institutionis adjunxit, dum hoc faciendum esse mandavit, scilicet ob memoriam sui, dicens: Hoc facite in meam commemorationem. Unde licet apostoli hanc adauxerint, dum super panem et vinum, non solum verba quae Dominus dixerat, sed etiam Dominicam orationem superaddendam statuerunt." *Mitrale*, l. 3, c. 1, *PL* 213: 91B-C. On Sicard and the *Mitrale*, see Macy, *Treasures*: 171.

[46] "Et hoc totum confertur in illis verbis Domini in coena prolatis, quae sacerdos subjungit. Sed ea dicturus sic prius incipit: *Qui pridie quam pateretur*. In his verbis sumit ab altari panem adhuc communem, et elevatum benedicit et signum crucis imprimit, et priusquam deponat repraesentat verba Domini dum dicit: *Benedixit et fregit*, et quae sequuntur. Postea tollit calicem et signat, et repraesentat verba Domini dicens: *Et dedit discipulis suis dicens: Accipite et bibite ex hoc omnes.* Hic fit illud insigne miraculum. In his verbis cibus carnis fit cibus animae. Per haec verba et per crucis signaculum novatur natura, et panis fit caro, et vinum sanguis." c. 7, *PL* 177:370C.

Premonstratensian, writing ca. 1150-1175, made the power of the cross the central theme of his entire spiritual commentary on the liturgy. According to Richard, "The power of the mass is the cross of Christ which consecrates and sanctifies the sacrament of the altar and all the sacraments of the church."[47] Further, it is "through the power of the cross that, first of all, those things placed [on the altar] are blessed." Once again, it is the Waldensians who seem to have put this teaching into practice in their liturgies, as they are reported by Alexander of Alexandria to have consecrated the bread and wine by means of the sign of the cross (Macy 1984, 57).

During the twelfth century at least, it appears that there was as yet no agreement as to what would be referred to as the "form" of the Eucharist. Many, if not most, theologians, most notably Peter the Lombard, would have agreed that the words of institution consecrate the bread and wine, transforming them into the body and blood of the Risen Lord.[48] As demonstrated above, however, there was not unanimous agreement on that question. Some theologians, based on a tradition stemming from Gregory the Great, would argue that the Lord's Prayer was at least at one time part of the words of consecration. Other theologians would put forth the theory that the sign of the cross was still part of the formula of consecration.

At the great Fourth Lateran Council of 1215, the first article adopted by Pope Innocent III and the others gathered together, was a creed directed against several heretical groups, including the Waldensians. In part, it reads:

> There is one Universal Church of the faithful, outside of which there is absolutely no salvation. In which there is the same priest and sacrifice, Jesus Christ, whose body and blood are truly contained in the sacrament of the altar under the forms of bread and wine; the

---

[47] "Virtus missae, crux Christi est, quae sacramentum altaris et omnia Ecclesiae sacramenta consecrat et sanctificat." *Sermo in canone misse, PL* 177:459A. On Richard and his work, see Macy, *Treasures*: 170.

[48] "Forma vero est, quam ibidem edidit dicens, Hoc est corpus meum; et post: Hic est sanguis meus. Cum enim haec verba proferuntur, conversio fit panis et vini in substantiam corporis et sanguinis Christi; reliqua ad Dei laudem dicuntur." l. 4, dist. 8, c. 4, 1981. *Sententiae in IV libris distinctae*, vol. 2. Grottaferrata: Collegii S. Bonaventurae ad Clara Aquas: 282.

> bread being changed (*transubstantiatis*) by divine power into the body, and the wine into the blood, so that to realize the mystery of unity we may receive of Him what He has received of us. And this sacrament no one can effect except the priest who has been duly ordained in accordance with the keys of the Church, which Jesus Christ Himself gave to the Apostles and their successors.[49]

This section of the creed and first canon of the Fourth Lateran Council held in 1215 arguably contains the most discussed and debated words from that Council. Scholars have particularly focused on the use of the term *transubstantiatiatis*, the first such use in an official church document.

Less noticed, but perhaps equally important, are the words which follow, "And this sacrament no one can effect except the priest who has been duly ordained in accordance with the keys of the Church, which Jesus Christ Himself gave to the Apostles and their successors." Most scholars assume that this statement merely repeats the standard orthodox position of the time. In fact, this statement may have been intended to quell twelfth-century debates on two issues: who could properly confect the sacrament and how that sacrament was confected. The creed of the Fourth Lateran Council could be seen not as a simple repetition of long-held Christian beliefs, but as a magisterial intervention to settle theological and pastoral discussions of real importance. The decrees of Lateran IV spread with remarkable speed throughout Western Christianity and the implementation of those decrees created a very different church from that which preceded the Council (Logan 2002, 193-201).

Seen in this light, Lateran IV provides a convenient demarcation between an older understanding of *ordination,* which included most of the functions and roles within the church, and a new understanding of *ordinatio,* which excluded all but those who lead the liturgy from orders. Along with and closely connected with this change, was an understanding of the priesthood which greatly enhanced its power by insisting that only a properly ordained priest could consecrate the bread and wine at the altar. The change was dramatic and very successful.

---

[49] Latin text is given in Denzinger, *Enchiridion*, no. 802: 260.

Not that Innocent III would have understood himself as introducing anything new. He would have seen himself as restoring an older order, basing himself on the texts of the Ambrioster as mediated by the *Glossa ordinaria*, by Peter the Lombard, and particularly by the *Decretum*. The teachings of Bernard and Thierry of Chartres, of John Beleth, and of the commentators on the liturgy mentioned above, were soon forgotten or explained away by later writers. Interestingly enough, none of these writers were ever accused of heresy, nor were their positions ever condemned either during their lifetimes or after. If the Waldensians were in fact carrying on what they may have felt were older traditions based on the above teachings, they were certainly condemned for holding them. The creed of Lateran IV was in part directed against them. What was a respectable, or at least acceptable, academic position before the end of the twelfth century, would become heretical in the thirteenth century. The church that emerged from Lateran IV was, despite the intentions of its creators, something new—a more clerical, more hierarchical, and more centralized church than that which preceded it.

Nor did the innovations of Gratian, the *Glossa,* and the Lombard come out of the blue. In many ways, they can be seen as the logical result, and in some sense the culmination, of reforms of earlier centuries, commonly known as the Gregorian Reform movement. Central to this reform was the insistence of the supremacy of the priesthood and of the papacy over the secular lords. Emphasizing the difference between laity and priesthood was essential to this claim. Throughout much of the twelfth century, the claims were at best tenuous, as claimants for the papal throne fought for control. Not until 1177 would there be one pope accepted by all of Europe. Only then could the Councils of Lateran III and Lateran IV begin to consolidate and enforce the claims of the Gregorian Reform movement. As in all human affairs, there are political factors that influence the choice of structures the Church uses to further its mission as the Body of Christ. In this case, the struggle for the control of the Church between lay lords and the papal office must be seen as the backdrop to the separation of clergy and laity effected in the late twelfth and early thirteenth centuries (Logan 2002, 105-115, 133-136).[50]

Of what practical importance can such an esoteric recitation of obscure and forgotten writers be to the present church? First and most importantly, it demonstrates that the present radical split between clergy and laity did not exist in its present form before the twelfth century. For most of Christian history, such a definitive split simply did not exist. Secondly, the Christianity of those early centuries was able to survive and thrive, and one assumes, mediate the life of the Risen Lord to all the faithful without the necessity of an exclusively ordained clergy. These conclusions are historical, for the most part. While not claiming to be the only possible interpretation of the sources presented, at least the presentation is plausible and cannot be dismissed without seriously engaging the evidence offered here. How and even whether they have theological or pastoral implications are theological, not historical questions.

A whole other set of mainly theological conclusions can also be reached, of course, and these are far more controversial and controverted. One could argue, for instance, that there is a development in the understanding of the church by which the Spirit guides the leadership of the Church to gradually uncover what the Spirit intended all along. In this understanding, the evidence offered above merely affirms the assertion that Innocent III as pope was fulfilling his role as adjudicator of the tradition. His position was the position of the Church and of the Spirit, and would remain so for all time, unless modified by his successors. The positions of John Beleth, of the Chartrians, and of the commentators were interesting speculation, but wrong: dead ends in the long history of the Church. The practices of the Waldensians were simply heretical and thus condemned as such.

A different theological approach, one long championed by Dr. Cooke, would argue that the Spirit speaks through each generation

---

[50] By far the best studies of the ecclesiology of this central period are those by Yves Congar, especially, chapters five through eight of *Die Lehre von der Kirche von Augustinus bis zum Ablendändischen Schisma, Handbuch der Dogmengeschichte.* 1971. vol. 3, fasc. 3c. Freiburg: Herder :53-174 and "La place de la papauté dans la piété ecclésiale des réformateurs du XIe siècle."1994. *Église et papauté.* Paris: Cerf: 93-114.

of the Church and each generation must respond to the Spirit in its own cultural, economic, and social setting. Central to that response is the understanding that all Christians are open to the Spirit. There is no theological necessity for a mediating body through which the Spirit must work. Such mediations are culturally conditioned and not divinely established ministries. Yet, to say this is not to deny the importance of structure in the Church. To be truly incarnated and working in the Church, the Spirit will certainly take a form that is human, and humans always structure themselves. No particular structure should be mistaken for the Spirit, yet to deny the inevitability of some structure would be to fall into the second of the distancings of God against which Dr. Cooke warns. We are not disembodied platonic entities immediately intuiting the divine will. We are saved with, through, and sometimes despite the communities in which we live and breath and have our being.

Here the theological conclusion might be that however necessary the separation of laity and clergy might have been to the independence (and hence prophetic role) of the Church in the twelfth and thirteenth century, such a separation might not be necessary or even desirable in the twenty-first century. The pastoral needs of the present are quite different from those of the thirteenth century, and may demand different models of leadership. The fact that such different models existed in the thought of John Beleth, of the Chartranians, and of the commentators, and in the pastoral practices of the Waldensians, suggests that there is more than one tradition from which the Church can draw in adjudicating the will of the Spirit. Different social, economic, and political settings require different responses from the Christian community, just as they have in the past.

The purpose of this article is not to settle these weighty and serious theological and pastoral problems.[51] It is simply to offer an alternative way of looking at Christian history; and thus, to offer an alternative way of understanding Christian tradition. As such, it is a footnote (literally "at the feet") to the scholarly, challenging, and prophetic work of Dr. Cooke, who has never let us forget that the Spirit is free and available

---

[51] My own view on the theological issues raised here is contained in *Treasures*: xi-xix, 1-19, 172-195.

to all Christians in their everyday human experience, whether those Christians lived in the twelfth or the twenty-first centuries. For this great gift, many thanks.

References

Audisio, Gabriel. 1999. The *Waldensian Dissent: Persecution and Survival, c. 1170 – c.1570*, transl. Claire Davison. Cambridge: Cambridge University Press.

Cameron, Euan. 2000. *Waldenses: Rejection of Holy Church in Medieval Europe*. Oxford: Blackwell.

Cooke, Bernard. 1976. *Ministry to Word and Sacrament: History and Theology*. Philadelphia: Fortress Press.

Congar, Cardinal Yves. 1977. "My Path-findings in the Theology of Laity and Ministries," *The Jurist* 32.

Logan, F. Donald. 2002. *A History of the Church in the Middle Ages*. London: Routledge.

Macy, Gary. 1984. *Theologies of the Eucharist in the Early Scholastic Period: A Study of the Salvific Function of the Sacrament According to the Theologians, c. 1080-1220*. Oxford: Clarendon Press.

Macy, Gary. 2000. "The Ordination of Women in the Middle Ages." *Theological Studies*. 61; reprinted with the Latin footnotes translated into English as the first chapter of Bernard Cooke and Gary Macy, eds. 2002. *A History of Women and Ordination: Volume 1: The Ordination of Women in a Medieval Context*. New York: Scarecrow Press.

9 Marriage: Covenant and Sacrament

Michael G. Lawler

Bernard Cooke argues that the most basic and universal sacrament of God's presence to men and women is human friendship and love. He further argues that, within the broad range of human friendships, the love between a wife and husband in Christian marriage is the ultimate paradigm of friendship and that marriage, not baptism, as is commonly assumed, is the basic ritual sacrament (Cooke 1983). This essay considers those claims and specifies them by reflecting theologically on friendship, love, marriage, sacrament, and covenant. The argument is cumulative; each succeeding section builds on what precedes it.

Friendship and Love

Aristotle and Cicero are witnesses that friendship is nothing new in human history. "No one," Aristotle argued, "would choose to live without friends, even if he had all the other goods" (Aristotle 2000, Book VIII, c. 1). In his commentary on Aristotle's *Nicomachean Ethics*, Aquinas argues that friendship is necessary for human living. It is necessary for the rich, for "there is no advantage to be derived from the goods of fortune if no one can benefit by them, but a benefit is especially and most laudably done for friends." It is necessary for the poor, for "in poverty people look upon friends as the one refuge." It is necessary for young men that "the help of friends may restrain them from sin." It is necessary for the old, "for assistance in their bodily infirmities" (Aquinas 1993). Cicero agrees. Friendship, "a complete accord of feeling on all subjects, divine and human, accompanied by kindly feeling and attachment" (Cicero 1890, 17), is to be preferred to all human possessions, and requires probation. Prudent people check their kindly feeling as they check their horses so that friendships, like horses, are fully proved.

As Aquinas worked to Christianize Aristotle's thought, Aelred of Rievaulx worked to Christianize Cicero's thoughts on friendship. Aelred follows Cicero's and Aristotle's threefold division of friendship: carnal, worldly, and spiritual. Carnal friendship is created by an agreement in vice, worldly friendship by hope of gain, and spiritual friendship by similarity of character and life-goals. Spiritual friendship is true friendship for Aelred. It develops when other persons are loved not for what they can offer in terms of erotic pleasure or material usefulness, but for what they are in themselves, images of God and reflections of the love of Christ. As for Cicero, true friendship is possible only for those who pursue good, and it finds its epitome in those who seek God to the fullest (Aelred 1994).

Aristotle's three kinds of friendship resonate with three Greek words for love: *eros*, love of another for my sake; *philia*, mutual love between two people; and *agape*, love of another for the other's sake. Aquinas makes a similar distinction with respect to love. He distinguishes between *amor concupiscentiae*, love or desire for my own good, and *amor amicitiae*, friendship or love for our mutual good. Their teleologies distinguish them: in love for my own good, I desire something or someone as *good for me*; in friendship I desire someone who is *good in himself or herself*. It is the latter, in all its charm and mystery, that is intended when one person says to another "I love *you*" and means it. Authentic, mutual human love is essentially ec-static, a going out of oneself to another. Aquinas makes a distinction between knowing and loving that underscores that fact.

"Knowledge is of things as they exist in the knower," he argues, "the will is related to things as they exist in themselves" (Aquinas 1947, Ia, 19, 3, ad 6). To know means to receive into oneself; to love means to go out of oneself to the other. To know someone is to know her within me; to love her is to love her as *she* is in her own uniqueness apart from me. In love, I go out of myself to another unique self like me, a second self, as Cicero said. If there is ever to be a second self, however, there must be a first self. For me, that first self is me; for you, it is you. If I am ever to grasp and cherish you as a second self, I must first consciously grasp and cherish me as a first self. It is this first self I love when I love myself; it is a similar, but distinctively unique, self I love when I love you.

Both Aristotle and Aquinas insist that friendship happens not when I love another, but only when my love is reciprocated: "Friendship requires mutual love, because a friend is a friend to a friend" (Aristotle 2000, 8, 2). Friendship is never one-sided; there is no real friendship, no real love, until love is reciprocated by the beloved. This mutual love between two selves, between a distinct I and a distinct Thou, creates between them the intimate communion that is the distinguishing characteristic of lovers. Communion is about common sharing, common possession, common responsibility and, in the communion between lovers, common nurturance of love. A frequent problem comes into focus here. In the loving communion between an I and a Thou, in which each loves the other *self*, communion cannot mean fusion of the two selves, it cannot mean identification of one of the lovers with the other. An element of *otherness* is central to the communion that arises from and is sustained by love. I love, not *my* self (though self-love is involved), but an *other*, unique self turned towards me. In the communion between lovers, a unique I and a unique Thou become an organic We, lovingly sharing in common their thoughts, their feelings, their dreams, their possessions and, as symbol of their personal sharing, their sexual bodies. The well-known biblical aphorism about a husband and a wife becoming "one body" (Gen. 2:24) is never to be interpreted as meaning that spouses merge their selves into one or the other. Such submergence and loss of self-identity sometimes happens in relationships, but it happens always with the loss not only of identity, but also of love and communion. Admired, valued, cherished otherness is integral to the relationship that is true love, even in marriage.

Marriage

Every reader of this essay will have been to a wedding. It may have been a civil wedding, it may have been a religious wedding, but it was always a solemn occasion. To establish a valid marriage, however, only one moment of the wedding counts, the solemn moment of giving consent: "I, Michael, take you, Susan, for my lawful wife, to have and to hold, from this day forward, for better, for worse, for richer, for poorer, in sickness and in health, until death do us part." When Susan had declared her free intention in the same words, you would have heard them pronounced married, "husband and wife." If that moment of free consent is missing or in any way flawed, there may be a wedding but there is no marriage. The outcome is called, legally, a null marriage, which may be verified, sooner or later, by a decree of annulment. It is this public, ritual commitment that makes married love quite different from unmarried love.

Not surprisingly, the wedding of Michael and Susan was conducted according to laws not of their making. Those laws have a long history in Western civilization, being rooted in the Roman Empire. Already in the sixth century, the Roman Emperor Justinian decreed that the only thing that was required for a valid marriage was the mutual consent of both parties. In many of the northern European tribes a valid marriage was created, not by mutual consent, but by sexual intercourse. That difference of opinion as to what constituted a marriage eventually created a widespread legal discussion in Europe, the solution of which has a major impact on every contemporary marriage. That solution was provided in the twelfth century by Gratian, the Master of the University of Bologna, who proposed a compromise solution. Consent initiates a marriage; subsequent sexual intercourse completes or consummates it. This compromise opinion settled the debate and is today still enshrined in the *Code of Canon Law* that governs marriages in the Roman Catholic Church (Can 1061).

Consent initiates marriage and consummation completes it. But what *is* marriage? Two definitions, again Roman in origin, have dominated the western discussion of this question. The first is found in Justinian's *Digesta* (23, 2, 1) and is attributed to the third-century jurist, Modestinus: "Marriage is a union of a man and a woman, and a communion of the whole of life, a participation in divine and human law." The second is found in the same emperor's *Instituta* (1, 9, 1), and is attributed to Modestinus' contemporary, Ulpianus: "Marriage is a union of a man and a woman, embracing an undivided communion of life." In 1996, the Congress of the United States, in the *Defence of Marriage Act*, felt constrained to underscore again the content of these two definitions. Though the "definitions" are really only generic descriptions of long-standing Roman social practice, they subsequently controlled discussions about marriage in western culture. They agree on the bedrock: marriage is a union (*coniunctio*) and, though the words are different in each definition, a union and a communion embracing the whole of life. That phrase, "the whole of life," is ambiguous, open to two different if not unconnected interpretations, and has been interpreted in two ways. It can mean as long as life lasts, and then implies that marriage is a life-long commitment. It can mean everything that the spouses have, and then implies that nothing is left unshared between them. Over the years, both meanings have been so interwoven that marriage is looked upon as the union of a man and a woman who commit to a lifelong sharing of all their goods, both material and spiritual. In the freshness of their love, Michael and Susan certainly approach it that way. Their mutually well-wishing love impels them to promise marital communion in everything "until death do us part."

One final consideration completes this section. We must ask, not what marriage *is* but what is it *for*? In both the Western and the Catholic traditions, which are not completely separable, marriage is held to have two purposes or ends. These ends are consistently articulated, from Augustine to the twentieth century, as they are in the 1917 *Code of Canon Law*: "The primary end of marriage is the procreation and nurture of children; its secondary end is mutual help and the remedying of concupiscence" (Can 1013,1). This explicit hierarchy of ends gave rise to a moral principle: where a conflict arises between the fulfillment of the primary end of procreation and the secondary end of marital love and support, the secondary end must always yield to the primary. In the Catholic Church, the second half of the twentieth century brought a significant change to that principle.

The Second Vatican Council met each fall from 1962 to 1965 to consider the teachings of the Catholic Church in the context of changed times. Among the many questions raised and answered was the one that concerns us presently, namely, the ends of marriage. In its *Pastoral Constitution on the Church in the Modern World*, the Council taught that both the institution of marriage and the marital love of the spouses "are ordained for the procreation and education of children, and find in them their ultimate crown" (GS 48). Given Western intellectual history, there is nothing surprising there. There is something surprising, however, in the Council's approach to the primary-secondary ends terminology. Despite insistent demands to reaffirm the traditional terminology, the Council refused to do so. Indeed, the Commission that prepared the final formulation of the *Pastoral Constitution* was careful to explain explicitly that the text cited above was not to be read as suggesting in any way a hierarchy of ends. The Council itself taught explicitly that procreation "does not make the other ends of marriage of less account" and that marriage "is not instituted solely for procreation" (GS 50). The intense debates that took place in the Preparatory Commission and in the executive sessions of the Council itself make it impossible to claim that the refusal to speak of a hierarchy of ends in marriage was the result of some geriatric lapse of memory. There is not the slightest doubt that it was the result of deliberate choice.

Any possible doubt was definitively removed in 1983 with the publication of the revised *Code of Canon Law*. The *Church in the Modern World* had described marriage, in language whose parentage in Justinian is obvious, in this way. It is an "intimate partnership of married life and love ...established by the Creator and qualified by his laws. It is rooted in the conjugal covenant of irrevocable personal consent. Hence, by that human act whereby spouses mutually bestow and accept each other, a relationship arises which by divine will and in the eyes of society too is a lasting one" (n. 48). The *Code* picked up this description and repeated it, declaring that "the marriage covenant, by which a man and a woman establish between themselves a partnership of their whole life, and which of its very nature is ordered to the well-being of the spouses and to the procreation and upbringing of children, has, between the baptized, been raised by Christ the Lord to the dignity of a sacrament" (Can 1055,1). These two documents resume the essence of marriage in the Catholic tradition. It is a partnership of love for the whole of life, ordered equally to the well-being of the spouses and to the generation and nurture of children. The discovery of this essence concludes this section and leads us into the next, for when such a marriage is between two believing Christians, the Catholic Church teaches, it is also a sacrament.

The Sacrament of Marriage

Since the twelfth century, the word *sacrament* has connoted certain ritual actions that contained and conferred grace. Catholics were frequently tempted to conclude too much by concluding that *only* those rituals were sacramental and grace-full or God-full, and that is far from the reality. All of God's creation is sacramental of God and grace-full (Rahner 1965), most especially the creation whom Genesis calls *'adam*, humankind, made in the image and likeness of God (Gen 1:26). It is not enough, however, simply to say that humankind is made in the image and likeness of God, for *'adam* is male and female, not only personal but also sexual. *'Adam's* human activities, therefore, men's and women's personal and sexual activities, provide a key image and sacrament of the nature and actions of God. As Cooke puts it, knowledge of the divine can be gained via the personal and sexual actions of men and women and, especially the relational actions of wives and husbands in marriage (Cooke 1983). Marriage is sacrament, not because it is a special ritual, but because men and women are created in the image and likeness of God (Schillebeeckx 1965), and that image and likeness is never more discernible than when they relate to one another as friends, lovers, wives, and husbands in marriage.

In the Bible there is an action called a prophetic symbol. Jeremiah, for instance, buys a potter's earthen flask, dashes it to the ground before a startled crowd, and proclaims the meaning of his action: "Thus says the Lord of hosts: so will I break this people and this city, as one breaks a potter's vessel" (19:11). Ezekiel takes a brick, draws a city on it, builds siege works around the city and lays siege to it. This city, he explains, is "even Jerusalem" (4:1) and his action "a sign for the house of Israel" (4:3). He takes a sword, shaves his hair with it, and divides the hair into three bundles. One bundle he burns, another he scatters to the wind, a third he carries around Jerusalem shredding into even smaller pieces, explaining his action in the proclamation: "This is Jerusalem" (5:5). The prophetic explanations clarify for us the meaning of a prophetic symbol. It is a human action that proclaims and makes explicit in representation the action of God. It is a representative symbol. The prophet Hosea creatively transformed his loving relationship to his wife Gomer into such a representative symbol of the loving relationship between God and Israel.

Self-understanding in Israel was rooted in the great covenant between the god Yahweh and the people Israel. It is easy to predict that Israelites, prone to prophetic action, would search for some human reality to symbolize and represent their covenant relationship with Yahweh. Hosea took the universal human reality of marriage between a man and a woman and established it as a prophetic symbol of the covenant. As a normal social reality, the marriage of Hosea and his wife Gomer is like many other marriages, though contemporary spouses could learn much from Hosea's loving fidelity to his wife. On a level beyond the superficial, however, the level on which men and women seek to discern the face of God, Hosea interpreted his marriage as a prophetic symbol, proclaiming and revealing in representation the covenant relationship between Yahweh and Israel. As Gomer left Hosea for other lovers, so too did Israel leave Yahweh for other gods. As Hosea waited in faithfulness for Gomer's return, as he receives her back without recrimination, so too does Yahweh wait for and take back Israel. Hosea's marital relationship to his wife is a prophetic symbol and image of Yahweh's relationship to Israel. In both covenants, the human and the divine, the covenant relationship has been violated, and Hosea's actions both mirror and reflect Yahweh's. In symbolic representation, they proclaim and reveal not only Hosea's faithfulness to Gomer but also Yahweh's faithfulness to Israel.

Hosea's casting of marriage as a prophetic symbol slowly changed two things important to Israelites. It altered, first, Israel's understanding of its covenantal relationship with God, deepening its grasp of the steadfast, faithful, and loving nature of this relationship, and it altered its view of marriage as this understanding of its relationship with God became part of its understanding of what marriage should be. Not only is marriage a universal human institution, it is also a religious institution, a prophetic symbol, proclaiming and revealing in the human world the relationship between God and God's people. Not only is it custom and law, it is also grace. Lived into in this context of grace, lived into in faith as we might say today, a marriage tells two stories. It tells the story of the mutually covenanted love of Hosea and Gomer, and of every wife and husband; it also tells, as prophetic symbol, the story of the mutually covenanted love of God and God's people. This two-storied view of marriage became the Christian view. Jewish prophetic symbol became Christian sacrament, with a change of *dramatis personae*, from Yahweh-Israel to Christ-Church.

The classical Roman Catholic definition of sacrament, "an outward sign of inward grace instituted by Christ," which took a thousand years to become established (Lawler 1987), can now be more fully explicated. A sacrament is a prophetic symbol in and through which the Church, the Body of Christ, proclaims and reveals in representation that presence and action of God, which it calls grace. To say that a marriage between Christians is a sacrament is to say, then, that it is a prophetic symbol, a two-storied reality. It tells a first story of the intimate relationship and communion of life and love between a husband and a wife and, embedded in this story, it tells a second story of the intimate communion of life, love, and grace between God and God's people and between Christ and Christ's people, the church.

A couple entering any marriage say publicly to one another, before the society in which they live, "I love you and I give myself to and for you." A Christian couple entering a specifically sacramental marriage says that too, but the couple also says more. The couple says, "I love you as Christ loves his church, steadfastly and faithfully." From the first, therefore, a Christian marriage is intentionally more than just the communion for the whole of life of this wife and this husband. It is more than human covenant; it is also religious covenant. It is more than law, obligation, and right; it is also grace. From the first, God and God's Christ are present in it, gracing it by their presence, modeling it by their steadfast relationship to their peoples. This presence of grace in its most ancient and solemn Christian sense, namely, the presence of the gracious God, is not something extrinsic to Christian marriage. It is something essential to it, something without which it would not be *Christian* marriage at all. Christian, sacramental marriage certainly tells of the love of a wife and a husband. It also tells of their faith in and their love for their God and for the Christ they confess as Lord. It is in this sense that marriage is a sacrament, a prophetic symbol, both a sign and an instrument, of the gracious presence of Christ and of the God he reveals.

In every symbol there are, to repeat, two stories. There is a foundational story and, built on this foundation, a second, symbolic story. The foundational story in a sacramental marriage tells of the loving communion for the whole of life of a man and a woman who believe in Christ and are members of his church. The symbolic or sacramental story tells, in and through their marital communion, the story of the communion between Christ and his church. This two-storied meaningfulness is what is meant by the claim that marriage between Christians is a sacrament. In a truly Christian marriage, which is always to be understood as a marriage between two *believing* Christians (Lawler 1991), the symbolic meaning takes precedence over the foundational meaning in the sense that the steadfast and faithful love of God and of Christ provides a model for the love of the spouses. In and through their love, God and God's Christ are present in a Christian marriage, gracing the spouses with their presence and providing for them models of steadfast and abiding love.

There is one final question. When the Catholic Church claims that *marriage* between baptized Christians is a sacrament, what precisely is the meaning of the word *marriage*? In ordinary language, the word is ambiguous. Sometimes *marriage* means the ritual wedding ceremony, in which a man and a woman freely consent and commit to one another "for the purpose of establishing a marriage" (Can 1057, 2). Sometimes it means the life that flows from their consent and commitment, the communion of life and love that lasts until death. Both these meanings of the word *marriage* are intended in the claim that marriage is a sacrament but, in terms of sacrament as symbol and image of the presence of God and God's Christ, the second meaning is more important than the first. Sacraments exist not only as ritual moments but also as ethical lives flowing from the ritual celebration. Baptism ritualizes the death and resurrection of Christ, not only to be celebrated but to be lived in daily actions; eucharist ritualizes communion in Christ, not only to be occasionally celebrated but to be constantly effected and lived; marriage ritualizes not only the commitment of the spouses to one another, but also their commitment to Christ as Lord and to a life modeled after the life of Christ. To focus on the sacrament of marriage only as a sacred ritual is to miss the point of sacrament, a symbol of the presence of the gracious God not only at one moment of time but always.

The Covenant of Marriage

Hosea introduced into religious history the idea of marriage as prophetic symbol of the covenant between Yahweh and Israel, an idea that was transformed by the early Christians into prophetic symbol of the covenant between Christ and the church. This talk of prophetic symbol and covenant gradually gave way in Catholic history to talk of sacrament and grace, and the idea of marriage as symbol of the covenant faded. John Calvin reintroduced it to the Reform tradition, but Catholics resisted it as a "Protestant" idea (Witte 1997; Stackhouse 1997). It was not until the Second Vatican Council and the publication in 1965 of the *Pastoral Constitution on the Church in the Modern World*, that the notion of covenant made its way back into the Catholic theology of Christian marriage. The Council describes marriage as "a communion of love" (GS 47), an "intimate partnership of conjugal life and love" founded in a "conjugal *covenant* of irrevocable personal consent" (GS 48). There is much to be learned about the sacrament of marriage by reflecting on the notion of covenant.

Hillers (1969) lists the standard elements in a covenant, which I will adapt here to marriage. First, there is a prologue that identifies the parties making the covenant ("I, Michael, take you Susan"). Second, the purpose of the covenant relationship is identified ("as my lawful wedded wife … wedded husband). Third, clauses specify the duration of the covenant ("until death do us part"). Fourth, blessings and woes are specified ("to have and to hold … for better of for worse, in sickness and in health"). Fifth, there is a publicly-sworn oath (the marital consent), and finally a public and permanent record of the covenant ceremony (the marriage certificate). Marriage clearly meets the requirements for a solemn covenant. It goes more to our point in this essay, however, to understand not just the structure of covenant but also its implications. I conclude this essay by reflecting on them.

To covenant is to consent and commit oneself radically and solemnly. When a man and a woman covenant in the sacrament of marriage, they commit themselves mutually to a life of equal and intimate partnership in loyal and faithful love. They commit themselves mutually to create and sustain a climate of personal openness, availability, and trust. They commit themselves mutually to behavior that will respect, nurture, and sustain intimate communion and steadfast love. They commit themselves mutually to explore together the religious depth of human life in general, and of their marriage in particular, and to respond to that depth in the light of their shared Christian faith. They commit themselves mutually to abide in love, in covenant, in marriage, and in sacrament for the whole of life (Yates 1985).

In a sacramental marriage, spouses consent and commit themselves to create a life of equal and intimate partnership in loyal and faithful love. When God created the heavens and the earth, when no plant had yet sprung up from the earth because God had not yet brought rain, a mist rose up and watered the earth. The mist turned the dry earth to mud, in Hebrew *'adamah*, and from that *'adamah* God formed *'adam* and breathed into her and his nostrils the breath of life. And *'adam* became a living being (Gen 2:4-7): "When the Lord Yahweh created *'adam*, he made *'adam* in the likeness of Yahweh. Male and female he created them, and he blessed them and he named them *'adam*" (Gen 5:1-2). This myth, for it is indeed a myth, responds to the perennial human question: where did we come from? We, in Hebrew *'adam*, in English *humankind*, came from God. Male and female as we are, we are from God, and together we make up humankind. This fact alone, that God names woman and man together *'adam*, establishes the equality of men and women as human beings. The further myth, which speaks of the creation of woman from man's rib, intends in the Hebrew metaphor to emphasize that equality, not their separate creation. The Catholic bishops of the United States underscore this fact in their pastoral response to the concerns of women in the church. Since "in the divine image … male and female (God) created them" (Gen 1:27), woman and man are equal in everything that is human; they are "bone of bone and flesh of flesh" (Gen 2:23). It is only because they are so equal, says the myth, that they may marry and "become one body" (Gen 2:24).

Christian marital covenant demands not only the creation of a life of equal partnership but also the maintenance of that life. As the God revealed in Jesus is not a God who creates and then abandons creation to its own laws, as Jesus is not a Christ who gives himself up for the church (Eph 5:25) and then abandons her, so no Christian believer creates a marriage, a sacrament, and a covenant and leaves them to survive by themselves. When a man and a woman marry, they commit themselves mutually to create rules of behavior that will nurture and sustain their marriage. As believing Christians, they will find those rules articulated in the Christian tradition.

Today, scholars across all Christian traditions are moving away from what may be called a "biblical rules" approach to morality. Realizing the difficulty of rigidly transposing rules from biblical times to our own, interpreters look for larger themes and ideals, which can inform moral reflection without determining specific practices in advance. Christian spouses will find the ideals to inform their covenant marriage succinctly summarized in the biblical Letter to the Ephesians. The author critiques the list of traditional household duties in first century Palestine, together with the inequality embedded in it, and challenges all Christians to "give way to one another because you stand in awe of Christ" (5:21). The critique both challenges the absolute authority of any Christian individual over another, including that of a husband over a wife, and establishes the basic attitude required of all Christians, even if they be husband and wife, namely, an awe of Christ and a giving way to one another because of it.

Since all Christians are to give way to one another, it is not surprising that wives are challenged to give way to their husbands (5:22). What is surprising, at least to husbands who see themselves as lords and masters of their wives and who seek to found this unchristian attitude in Ephesians, is the challenge to husbands. The challenge is that "the husband is the head of the wife *as* (that is, in the same way as) Christ is head of the church" (5:23). In immediate response to the obvious question "How is Christ head of the church?" the writer explains, "he gave himself up for her" (5:25). There is here clear echo of a self-description Jesus offers in Mark's gospel: "the Son of Man came not to be served but to serve" (10:45). There is loud echo also of what Jesus constantly pointed out to his power-hungry disciples, namely, that in the kingdom of God the leader is the servant of all (Luke 22:26). The Christian way to exercise authority is to serve. Christ-like authority is not domination of another human being; it is not making unilateral decisions and transmitting them to another to carry out; it is not reducing another to the status of a slave. To be head as Christ is head is to serve. The Christian husband, as Markus Barth puts it so beautifully, is called to be "the first servant of his wife" (1974, 618), and she is equally called to be his first servant. One rule of behavior by which Christian spouses may nurture both their marriage and their sacrament is the Christian rule of service, of God, of one another, and of the needs around them.

Another Christian rule for behavior, in and out of marriage, is the great commandment: "You shall love your neighbor as yourself" (Lev 19:18; Mark 12:31). Husbands, the Letter to the Ephesians instructs, are to "love their wives as their own bodies," for the husband "who loves his wife loves himself" (5:28). We can rightfully assume that the same instruction is intended also for wives. The great Torah and Gospel commandment to love one's neighbor as oneself applies in marriage to one's spouse who, in that most beautiful and sexual of Jewish love songs, the *Song of Songs*, is addressed nine times as *plesion*-neighbor (1:9, 15; 2:2, 10,13; 4:1, 7; 5:2; 6:4), suggesting that *neighbor* is a term of endearment for the beloved. A paraphrase of Paul clinches the rule of love for Christian spouses: those who love their spouses have fulfilled all the rules of behavior for nurturing and sustaining a Christian marriage (Rom13:8).

A sacramental marriage, as we have argued, is not just a wedding to be celebrated. It is more critically an equal and loving partnership to be lived for the whole of life. When spouses covenant to one another in the sacrament of marriage, they commit themselves to explore together the religious depth of their married life and to respond to that depth in the light of their mutual covenant to Christ and to the church in which he abides. A central affirmation of Christian faith is the affirmation of discipleship: "Follow me" (Mark 1:17). *Disciple* is a gospel word, implying both a call from Jesus and a response from a believer. Disciples learn from their Master, and the disciples of Jesus are learners of mystery. They ponder the mystery of God as Spirit who calls them to know, to love, and to serve the mystery of the Christ in whom this God is embodied and revealed, the mystery of the church, the Body of Christ (Eph 1:22-23; Col 1:18, 24), which calls them to communion and to service. Christian spouses, members of the church, disciples of the Christ, and believers in the God he reveals, consent in covenant to ponder together these mysteries, to uncover their implications for their marital life, and to live accordingly. It is that marital life, lived in faith, friendship, and love, that is ultimately the sacrament of the presence of God and God's Christ in the world.

Marriage does not isolate the spouses from life. It immerses them in life, and confronts them with the ultimate questions of life and death that are the stuff of religion. Sometimes the questions are easy, concerning things like happiness, friends, success, the birth of children; sometimes they are difficult, concerning pain, suffering, alienation, fear, grief, and death. Always life demands that sense be made of the questions; marriage demands that the spouses make sense of them together; Christian marriage demands that they make sense of them in the light of their shared Christian faith. As spouses find adequate Christian responses to the questions that life and marriage impose on them, they mutually nurture one another in Christian discipleship. They learn and grow together in Christian maturity. The more they mature, the more they come to grasp the ongoing nature of their marriage as sacrament. They come to realize that though their marriage is already *a* sacramental sign of the covenant between Christ and his church, it is not yet the *best* sign it can be. That best sign takes time. In Christian marriage, even more than in any other marriage, the answer to the age-old question of when are two people married is simple: a lifetime after they exchanged consent.

In our age, when marriage and family are in such disarray (Lawler 1998), followers of Christ have to learn and decide what sign their marriage will offer to a world that is sinful, broken, and divided by racism, sexism, and classism. Since they are believing Christians, that sign will depend, at least in part, on Jesus' assertion, already considered, that he came "not to be served but to serve" (Mark 10:45). Nobody claiming to be Christian, no individual, no couple, no church, can be anything less than for others. No Christian family can be anything less than a "domestic church" (LG 11) for others, reaching out to heal the brokenness in the communities in which it exists (Lawler and Roberts 1996). Service to the society in which they live is the responsibility of all Christians, married or unmarried. Sacramental, covenant marriage adds only the specification that the spouses exercise their service as part of their marital life.

This section concludes as it began, with a characterization of marriage, only now a more fully elaborated characterization of *Christian* marriage. Christian marriage is an intimate and equal partnership of life and love. Its origin is, ultimately, in God's act of creating *'adam* male and female, proximately, in the covenant of the spouses' free consent; its goal is the continuation of Christ's mission to establish the reign of God in the lives of the spouses, their family, and in the world in which they live. Spouses are instructed about such marriage in the prayers of their wedding service: "Father, keep them always true to your commandments. Let them be living examples of Christian life. Give them the strength which comes from the gospels so that they may be witnesses of Christ to others" (Rites 1976). If ritual prayers are always the best indicators of ritual meaning (and they are) there can be no doubt about the meaning of Christian covenant and sacramental marriage.

Summary

This essay considers and seeks to specify Bernard Cooke's claims that the most basic and universal sacrament of God's presence in the world is human friendship and love, and that the love between a husband and a wife in marriage is the ultimate paradigm of love and, therefore, also the ultimate sacrament of God's presence. The analysis of friendship and love supported Cooke's claim that they provide the most universal human matrix for sacrament, that is, they are "the human conduct … that is taken and made into sacrament" (Mackin 1989, 11). Every sacrament is a graced interaction with three components: God, believers, and the human action in and through which they interact. Believers' actions are sensible and immediately accessible, God's actions are non-sensible and not immediately accessible. In the interaction that is sacrament, however, believers' actions are signs of the presence and the grace of God; human friendship and love are context and the media in and through which God offers Godself as gift and believers freely and intentionally accept this gift of grace and offer themselves in return. Friendship and love, in short, provide the matrix of sacrament.

Cooke, therefore, is correct, in his claims and he may have the last word: "The sacrament of Christian marriage is much more than the ceremony in the Church; that ceremony is only one important element in the sacrament. Christian marriage is the woman and the man in their unfolding relationship to each other as Christians; they are sacrament for each other, sacrament to their children, and sacrament to all who come to know them" (Cooke 1983, 93). They create that sacrament when they create a marriage in the Lord by covenanting in faith, friendship, and love and by faithfully living into that covenant throughout their marital life.

References

Aelred of Rivaulx. 1994. *Spiritual Friendship*, translated Mark F. Williams. Scranton: University of Scranton Press.

Aquinas, Thomas. 1947. *Summa Theologica*. New York: Benziger.

Aquinas, Thomas. 1993. *Commentary on Aristotle's Nicomachean Ethics*. Notre Dame: Dumb Ox Books.

Aristotle. 2000. *Nicomachean Ethics*, translated and edited by Roger Crisp. Cambridge: Cambridge University Press.

Barth, Markus. 1974. *Ephesians. The Anchor Bible*. New York: Doubleday.

Cicero, Marcus Tullius. 1890. *Friendship*. translated Cyrus R. Edmonds. Chicago: Albert and Scott.

Cooke, Bernard. 1983. *Sacraments and Sacramentality*. Mystic: Twenty-Third Publications.

Hillers, Delbert R. 1969. *Covenant: The History of a Biblical Idea*. Baltimore: Johns Hopkins University Press.

Lawler, Michael G. 1987. *Symbol and Sacrament: A Contemporary Sacramental Theology*. New York: Paulist Press.

Lawler, Michael G. 1991. "Faith, Contract, and Sacrament in Christian Marriage: A Theological Approach." *Theological Studies* 52: 712-731.

Lawler, Michael G. and William P. Roberts. 1996. *Christian Marriage and Family: Contemporary Theological and Pastoral Perspectives*. Collegeville: Liturgical Press.

Lawler, Michael G. 1998. *Family: American and Christian*. Chicago: Loyola Press.

Mackin, Theodore. 1989. *The Marital Sacrament*. New York: Paulist Press.

Rahner, Karl. 1965. *Theological Investigations I*. London: Darton, Longman and Todd.

Schillebeeckx, Edward. 1965. *Marriage: Human Reality and Saving Mystery*. New York: Sheed and Ward.

Stackhouse, Max L. 1997. *Covenant and Commitments: Faith, Family, and Economic Life*. Louisville: Westminster John Knox Press.

The Rites of the Catholic Church. 1976. New York: Pueblo Publishing.

Witte, John, Jr. 1997. *From Sacrament to Contract: Marriage, Religion, and Law in the Western Tradition*. Louisville: Westminster John Knox Press.

Yates, Wilson. 1985. "The Protestant View of Marriage." *Journal of Ecumenical Studies* 22: 41-54.

III. Applied Theology

10 Resisting Amnesia: Theology and Human Rights after Globalization

John K. Downey

Theology is no private affair. Christian theology must be a theology of the world, a theology of engagement, a theology of incarnation. As an academic university discipline and an intellectual manifestation of a missionary religion, theology remains public at its core (Tracy 1975, 3-21; Tracy 1987; Ogden 1996, 80-91; Geffré 1994). And that also has meant that theology must engage and collaborate with other disciplines. The Incarnation did not crush humanity, but transformed it. Much recent theology assumes human beings exist in connection to the world and find a fundamental dignity in their concrete historical existence. Many Christian images and concepts advance the commitment to human dignity and to political and social rights: Christianity is a religion of involvement (Cooke 1966, 39-47; Thompson 1997, 88-111; John Paul II 1999). The theological contribution to the commonweal functions within the rules and methods of the intellectual community to faithfully integrate identities, cultures, and sources. Contemporary theologies, then, are responsive to globalization (Sanks 1999, 625-51).

Globalization razes the walls that divided us, that blocked our vision, and that cushioned our impact on each other. This worldwide flow of connections alters the primacy of the nation state in international relations, exposes powerful economic interests, and challenges social, religious, and political differences. Globalization fosters a new cultural grammar for self-understanding and action. New amalgams emerge within and across established borders. With a widening net of ambiguity and pluralism, modernity and postmodernity loosen our innocent metaphysical grasp of nation, "race," class, and way of life. We live confidently–if ironically–in a socially constructed, contingent weave (Lakeland 1997; Downey 1998, 239-247). We have the technological means to know and appreciate variety; we are committed to honoring differences; and yet, simultaneously, our diversity has become threatened.

The discussion of human rights provides a crucial attention to issues of identity and dignity within the tensions of globalization; moreover, the fear of a hidden cultural hegemony troubles human rights discussions. To discuss humanity and rights across cultural lines risks denying difference. Talk of universals or transcultural human identity is suspect since many so-called universals simply impose one local practice or philosophy on many others. Is the discussion of human rights merely a Trojan Horse for sneaking in the values of Western culture, economy, or religion? So, for example there has emerged an Asian values debate which asks whether human rights talk might be a version of Western individualism and a covert assault on the equally humane but communal Confucian notions (Mahbubani 1998; Bauer and Bell 1999). Even using the phrase "human rights" might be a trap, a cover for dominating different local traditions. At the same time, the actual international discussion of human rights has never been more universal. At the World Conference on Human Rights sponsored by the United Nations in June of 1993, 171 nations affirmed by consensus the "universal nature" of those "fundamental freedoms" and "human rights" articulated in the Universal Declaration of Human Rights. In 1948 that Declaration was approved forty-six to zero with eight abstentions (Alves 2000, 481-83). The human rights discussion, then, has become less a Western melody and more a global polyphony.

Discussing human rights after globalization requires finding universal grounds while continuing to affirm local identities and contexts. If we cannot talk across real cultural, social, gender, and political particulars–across our difference and otherness–we cannot talk about human rights. But talking across these borders has proven risks: local knowledge may masquerade as common knowledge and domination may present itself as friendly interpretation. In this essay, I want to argue that some theological moves might serve the political conversation on human rights.

The most useful theological conversation partner on the issues of globalization and universal common ground will be the sub-discipline of fundamental or philosophical theology; this branch of the theological enterprise concerns itself less with particular doctrines than with the rules for theological discourse. Oriented outward, it is rooted in the public demonstration of our hope (1 Peter 3:15; Downey 1999, 1-9). It addresses methodological issues and asks how diverse sources and situations can talk to each other. It finds common frameworks by which to enter public conversations. One of the new fundamental theologies—a reorientation to social roots called political theology[52]—can help by suggesting some common criteria for a conversation that respects the paradox of globalization. Here theology may make a contribution to human rights and so to our political imagination.[53]

The Paradox of Globalization

Pluralism among and within human communities is a fact. Meanings in a culture naturally come into focus relative to the structures and assumptions of that culture: it is important to know the rules of the game. But this contextual relatedness and difference, this relativism,

---

[52] Liberation theologies arose from the work of Latin American theologians such as Peruvian Gustavo Gutierrez and have found expression in Asian, African, and feminist idioms. For examples, see Curt Cadorette, Marie Giblin, Maryilyn Legge, and Mary Snyder, eds., 1992. *Liberation Theology: An Introductory Reader.* Maryknoll, New York: Orbis Press. Political theologies address social issues from a different context, class and culture, but no less aggressively. This theological approach arose in affluent West Germany in late 1960's with the work of Johann Baptist Metz, Jürgen Moltmann, and Dorothee Sölle. For recent examples, see Metz and Moltmann. 1995. *Faith and the Future: Essays on Theology, Solidarity and Modernity.* Maryknoll, New York: Orbis Press; Sölle. 1995. *Theology for Skeptics: Reflections on God.* Minneapolis: Fortress Press. The Womanist theology of African-American feminists also moves in this direction. See, for example Emilie Townes. 1995. *In a Blaze of Glory: Womanist Spirituality as Social Witness.* Nashville: Abingdon Press.

[53] I do not wish to argue here that human rights imply religious justifications. For that argument see Michael J. Perry. 1998. *Human Rights: Four Inquiries.* New York: Oxford University Press: 11-41. Also see Max L. Stackhouse. 1999. "Human Rights and Public Theology: The Basic Validation of Human Rights," in Carrie Gustafson and Peter Juviler, eds., *Religion and Human Rights: Competing Claims?* Armonk, New York: M. E. Sharpe: 12-30.

may include interchange, argument, or change. Globalization supports both the concrete language-game being played and its potential transformation in interaction.

Diverse cultures are moving closer in language, values, economics, and politics. Across our borders we interact, ideas cross-pollinate, and people reconfigure their standpoints. Like Internet transmissions, these new connections move rapidly in many directions and cannot be regulated. Globalization—global cultural relativity—reshapes our dialogue; it does not deny it. We live in paradox, in the tension of the universal and the particular, in a space occupied at once by respect for difference and mutual alteration. Cultural relativity locates meaning in the context of local language-games and yet denies the isolation of these games. It is a mistake to stretch the notion of cultural relativity from a contextual anchor of meaning to the impossibility of naming any common ground (Perry 1997). While all meaning emerges only in the context of the game, contexts are in flux, and they influence each other in increasingly substantive ways and in faster, more intense connections. "Culture" designates not romantically preserved specimens with exact edges, but dynamic networks of people, places, activities, and visions. Relations can best be spoken of as flows; borders are permeable, overlapping, melding (Schreiter 1997, 4-21). This new culture alters the political, economic, and social context for claiming human rights. How does one appeal to common ground after globalization?

Globalization need not cancel the particular, nor does it automatically homogenize the universal. The very fact of our conversations shows there are commonalities, yet these must emerge in particular settings. Roland Robertson argues that in addition to local and national cultures, a global culture is now forming and this culture is much more than a Westernization of other cultures. Robertson describes this dialectical culture as an ongoing presence of "the two-fold process involving the universalization of particularism and the particularization of universalism" (1992, 100). The tension of the universal and particular generate a global consciousness, which affirms the local consciousness and retains its identity within the global. It is not a matter of either universal or particular. Local traditions are noted and described within the stream of global connections and comparisons.

Globalization exists as a tensive interplay between the global and the local, what Robertson dubs *glocalization* (2000, 53-68).

Like the religious conversation across cultures, the conversation over human rights must be credible, not credulous. One must be vigilant lest the conversation shift to a monologue. A global awareness that notices differences can still become a "discourse of hegemony" suppressing difference (Aziz 1999, 32-55). Students of religion have learned that persons, groups, and nations can use the mantle of their communal tradition to cloak pathologies of power, fear, wealth, or myopia. So also in the political realm.

Global vision can be monochromatic. If enjoyment of the free market and the instant communications of computer life are typical, then globalization describes only one-third of the world. The other two-thirds experience only disruptive side effects. The poor continue to be pushed to the margins of the economy, their risky lives simply a natural part of the developed world's competitive edge. The poor are a drag on progress and deserve their poverty. Overpopulation is Asian or Latin American, AIDS is African, terrorism is mostly a Moslem problem, in spite of American white supremacy and neo-Nazi movements, and drug traffic results from third world production rather than global demand. Others are compelled into financial and military disasters. World media preempt the normative traditional narratives that have shaped social identity. Globalization names a web of connections, but it does not make them humane (Alves 2000, 484-86; Friedman 2000, 255-64).

The simple fact that China or Singapore asserts its cultural difference—their Asian values—does not make that difference accurate, contrary, or essential. For example, Neil Englehart discovered that when the government of Singapore attempted to engage its people in a reclaiming of their Confucian ethics, they weren't much interested (2000). Instead of presuming that differing cultural language-games are absolutely incommensurate, one could draw points of contact from within Chinese culture as, for example, philosopher Chenyang Li does (1999,163- 89). Cultures are not monolithic: one can often find internal criteria of legitimacy in a particular culture to support particular human rights (An-Na'im 1992, 19-42; Friedman 1999, 56-79). Globalization itself presents resources that transform the simplistic apocalyptic notion of the "West and the rest" (Huntington 1996, 183-206, 301-21). The local and the global touch, and they need not always collide.

The human rights discussion surely developed in Western categories, but that fact does not *a priori* mean that it cannot, *mutatis mutandis*, function in other cultures (Donnelly 1999, 60-87). Diverse sources and situations do converse. It is possible to learn global lessons, however tentative or partial, from a particular tradition, voice, or idiom. Though political theologies accept the context of globalization, they make universal claims. Some of these moves can be useful in suggesting *glocalized* criteria for the global human rights discussion. One preserves a particular identity while engaging claims of universality with a strategic commitment to honor the "other," to value the different one and the stranger. Further, a key tactic for remembering the other will be attention to concrete suffering. These proposals come from Christian and Western thought, but without any claim to exclusivity. Within the paradoxes of globalization, solutions will only emerge from particular stories striving for wider resonance.

Awakening to the Other: Political Theology

Political Theology is a major strand of contemporary Christian thought. Accepting the issues of historicity and contextuality, it moves to the praxis mode for its truth criterion. It is not a new list of doctrines, but a new fundamental theology, that is, a new way to construe the foundations for doing theology. It is a corrective to notions of religion as a private affair. Johann Baptist Metz, founder of this new political theology,[54] insists that Christianity is both mystical and political. Not only do theologians admit religious experience, but they also see that experience as intertwined with the social, political,

---

[54] Johann Baptist Metz (b. 1928) is a Roman Catholic diocesan priest from Bavaria. He holds degrees in both theology and philosophy and is Ordinary Professor of Fundamental Theology, Emeritus, at Westphalian Wilhelms University in Münster. He has also been Visiting Lecturer in Politics and Religion at the Institute for Philosophy at the University of Vienna. Metz has consistently sought to view theological and philosophical problems through the lens of human suffering. His political theology should not be confused with that of Nazi legal theorist Carl Schmitt who sought to justify the political as polemical.

economic agenda of all human enterprises. This new political theology insists on turning our attention to particulars and highlighting the baggage hidden in culture, science, and society. This attention calls us to remember who we human beings are by evoking our past suffering and recalling our future possibilities. And this remembering requires appropriate action.

Far from being a calming opium or a path of escape, this theology connects humankind through disruption and dissension: it names evils and calls on human beings to change the world. It is an antidote to the shift of religion into the private sphere. A theology that abstracts from concrete human lives, that pretends to be situation-free, is naïve. In response to Enlightenment reason, Christianity downplayed its controversial social dimension and reduced its heritage to the realm of private, intimate, apolitical decision. But the Enlightenment itself implies the political. If, as Kant says, human beings must be free to use their reason publicly, then it follows that they must also construct social situations in which these reasoning people can flourish. Concrete social settings for hope and suffering are central.

Metz's actual strategy is to acknowledge "the other." The universalism suggested here is a universalism of responsibility for other human beings. Attending to unreasonable human suffering, especially to others' suffering, provides direction for reasonable human praxis. The memory of suffering and the acknowledgment of the other have a practical intent. Metz uses this memory as an interruption that honors otherness. In this way the victims of structures and policies are not erased from the conversation. Metz cautions against living off a "bread of domination" that disconnects people: subjugation does not give lives their value (1981, 34-44). Political theology focuses on hearing the voices of the marginal, those who have disappeared behind the projection of universal essences. Christian discipleship offers human solidarity rather than domination as its hope. All human beings are called to be subjects, that is, to be agents of human value in the world, actors who declare human value in their action.

Remembering this call to act humanly, as well as remembering the suffering from particular actions and structures, can be dangerous. These dangerous memories of our hope and our grief position us to build a humane future. These memories shape a resistance and an agenda that spring not from a theoretical naiveté, but from memory and narratives of pain, suffering, and invisibility. Noticing and norming by concrete human suffering brings an anthropological revolution. The memory of suffering makes concrete the value of the other and helps one resist the culture's homogenizing amnesia.

Metz's focus on suffering decenters the controlling ego: "I begin not with the question 'What happens to me when I suffer, when I die?' but rather with, "What happens to you when you suffer, when you die?'" The classical question of theodicy, of how to justify God in the face of human suffering, should not be a question about our own sufferings. The question "What dare I hope?" turns around what I may also hope for you:

> "To dare to hope in God's Kingdom always means entertaining this hope for others and therefore also for oneself. Only when our hope is inseparable from hope for others, in other words, only when it automatically assumes the form and motion of love and communion, does it cease to be petty and fearful, a hopeless reflection of our egotism." Our hope, then, is not a faceless metaphysical hope (1987, 40).

It is important to bring victims into the foundations of knowing and acting. The usual story must be interrupted by connecting with others in a strategic love that sides against human agony. Victims show us the edges of society and call for a response. Metz wants to interrupt the ordinary by bringing the faces of the victims to mind. Narratives about the suffering of others, including Jesus, work to highlight and disable dehumanizing structures and behaviors: "We have a duty to face these catastrophes and remember them with a practical-political intention so that they might never be repeated" (1987, 42). Thus theological investigations and constructions done before the eyes of the victims will value difference.

The focus on the other, then, interrupts our fascination with the camouflage of sameness. For Metz, this interruption reorients the hope for a new life and a new world. The drive for justice, for the dignity of the other as other, is the heart of any version of Christianity. The world emerges in difference, difference that the theological enterprise has habitually overlooked. They put a face on "human being": the call of other can be heard only from particular persons. This limited, concrete face-to-face is the universal starting point. It is founded on a hope that the human heart will naturally turn outward.

Jesus followed his Jewish tradition by joining the love of God and love of neighbor. His parables of the Last Judgment (Matthew 25: 31-46) and the Good Samaritan (Luke 10:30-36) shape this tradition into the authority of others' suffering. In Matthew's parable, we discover that "sheep go to heaven and goats go to hell" largely because they do or do not care for others, for those different ones: the hungry, the thirsty, the sick, the naked, prisoners, and strangers. Luke's story of the man who helped the stranger who had been robbed and thrown into a ditch argues that one may not delimit who counts as a neighbor. The obligation is universal. It is not just remembering one's own suffering that matters but, as Metz points out, remembering the suffering of others, *even the suffering of one's enemies.* Jesus focuses not on the sin of others, but on the suffering of others. Sin is "a refusal to participate in the suffering of others, a refusal to see beyond one's own history of suffering. Sin is, as Augustine put it, turning the heart inward" (1999a, 230).

Metz proposes a new type of reason for the post-Enlightenment age: reason endowed with the power of memory: "The Enlightenment has never overcome a deeply rooted prejudice in the model of reason that it developed: the prejudice against memory. The Enlightenment promotes discourse and consensus, but—in its abstract, totalizing critique of traditions—underestimates the intelligible and critical power of memory" (1998, 142). Thinking critically is more than logical coherence, instrumental reason, or the following of procedures; it includes remembering others and their suffering. This socially oriented reason focuses on not forgetting (an-amnesia) and on actions of recollection or remembrance. This epistemological mediation of human suffering is practical in that it responds in ways that prevent abstract ideas of freedom or peace from erasing the concrete history of others' suffering. Anamnestic reason recovers memory as a resource for critical thought and political life: "Remembrance allows later generations to enter into solidarity with the dead in the act of recollection that brings the suffering of the past to light today" (Hewitt 1994, 77).

Reason endowed with the power of memory, a *memoria passionis* rooted in the memory of someone else's suffering, demands more than mere assent. This reason is not just a feeling, not simply compassion, but also a claim on us: it is a call to responsibility. The solidarity encouraged by our memories and hopes entails an impulse to action. After all, Christianity and Christian theology are practical at the core: "Ultimately, it is of the very essence of Christian faith to be believed in such a way that it is never just believed, but rather—in the messianic praxis of discipleship—enacted" (Metz 1999b, 47). It is so simple to merely believe in compassion—who can be against that great virtue?—but anamnestic reason asks for more: solidarity and resistance that transform the world.

Awareness of others' suffering provides a common ground that survives in the midst of globalization as an antidote to any abstract totalitarianism of rights. In addition, the memory of suffering, *memoria passionis,* might be a control on the negative aspects of fundamentalism. For Metz the dominating subtext of these discussions could be modulated by refusing to separate the authority of God from the authority of others' suffering (1999a, 233-35). Xenophobia, ethnocentrism, and religious arrogance generate human misery. Various religions and cultures might come together to resist the sources of unjust suffering in the world. This call to memory and to resistance would function as the criterion for judging moral visions and their concrete tactics.

Human Rights and *Memoria passionis*

The theological category *memoria passionis*—the memory of others' suffering—jars people's amnesia and awakens them to a universal responsibility for others. This interruption necessarily reshapes the political imagination. Human rights are not only particular legal and political proposals, but also a vision of the human good. When political scientists Jack Donnelly and Rhoda Howard distinguish between human rights and human dignity, they are pointing to the same sort of differing layers in the human rights discussion (Donnelly 1989, 66-87; Moltmann 1995, 178-93). Though certainly not allied with the Donnelly-Howard camp, Chandra Muzaffar likewise notes that human rights notions are embedded in specific cultural worldviews that norm the picture of the human being, human relationships, and the good society. After excoriating the West for its deteriorating human rights standards, Muzaffar asks for some universal vision of human dignity: "Without a larger spiritual and moral framework, which endows human endeavor with meaning and purpose, with coherence and unity, wouldn't the emphasis on rights *per se* lead to moral chaos and confusion" (1999, 28-29; see also Küng 1998, 114-56)? Interjecting some common criteria will prevent appeals to human dignity from degenerating into a disguise for other basic commitments to communication, political structures, or economic theories.

If globalization is not homogenization, then commonalities among groups originate in a particular tradition, a local culture or—as Ludwig Wittgenstein puts it—a particular language-game. It also means we can hope to discover some universal, classic expressions within the particular and local. Globalization need not be seen as submission of human beings and human societies to automatic laws of economic markets, culture wars, or political evolution. Rather, the globalized world must be interwoven with the pattern of human identity and value. Globalization is a human creation and so must be fashioned as a process of humanization.

Concrete dangerous memories, memories of real suffering and hope, provide the key. They are anamnestic: they interrupt in order to awaken and reorient people: "With its creed—'suffered under Pontius Pilate'—[Christianity] is and remains bound to concrete history, to that history in which people have cried and loved, but also hated, tortured, crucified, and massacred" (Metz 1989, 6). Political theology points to a common ground for intercultural and interreligious collaboration. This common ground is found not in a theory or policy, but rather in the common human response to others' suffering. This response-ability is a human imperative confirmed, demanded, and maybe enhanced by Christian hope. It is specific—though not exclusive—to Christian identity (Soko 1999). The attention to suffering Metz advocates comes from the stories and traditions of Christianity, and it also highlights a basic feature of human being. It does not require acceptance of the Christian scriptures or doctrines: the authority of suffering can cross borders. For example, recognition of the suffering of the Holocaust was a major factor in generating the cautions and hopes of the "Universal Declaration of Human Rights" in the United Nations (Morsink 1999, 36-91).

Prior to every theory, prior to every relationship of exchange and competition, should be the meta-political turn to the other. The best way to effect this turn concretely is through contact with the suffering of others (perhaps this was one benefit of the South African Truth Commissions). In this way, the whisper of human suffering keeps the political imagination alive in the face of the giants of technology and economics. The point of solidarity is not just to remember suffering, but to enforce the changes needed to end it: "The catastrophes must be remembered with a practical-political intention so that this historical experience does not turn to tragedy and thus bid the history of freedom farewell. That is a great seduction: to face these catastrophes and then end up with a kind of tragic consciousness" (Metz 1987, 42).

The West has, for example, the dangerous memory of Auschwitz as a warning. Its ignominy teaches that compassion without any entailed action cultivates the disconnectedness that allows Christians to go on untroubled "believing and praying with our backs to Auschwitz." Christians, as Dietrich Bonhoeffer put it, were able "to go on singing Gregorian chant during the persecution of Jews without at the same time feeling the need to cry out in their behalf" (Metz 1999b, 48).

The human rights discussion is not grounded finally in a consensus about definitions, laws, ethics, or rights. Rather, those arguments must be anchored in something prior to any consensus: suffering. Talk about human rights functions as an interruption, prodding communities to improve human life on the planet. The conversation itself challenges personal apathy and disrupts social amnesia by keeping the faces of suffering people before our eyes and posing questions about our responsibilities toward them. Rights are ways of acting on the responsibilities made clear by the authoritative claims of others' suffering. On this, we can build a constellation of values and ultimately specific tactical policies.

This turn to suffering is not grounded in a fixed "norm"; it is not a defined theoretical or metaphysical essence, but rather a contextually-normed imperative that honors particular settings. In current discourses, the turn to interpretation and to the social roots of human constructions undermines the pretensions of any so-called pure, disconnected essence. The sensitivities of the academy—hermeneutic, social sciences, ethnography, postmodernity—have raised suspicions about the unmediated knowing of some "already-out-there-now- real" (Preis 1996; Rosaldo 1993). But one could speak descriptively of culturally diverse, yet overlapping discussions about humane behaviors and postures. One might, with Ludwig Wittgenstein, speak not of sharply defined borders and essences, but of "family resemblances" which crisscross in our discussions.[55] Anthropologist Ann-Belinda S. Preis seems to agree when she claims, "Human rights increasingly form part of a wider network of perspectives which are shared and exchanged between North and South, centers and peripheries, in multiple, creative, and sometimes conflict-ridden ways. Human rights have become 'universalized' as values subject to interpretation, negotiation, and accommodation. They have become 'culture'" (1996, 290). Such a socially described commonality can enable a global discussion of human rights and human suffering.

Acknowledging a cultural location does not mean that unique persons and communities cannot agree and converse. An appeal to the authority of suffering, especially the "unreasonable" suffering of the innocent, is both universal and particular. As Michael Perry puts it, "No one believes that rape, or slicing off breasts, or ripping out wombs, or decapitating a child in front of its mother (who has just been raped), or castrating a prisoner (or forcing another prisoner to do so), or throwing a prisoner into hot oil—no one believes that such acts are or might be good for those on whom the horror is inflicted" (1998, 71). The starting point for discussion of human rights is not any sort of alternative theory or political system, but a negative critique

---

[55] *Philosophical Investigations*. 1966. New York: The Macmillian Company: paragraphs 66 and 67 reveal Wittgenstein asking what is common to all games. He shows that while there is no invariable core to the word "game," there are overlapping and crisscrossing similarities. He calls these similarities "family resemblances" because in a family "build, features, colour of eyes, gait, temperament, etc., etc., overlay and criss-cross in the same way—and I shall say: 'games form a family.'" No tightly patrolled concept defining an essence allows us to communicate exactly, but rather patterns of use and usage in the stream of life. "Human rights" gathers its meaning from this practiced weave in overlapping language-games.

flowing from a practically oriented empathetic reaction to truncated humanity.[56]

Remembering not just one's own or one's people's suffering, but also the suffering of others becomes a local criterion for global political dialogue. Political theology voices a common human call to respond, to connect, and to imagine new political relations. It calls for an interruption that promotes the imagination of new possibilities. Discussing human rights is similarly disruptive. The radical goal of human rights talk is to change the vision. Human rights discourse has a protest character: the conversation itself is a strategy of protest, as well as a preemptive strike aimed at changing the weave of life. Appealing to an anamnestic reason that faces others' suffering protects the integrity and mutuality of the conversation. Here lie the foundations; here "our spade is turned."

This conversation calls us to act on our hope and memory by changing damaging social structures of domination. Political discourse needs a shock, an interruption that reorients: it needs to touch the authority of suffering. Putting people in contact with the suffering of others may generate new ways of acting, thinking, and living. Here is a common criterion which at the same time can be internal to particular cultures. Political scientist Richard Falk agrees that "taking suffering seriously is the Archimedes point for intermediation between the universal claim and the particular practice when it comes to resolving antagonisms between widely endorsed human rights norms and culturally ordained patterns of behavior" (1992, 49). Or in theological terms, "Articulating others' suffering is the presupposition of all universalist claims" (Metz 1998, 145).

We must name human suffering, we must be in solidarity with those who suffer, and we must grieve. But these practices are not

---

[56] If all these things are so spontaneously horrible, one may ask, how people can do them. There is, of course, pathology. But psychologists have also noted the ordinary human drive to reduce any dissonance between actions and values. See, for example, James E. Waller. Spring 1996. "Perpetrators of the Holocaust: Divided and Unitary Self Conceptions in Evildoing." *Holocaust and Genocide Studies* 10: 11-33. Waller argues that the need to form a unitary self-concept brings those who act inhumanely eventually to adjust their thinking about themselves and their victims. "The evildoing becomes justified or rationalized when its effects, however atrocious, are no longer empathically considered by the evildoer" (18).

enough to change the world. We also need expectations. We need hope. A solidarity that feels the claim of the other and responds in the real world provides not just empathy or identity with the past, but a chance to transform the future. When the memory of suffering is merely the memory of one's own or one's people's suffering, it can be harmful, as in the former Yugoslavia. The suffering of others must be acknowledged in political negotiations. There is no place for silence, no place for turning away from the *memoria passionis*, no place for forgetfulness of our human communion. The authority of suffering interrupts our banality, our control, and our egocentrism. It is both universal and particular: universal without falling into abstract idealism and particular without being myopically egocentric or ethnocentric. It grounds a realistic hope, hope in the face of the radical denial of humanity in Auschwitz and other places of misery. It calls for a political imagination that trusts in the future, that has expectations, that transforms societal structures accordingly: "There can be no peace without hope" (Camus 1948, 263).

Talk of human rights is talk of universals, and such talk is suspect in this era of globalization. Relativity and honoring diversity seem automatically to challenge this conversation. But Christian political theology offers us a foundation to build on, acknowledging others in their otherness and recognizing the authority of their suffering. This *memoria passionis* demands concrete social actions and structures. No conflicts on issues and cultures are peremptorily settled by this fundamental methodological commitment; rather, this commitment provides a touchstone for justifications internal to particular cultures. The non-theoretical universal starting point offered by political theology is not a particular human rights formulation, but the experience of the authority of those who suffer: "Is there any suffering at all in the world of which we might say that it does not concern us all? Is there a single cry of suffering that is not meant for every ear?" (Metz 1996, 51).

The authority of suffering can function within a globalized world. Not only does it provide concrete and universal measures for any human rights policy, but the conversation alone is a exercise in the practical memory of our common ground. Political theology and talk about human rights both succeed when they remind us who we are. They are one way we resist our own disappearance: "Perhaps in this fluid situation, theology's main function is to help people dream the truly human dreams and see truly human visions of the future" (Cooke 1980, 46).

References

Alves, José A. 2000. "The Declaration of Human Rights in Postmodernity." *Human Rights Quarterly* 22: 478-500.

An-Na'im, Abdullahi A. 1992. "Toward a Cross-Cultural Approach to Defining International Standards of Human Rights: The Meaning of Cruel, Inhuman, or Degrading Treatment or Punishment." In Addullahi A. An-Na'im, ed. *Human Rights in Cross-Cultural Perspectives: A Quest for Consensus*, 19-43. Philadelphia: University of Pennsylvania Press.

Aziz, Nikhil. 1999. "The Human Rights Debate in an Era of Globalization." In Peter Van Ness and Nikhil Aziz, eds. *Debating Human Rights: Critical Essays from the United States and Asia*, 32-55. London: Routledge.

Bauer, Joanne R. and Daniel A. Bell. 1999. *The East Asian Challenge for Human Rights*. Cambridge: Cambridge University Press.

Camus, Albert. 1948 [1947]. *The Plague*. Trans. Stuart Gilbert. New York: Modern Library.

Cooke, Bernard. 1966. *Christian Involvement*. Chicago: Argus Communications.

Cooke, Bernard. 1980. "Truly Human Dreams." In Michael Novak, ed., *The Denigration of Capitalism*, 39-46. Washington, D.C.: American Enterprise Institute for Public Policy Research.

Downey, John K. 1998. "Postmodernity and Pedagogy: Connecting the Dots." *Horizons* 25: 238-57.

Downey, John K. 1999. "Risking Memory: Political Theology as Interruption." In John K. Downey, ed. *Love's Strategy: The Political Theology of Johann Baptist Metz*, 1-9. Harrisburg, PA: Trinity Press International.

Donnelly, Jack. 1999. "Human Rights and Asian Values: A Defense of 'Western Universalism.'" In Joanne R. Bauer and Daniel A. Bell, eds., *The East Asian Challenge for Human Rights*, 60-87. Cambridge: Cambridge University Press.

Donnelly, Jack. 1989. *Universal Human Rights in Theory and Practice*. Ithaca, NY: Cornell University Press.

Englehart, Neil A. 2000. "Rights and Culture in the Asian Values Argument: The Rise and Fall of Confucian Ethics in Singapore." *Human Rights Quarterly* 22: 548-68.

Falk, Richard. 1992. "Cultural Foundations for the International Protection of Human Rights." In Abdullahi Ahmed An-Na'Im, ed. *Human Rights in Cross-Cultural Perspectives: A Quest for Consensus*, 44-64. Philadelphia: University of Pennsylvania Press.

Friedman, Edward. 1999. "Asia as a Font of Universal Human Rights." In Peter Van Ness and Nikhil Aziz, eds. *Debating Human Rights: Critical Essays from the United States and Asia*, 56-79. London: Routledge.

Friedman, Thomas L. 2000. *The Lexus and the Olive Tree*. New York: Random House.

Geffré, Claude and Werner Jeanround, eds. 1994. *Why Theology?* Maryknoll, NY: Orbis Books.

Hewitt, Marsha. 1994. "The Redemptive Power of Memory: Walter Benjamin and Elisabeth Schüssler Fiorenza." *Journal of Feminist Studies in Religion* 10: 73-89.

Huntington, Samuel. 1996. *The Clash of Civilizations and the Remaking of World Order*. New York: Simon & Schuster.

John Paul II. 1999. *Respect for Human Rights: The Secret of True Peace*. Washington, D.C.: United Catholic Conference.

Küng, Hans. 1998. *A Global Ethic for Global Politics and Economics*. New York: Oxford University Press.

Lakeland, Paul. 1997. *Postmodernity: Christian Identity in a Fragmented Age*. Minneapolis: Fortress Press.

Li, Chenyang. 1999, *The Tao Encounters the West: Explorations in Comparative Philosophy*. Albany: State University of New York Press.

Mahbubani, Kishore. 1998. *Can Asians Think?* Singapore: Times Books International.

Metz, Johann Baptist. 1981. *The Emergent Church: The Future of Christianity in a Postbourgeois World*. New York: Crossroad.

Metz, Johann Baptist. 1987. "Communicating a Dangerous Memory." *Lonergan Workshop* 6: 37-53.

Metz, Johann Baptist. 1989. "The 'One World': A Challenge to Western Christianity." *First Hunthausen Lecture*, October 9, Saint Martin's College, Lacey, WA. Unpublished typescript.

Metz, Johann Baptist and Jürgen Moltmann. 1995. *Faith and the Future: Essays on Theology, Solidarity, and Modernity*. Maryknoll, NY: Orbis Books.

Metz, Johann Baptist. 1996. "The Last Universalists." In Miroslav Volf, Carmen Krieg, and Thomas Kushcarz, eds., *The Future of Theology: Essays in Honor of Jürgen Moltmann*, 47-51. Grand Rapids, MI: William B. Eerdmans Publishing Company.

Metz, Johann Baptist. 1998. "Monotheism and Democracy: Religion and Politics on Modernity's Ground." In J. Matthew Ashley, ed., *A Passion for God: The Mystical-Political Dimension of Christianity*, 136-49. New York: Paulist Press.

Metz, Johann Baptist. 1999a. "In the Pluralism of Religious and Cultural Worlds: Notes Toward a Theological and Political Program. *Cross Currents* 49: 227-36.

Metz, Johann Baptist. 1999b. "Christians and Jews After Auschwitz." In John K. Downey, ed., *Love's Strategy: The Political Theology of Johann Baptist Metz*, 39-52. Harrisburg, PA: Trinity Press International.

Moltmann, Jürgen. 1995. "Human Rights, Rights of Humanity, Rights of Nature." In Johann Metz and Jürgen Moltmann, eds., *Faith and the Future: Essays on Theology, Solidarity, and Modernity*,178-193. Maryknoll, NY: Orbis Books.

Morsink, Johannes. 1999. *The Universal Declaration of Human Rights: Origins, Drafting, and Intent.* Philadelphia: University of Pennsylvania Press.

Muzaffar, Chandra. 1999. "From Human Rights to Human Dignity." In Peter Van Ness and Nikhil Aziz, eds. *Debating Human Rights: Critical Essays from thte United States and Asia*, 25-31. London: Routledge.

Ogden, Schubert M. 1996. *Doing Theology Today*. Valley Forge, PA: Trinity Press International.

Perry, Michael. 1997. "Are Human Rights Universals? The Relativist Challenge and Related Matters." *Human Rights Quarterly* 19: 461-509.

Perry, Michael. 1998. *The Idea of Human Rights: Four Inquires*. New York: Oxford University Press.

Preis, Belinda S. 1996. "Human Rights as Cultural Practice: An Anthropological Critique." *Human Rights Quarterly* 18: 286-315.

Robertson, Roland. 1992. *Globalization: Social Theory and Global Culture*. London: Sage Press.

Roberston, Roland. 2000. "Globalization and the Future of 'Traditional Religion.'" In Max L. Stackhouse and Peter J. Paris, eds. *God and Globalization: Religion and the Powers of the Common Life*, 53-68. Harrisburg, PA: Trinity Press International.

Rosaldo, Renato. 1993 [1989]. *Culture and Truth: The Remaking of Social Analysis*. Boston: Beacon Press.

Sanks, T. Howland. 1999. "Globalization and the Church's Social Mission." *Theological Studies* 60: 625-51.

Schreiter, Robert J. 1997. *The New Catholicity: Theology Between the Global and the Local*. Maryknoll, NY: Orbis Books.

Soko, Keith. 1999. "Human Rights and the Poor in the World Religions." *Horizons* 26: 31-53.

Thompson, J. Milburn. 1997. . *Justice and Peace: A Christian Primer*. Maryknoll, NY: Orbis Books.

Tracy, David. 1975. *Blessed Rage for Order: The New Pluralism in Theology*. New York: Seabury Press.

11 Practical Theology and Congregational Studies

John A. Coleman, S.J.

The book by Bernard Cooke I have most frequently read, consulted, or directed students to study first hand is his magisterial, *Ministry to Word and Sacraments: History and Theology* (1976). By any reckoning, it should make most people's short list for the outstanding work in American Catholic theology in the last fifty years. Cooke's study contends that there are five major modalities of ministry that need to be found wherever the church, as such, exists. They represent ecclesial exemplifications derived from Christ's own ministry and/or from foundational and scriptural models of the church. The five facets of ministry include (1) *Koinonia*—ministry as formation of community; (2) *Kerygma*—the ministry to God's word; (3) *Diakonia*—the ministry of service in the works of mercy; (4) Ministering to God's judgment of reconciliation; and (5) *Leiturgia*—ministry to sacraments and worship.

Cooke is a systematic theologian. But I have mainly culled and re-appropriated his material in *Ministry to Word and Sacraments* for courses in practical theology, most especially for courses on ministry and on the theology of the parish. Because I am trained as a sociologist, I also always have drawn generously, in these practical theology courses, on

---

⁵⁷ For a brief introduction to congregational studies see Wind, James and Lewis, James, eds., *American Congregations* 2 vols., 1994. Chicago: University of Chicago Press, and Nancy Ammerman. 1997. *Congregation and Community.* New Brunswick, New Jersey: Rutgers University Press

material from sociology of religion, especially the burgeoning sub-area of congregational studies.[57]

In this essay, I want to (1) state what I understand by practical theology; (2) show the essential nexus between practical theology and sociology of religion, especially congregational studies; (3) examine how Cooke's categories about the essential modalities of ministry—wherever the church, as such, exists—might get re-figured when parsed through the lens of congregational studies.

What is Practical Theology?

Historically, until quite recently, practical theology may have been, in ways, the most unfairly beleaguered and "minimized" of the theological disciplines. At times, it has been reduced to an amorphous "pastoral theology." In the United States especially, it has often been trivialized to a kind of "skill-building" discipline, focused on preaching, worship, pastoral care, and religious education. Yet practical theology deserves to be ranged with systematic and historical theology as one of the three main arches in the edifice of theology. In a profound sense, practical theology reminds *all* of theology that theology must be a reflection on the praxis of the church. All of theology should be practical, in some real sense. If the *lex orandi* (the rule of prayer and, more broadly, the rule of lived faith) is the legitimate *lex credendi* (the rule for orthodox believing), then all of theology must be rooted, more generally, in a critical reflection on the actual practices of the church.

In his classic statement about the triadic branches of theology, Friedrich Schleiermacher organized the discipline into philosophical, historical and practical theology. Schleiermacher saw the latter primarily as theological reflection on the task of the ordained ministers or the leadership of the church—a kind of systematic analysis of the ministerial role as preacher, catechist, liturgical leader, and specialist in congregational care. Schleiermacher, however, held a deductive and subordinate view of practical theology. One simply "applied" the theory, derived ultimately and uniquely from philosophical and historical theology, to shape the lived praxis of ministry (Schliermacher 1966). Practical theology, in this view, is merely applied theology, lacking any independent role as an independent source for theology, as such.

More recently, practical theologians such as Germany's Norbert Mette and North America's Don S. Browning, Thomas Groome, and David Kelsey have challenged some of the received notions about practical theology deriving from the inherited paradigm of Schleiermacher (Browning 1991; Mette 1980; Kelsey 1992; Groome 1991). They have broadened the scope of the field, beyond the minister's role, to a "critical reflection on the church's ministry to the world" (Browning 1991, 35). They have explicitly added and included social-action ministry to the earlier canonical sub-fields of practical theology: liturgics, homiletics, pastoral and congregational care. This addition makes quite explicit that practical theology does not focus exclusively on the inner life of the church (Browning 1991, 57).

The new practical theologians have insisted that, rather than a deductive move from theory (supplied by historical and systematic theology) to praxis, as in Schleiermacher, the preferred move is from a beginning in praxis to an explicit theorizing about it (since all praxis is implicitly theory-laden) and a subsequent return to praxis. Praxis does not get all of its theory from the outside. It congeals its own variant of practical reason:[58] some things we only know from and in the doing.

Don Browning sees practical theology as "critical reflection on the church's dialogue with Christian sources and other communities of experience and interpretation, with the aim of guiding its action toward social and individual transformation" (Browning 1991, 37). Practical theology, then, inquires into how the present practices of the church form the very questions we bring to the historical sources of Christian faith. Theological understanding—indeed, all understanding—is also a moral conversation, shaped throughout by practical concerns about application that emerge from our current situation. Thus, application to practice is not an act that simply follows on understanding. It guides the very interpretive process from the beginning, often in subtle and

---

[58] For practical reason as an ingredient of practical theology see Browning, Don. 1991. *A Fundamental Practical Theology*: 34-54. A more generalized account of practical reason can be found in Toulmin, Stephen. 2001. *Return to Reason*. Cambridge, Mass.: Harvard University Press. For an argument that the social sciences employ a variant of practical reason see Bellah, Robert, et.al. 1985. *Habits of the Heart*. Berkeley: University of California Press: 297-307.

overlooked ways. Even the return to and retrieval of historical sources is not simply "objective." Our situation, our interests, and current problematic inform our very recourse to historical texts and roots. Practical theology is concerned with testing the lived validity claims of the Christian faith. It envisions transformations of persons and structures. Conversion is one of its key categories. Practical theology inverts the hoary maxim about theology being *fides querens intellectum* (faith seeking understanding) to a *fides querens transformationem* (faith seeking transformation or conversion).

Practical theology involves the following three sequential steps:

1 A doing of theology in close connection
with the description of situations

As Robert Schreiter notes, "describing the situation is part of theological reflection itself, not just a prelude to it." Thus, in his view, "Theology does not exist in the abstract; it is always rooted in a context. Knowledge of the context is part of the theology itself. Second, how we read the environment and the practices and beliefs of a congregation is never a neutral process" (1998, 26).

Something akin to a sociological analysis of the situation for the church—what the anthropologist Clifford Geertz calls 'thick description'—is a necessary component of practical theology. Thomas Groome has called this moment "naming the present praxis," while Browning dubs it "descriptive theology" (Geertz 1973, 412-413). It entails much more than a positivistic map of "facts," since practices embody congealed wisdom, a practical reason. Some things we know only in their concrete doing, in praxis. By praxis more is meant than a mere attention to practice, as such. Praxis "is practice that is self-aware of the theory that shapes or informs it." (Groome 1991) Practical theology, then, is done in close dialogue with the social sciences. It may even generate its own sociology! (Schreiter 1998, 39).[59]

---

[59] Browning does generate his own substantive sociological surveys in Browning, Don S, et.al. 1997. *From Culture Wars to Common Ground*. Louisville, Kentucky: Westminster/ John Knox.

2 An honest and explicit situating
of the researcher's social location

Practical theology is hermeneutical through and through. It knows that we are interested knowers and that our initial situation shapes the kinds of questions we ask. Our social locations and situations for appropriating meaning contour the very questions we ask, as we meet quite different horizons of meaning embedded in historical texts and traditions. Practical theology cannot remain sociologically naïve about the impact of social location on the cultural constructions of reality.[60] Robert Schreiter says of this second step in practical theology: "ideas and images that have been passed down through the ages need to be made accessible for each group of faithful people. Here you are looking especially for parallels to your current situation and instances in the tradition that illumine and challenge the situation" (Schreiter 1998, 24).

3 A privileged focus on the concrete praxis of the church

The sociological component stems from this step in order to describe that practice accurately. But the assumption is that the theologian does more than merely describe. He or she also looks to the deeper wisdom ingredient in practices, as well as at their deformations and needed transformations. What begins in practices finally moves, once again, to practical interventions to sustain, retrieve, or challenge current practice.

Schreiter claims that this third step in practical theology greatly differs from much traditional theological work. Instead of simply using historical sources as the guideposts to critique current situations in the church, practical theology calls for a mutual correlative conversation between sources and current practice. If the narratives of the tradition sometimes critically call current practices to account, the things we discover about God in current practices also bring a new theological understanding. There is a dialectical conversation between the sources of the tradition (which may be truncated or distorted) and current

---

[60] The classic statement on social location and the construction of knowledge is Mannheim, Karl. 1936. *Ideology and Utopia*. New York: Harcourt, Brace & World.

practice (which also may be distorted or truncated). Current experience, nevertheless, can become a genuine locus or source for theology (Schreiter 1998, 26).

I have found Yale theologian David Kelsey's work on refiguring theological education around a focus on concrete study of congregations very helpful. Kelsey proposes two terms for our inspection: practice and action. By a practice, Kelsey means "any form of socially established cooperative human activity that is complex and internally coherent, is subject to standards of excellence that partly define it, and is done to some end but does not necessarily have a product" (1992, 118). For its part, action is seen as "intentional, done on purpose and having an end or motive" (1992, 118). Actions are not, as such, practices. But practices are cooperative human activities. Thus, practices have two inter-related features. They are social and inter-active. Secondly, they are governed by rule-like customary regularities. One learns how to engage in a practice by learning its implicit rules through cooperative behavior.

Because practices are socially established activities, they have a history. Practices distinguish, but do not totally separate, traditions of human action from traditions of thought. Practical theology, consequently, must be in dialogue with historical theology in order to understand the roots of practice. As cooperative and complex activities, practices are necessarily institutionalized, at least to some degree. Thus, practices and institutions entail one another. They ought not to be contrasted to each other as opposites. Indeed, through institutions, practices cohere with other related practices to form a constellation of practices. Precisely because of this linking of practices, the "need for practices to maintain the institutionalization of other practices [to which they are institutionally linked], creates one of the possibilities for practices becoming deformed" (Kelsey 1992, 122).

Practices as forms of cooperative human action, which are institutionalized inescapably, also have a 'material' base. Practices involve bodily actions. They entail access to varying kinds of tools and instruments to instantiate and express them, and to cultivate communication among the cooperators in the practice. Practices need to be sustained in places or locations, through communication patterns that cost money, depend on resources, and need defense against opponents of the practice. Kelsey draws out some important implications of this point:

> It would be a mistake to look at this material base of practices as merely a 'precondition' for practices but not really 'part' of any practice. The two are not logically distinct. One can see this by noting the impossibility of defining any given practice without including in the definition either a reference to bodily action or reference to physical media of communication among practitioners and the physical tools they employ in the practice. This is an important point to stress because it underscores that practices have concrete social and cultural locations in their larger host societies. Access to the sorts of material base that different practices require is determined by the ways those host societies arrange social, economic and political power. Consequently, practices will tend to have some interest in preserving social arrangements that give them access to the resources they need and some interest in resisting changes in those societal arrangements that might limit their access to the resources they need. This obviously creates another possibility for practices becoming deformed; inherent within them is the possibility of their coming to fill an ideological role (1992, 122-123).

One consequence of a religious parish/congregation or denomina≠tion's social location is the concomitant threat of ideological distortions: "Precisely because a congregation [or denomination] has 'material' bases and is necessarily located at some point in conflicts with a society which may tend to privilege its access to the material sources it needs, a congregation's [or denomination's] practices are always in danger of serving to preserve the social arrangements from which they profit and of obscuring the inequalities inherent in those arrangements. When that happens the practices are filling an ideological function" (Kelsey 1992, 140-141).

The material interest being protected displaces God as the one to whom response is being made. In this case, the critique of the practice calls for creative reflection about how to avoid ideological captivity and idolatry *in the concrete setting*. Gary Will's recent book, *Papal Sin*, illustrates for Roman Catholicism this kind of idolatrous replacement of God by the shoring up of institutional interests that protect some practices (perhaps laudable ones), but distort and betray others (perhaps more fundamentally religious ones) (Wills 2000). Finally, Kelsey notes that since practices are ordered to ends and partly are defined by certain standards of excellence, attention to practice inherently requires self-critical reflection.

So, current practices can be deformed. They need to be juxtaposed to and correlated with normative and ideal standards. Church practices of ministry, for example, need to be judged, to be sure, against the normative standards for ministry that Cooke has drawn for us in *Ministry to Word and Sacraments*. But deformation runs in both directions. One consequence of practices being *always* historically and culturally situated and relative is that "practices shaped by one cultural and historical setting may become increasingly esoteric, private, and disengaged from the public realm as its host society goes through historical and cultural changes" (Kelsey 1992, 140). The increasing unintelligibility and inappropriateness of practices to the public realm and cultural categories may require, then, a critique of the effective tradition and attempts to re-imagine and retrieve it. Traditions, as well as current practices, have their deformations. The sociologist Thomas O'Dea, in a classic essay in sociology of religion speaking of the dilemmas in the institutionalization of religion, calls this distortion "the dilemma of the objectification of symbols" (1961, 30-39). Symbols need to be concretely objectified in historically given cultural categories in order to give them concrete meaning. But, over time, that very objectification may alienate people from the real and deeper meaning of the symbol.

Don Browning suggests that a practical theology will ask the following four questions:

> 1. How do we understand the concrete situation (in all its particularity) in which we must act?
> 2. What should be the praxis in this concrete situation? Sometimes this entails merely a 'pastoral' application of a normative traditional practice. At other times, however, the new concrete situation calls forth a new sense of praxis for the universal church.
> 3. How do we critically defend the norms of our praxis in this concrete situation?

4. What means, strategies and rhetorics should we use in this concrete situation? (1991, 55)

In the concrete, the practical theologian gains an entry into and a lens on to the field by an immersion in one or other of the main disciplines of church practice: liturgics, religious education, congregational care, pastoral care, and preaching. For example, in his book on practical theology, Browning strongly focuses on congregational care. He also draws on his expertise as a pastoral psychologist. Thomas Groome, however, mainly builds on his expertise as a catechist and religious educator. Virgil Elizondo roots his practical theology in a pastoral and anthropological immersion in an ethnic sub-group of Mexican Americans.[61] But several of the proposals for practical theology, among them Browning's and Kelsey's and, by implication, Schreiter's, seem to suggest *a privileging* of congregational study as the prime site for the analysis, critique, and renewal of church practice. How can this choice be justified?

Congregational Study as the Privileged Site for the Study of Church Practice

Differing claims for a nexus between practical theology and congregational studies vary in their forcefulness. Browning, in his *A Fundamental Practical Theology*, richly exemplifies his treatment of practical theology by appealing to studies of concrete congregations. At least in one place, he seems to suggest that the main question for historical theology—"What do the normative texts that are already part of our effective history *really* imply for our praxis when they are confronted as honestly as possible"—is best answered in a congregation, in a discernment in a concrete community (Browning 1991, 49). Nowhere does Browning simply equate practical theology with congregational studies. Schreiter shows the aptness of a turn to a study of the congregation in practical theology, yet makes no exclusive

---

[61] For Browning's appeal to psychology see Browning, Don S. 1987. *Religious Thought and the Modern Psychologies*. Philadelphia: Fortress Press; for Virgil Elizondo as practical theologian see my "Virgil Elizondo: Practical Theologian, Prophet and Organic Intellectual" in ed. Timothy Matovina. 2000. *Beyond Borders* Maryknoll, New York: Orbis Press: 235-245.

claims for that site as the primary locus for doing practical theology. Groome does not do his practical theology primarily in dialogue with congregational studies.

Kelsey and others, such as Joseph Hough and Barbara Wheeler, however, privilege congregational study for practical theology for focusing theological education as a whole (Hough 1988). Objections to this proposal abound. The congregation, after all, is not identical with the Christian church or Christian tradition, which is wider and richer than any congregation. The focus on congregational study may be too complacent, since most congregations fall far short of the normative ideals of the Christian tradition for ministry and community. Yet, as Kelsey argues, the "tradition is nowhere concretely actual except as practiced in particular congregations." What one studies independently of congregational life—the history of dogma or the sacraments or the liturgy—are relative abstractions from the concrete reality of local church life: "The abstractions from concrete social reality in each case tend to create the illusion that theological ideas or practices of worship or church legal systems have ghostly lives of their own that transcend the concrete particulars of the communities, which more or less believe the dogmas, practice the liturgies, and follow the rules" (Kelsey 1992, 134). We see here a variant of an old argument in ecclesiology about the universal and local church.

Since Vatican Council II, many Roman Catholic theologians have tried to mine the remarks in *Lumen Gentium* (The Dogmatic Constitution on the Church) to build up a theology of the local church:

> This church of Christ is truly present (*vere adest*) in all legitimate local congregations of the faithful, which united with their pastors, are themselves called churches in the New Testament. For in their own locality these are the new people called by God, in the Holy Spirit, to much fullness (1 Thes 1:5). In them the faithful are gathered together by the preaching of the gospel of Christ, and the mystery of the Lord's supper is celebrated, "so that the whole fellowship is joined together through the flesh and blood of the Lord's body." In these communities, though frequently small and poor, or living far from each other, Christ is present. By his power the one, holy, catholic and apostolic church is gathered together (Lumen Gentium #26).

The "universal" church is found wherever the true church of Christ is present. It is always present where the eucharist is authentically celebrated—most typically in the local congregation. Drawing on a rich theology of the church as a communion, mirroring in the community the life of the Trinity, a number of theologians have probed the ecclesial reality of the local church. They have argued that the universal church is not some over-arching mosaic of particular churches, because the universal church is found and realized in each local church. The church universal exists in and out of local churches. It does not float freely as some abstract universal above all its concrete embodiments. Local congregations 're-present,' make present, the worldwide church. They realize it—make it real—whenever the congregation with its pastor celebrates the eucharist on Sunday. Indeed, as Karl Rahner once argued, inasmuch as the church is and ought to be not only institution but event, the local congregation is *the primary* realization of the church as event.

In his *Ministry to Word and Sacrament*, Bernard Cooke gives us the formal ministerial components or elements, which must be present wherever the church authentically exists: the call of God, the word of Christ, the presence of the Spirit in word and sacrament and community, the celebration of the eucharist, and the fellowship of love and apostolic ministry. As James Coriden has noted: "Where these principles generate a community, it is the church, not merely a part of the church, but the full reality of the people of God and the dwelling place of the Spirit. In terms of spiritual reality, nothing more is realized in any wider or higher level of the church's life than is realized in an authentic local church" (1997, 49). Where the eucharist is celebrated, there is the church. Where the eucharist is celebrated, there must be the church in its fullness: in the scriptures proclaimed, the sacraments celebrated, in religious catechesis and pastoral care for the poor or sick, in social justice outreach, and the ministry of judgment, since these are ministries of the church.

The adjective Coriden employs, however, is telling. There are 'authentic' and less authentic, faithful and less faithful local churches. Kelsey knows this, too. So his proposal to do theology through congregational studies addresses the issue of authentic faithfulness: "To address the norms of congregational faithfulness is to do constructive dogmatic theology and moral theology. To engage in the critique itself is to do a theology of culture, and to undertake 'prophetic' judgment of congregations' common life" (1992, 157). Kelsey proposes that the congregational studies that he wants to make the heart of theological education be done in a comparative perspective. Precisely in and through a comparative study of congregations, one can probe how different construals of the Christian faith make real differences in the ways people's lives and identities are shaped and empowered. Practices of the Christian faith, to be sure, are encountered elsewhere than in local congregations, e.g., in exemplary lives or in personal spiritualities. But no other group besides the local congregation so insistently claims for itself that it enacts and instantiates the Christian faith. No other is found, in analogous forms, across cultures, ecclesial traditions, or even in inter-faith contexts. No other is so salient for the concrete faith life of Christians.

For Kelsey, practical theology, focused on local congregational life, redounds back to and correlates with a wider historical and ecumenical theology. Nor does Kelsey propose a narrowly sectarian or reductively congregational understanding of the church:

> If congregations are constituted by the enactment of a more broadly practiced worship, then study focused by questions about congregations must locate the congregations it studies in history. It must study them diachronically or through time. Study of the particular congregation is thus inescapably study of it *in* its own tradition, in its likeness to other congregations in previous historical periods who share its basic construal of what the Christian thing is all about, what it is to understand God. . . At the same time, study of that same congregation also involves comparing it with congregations in earlier periods whose enactments of the universally practiced worship of God are markedly different (1992, 151).

It is evident, secondly, that if congregations are constituted by sharing in more broadly practiced worship of God, study focused by questions about them must compare and contrast congregations that are contemporaneous. It must study them synchronically, or at the same time, in a cross-cultural way to probe ways in which the broadly practiced worship may be enacted in quite different dialects.

We need to ask about congregations: how do they see themselves as church and how do they hold themselves accountable to the forms of ministry incumbent on the church? We also need to identify how Christian congregations, for all their differences from one another, are somehow one, part of a more embracing whole. We need to specify, too, how congregations are not only located within traditions of faith, but located within and somehow integral to the larger social and cultural systems of their society. Thus, for example, the authoritative handbook for the study of congregations, *Studying Congregations*, contains chapters and specific methods for probing the social ecology of congregations, the culture and identity within congregations, and differing leadership styles and resources (both within congregations and in the ways congregations, themselves, become resources for their wider social settings) (Ammerman 1997). *Studying Congregations* is a veritable *vade mecum* guide to how even ordinary parishioners can do practical theology within their own congregations.

The Proliferation of Congregational Studies in Theology and Sociology

Fortuitously and fortunately, this call for a new turn toward congregational study as a privileged site for doing practical theology comes just at a time when studies of congregations, in sociology and elsewhere, are proliferating. University of Illinois sociologist R. Stephen Warner notes that the congregation remains the bedrock of the American religious system. Arguably, with the decline of the salience of denominational identities in America (people sit lightly with denominational loyalties and switch, over a lifetime, more frequently to new denominations, largely due to attraction toward alternative congregations and the ministries they provide), the significance of congregations in American life is actually increasing. There are nearly 300,000 congregations in America, one, on average, for every 400 church-goers. Warner argues that there exists a kind of *de facto* congregationalism, even in denominations, such as Roman Catholicism, which are hierarchical and not congregational in polity (Warner, 54-99).[62]

[62] See also Warner, R. Stephen. March 1993. "Work in Progress: Toward a New Paradigm for the Sociological Study of Religion in the United States" in *American Journal of Sociology* 98: 1044-93.

Recent studies have focused on the role of the local congregations for new immigrant groups, serving both as a buffer and as a resource and legitimate locale for ethnic sustenance and negotiation with the new culture (Warner 1998; Yeng 2001, 367-378). Such congregations have grown apace. Other studies—such as Nancy Ammerman's path-breaking work, *Congregation and Community*—attend to case studies of innovation, relocation, adaptation, and resistance to change by congregations, as inner city neighborhoods undergo drastic demographic shifts or as new congregations build in expanding suburbs (1997). In-depth case studies have been done of particular Presbyterian, African-American, Jewish, or mainline Protestant congregations (Warner 1998; Freedman 1984; Dorsey 1995; Wilkes 1994). A recent new overview of successful Catholic parishes gives hints for strategies for renewal and niche marketing among a Catholic population (Wilkes 2001).[63]

Another important sociological study of congregations focuses on a typology of self-understandings of the congregation as, alternatively, a set-apart house of worship, a family, an internally collegially organized community, and a civic leader. This study carefully details the ways conflicts arise within each type of congregation and how they get resolved (Becker 1999).

University of Arizona sociologist Mark Chaves has undertaken a massive national survey of congregations to find out their size, location, polity, and range of programs and resources (2000, 261-272). Chaves' study will eventually turn out to be a goldmine in comparative congregational studies. Other studies have focused on a typology of various construals of the social mission of congregations—their sense of presence to their communities—arguing that theological stances about the church's mission to the world, at local levels, have perduring impact on a congregation's positions on issues of social outreach and civic engagement (Roozen 1983). The new concern for faith-based initiatives in social services has led to broad studies of congregations' concern for and actual deliverance of social services to the community (Cnaan 1999).

---

[63] See also Gremillion, Joseph and Jim Castelli. 1987. *The Emerging Parish: The Notre Dame Study of Catholic Life.* San Francisco: Harper and Row.

New works have probed, in depth, the rooting of community organizing in congregations and how congregations generate social capital for entire neighborhoods and cities in which they are located (Warren 2001; Wood 2002). Several sociological studies have done comparative research on stewardship and the giving of money in local congregations (Wuthnow 1994; Hoge 1996). Still other studies have focused research on the mega-church phenomenon (Eisland 1998).

Besides these strictly sociological accounts that demonstrate that parishes are micro-organizations of considerable complexity and subtlety (with important links to other congregations, community organizations, and primary sources in American society, beyond the family, of community feeling), theologically sophisticated practitioners of church research or proponents of church growth programs, through amalgam research using social science, provide needed research tools to help local members of a congregation to focus anew on their mission statements, self-images, pastoral councils, planning processes, leadership styles, ministry engagement, and narratives and histories (Dudley 1993; Dudley 1983; Dudley 1978; Hopewell 1987; Carroll 1991). Historians have tried to retrieve American religious history by a unique focus on congregational histories (Wind 1987; Dolan 1987). Various specialized centers for research on congregational ministry now exist: The St. Alban's Institute, the Willow Creek Association for the study of mega-churches, the Yokefellow Institute connected with the work of pioneering congregational researcher, Lyle Shaller, The Institute for Church Growth at Pasadena's Fuller Seminary, and the Center for Social and Religious Research at the Hartford Seminary. The Center for the Applied Research in the Apostolate (CARA) and Monsignor Philip Murnion's National Pastoral Life Center provide similar resources for the study of Catholic parishes.

So, the tools are roughly in place to follow the promptings of those, such as Kelsey, who would turn to congregational study as the privileged site for practical theology. How might Cooke's categories for ministry (derived from historical and systematic theology) look different, when seen through the lens of congregational study? How might practical theology attend to ministry as formation of community, ministry to God's word, ministry as service to the people of God, and ministry to the church's sacramentality? A full answer would involve writing an entire book. I want merely to sketch some of the ways congregational studies tackle these elements that Cooke contends are constitutive for the ministry of God's church.

Ministry as Formation of Community

Cooke reminds us in *Ministry to Word and Sacraments* that Jesus gathered together a community of disciples. In the New Testament, the minister was seen as a worker with/ ambassador of Christ who introduces others to the life of Christ and exercises the authority of Christ himself. The minister is to build up the body by giving witness to Christ, effecting reconciliation, giving life, and redeeming from wickedness. One of the aims of ministry is the formation of a community that will be an extension of Christ's work in ministry. As Cooke puts it, "The community envisaged by the New Testament writers as a goal of Christian ministry (including the ministry of Christ himself) is not basically a matter of social arrangement. Rather it is the deeper reality involved in people sharing a common insight—animated by the spirit—into the meaning of life" (Cooke 1976, 41). Ministries of building community are not self-initiated: God is the great community organizer. But, in concrete fact, congregational communities do take on one or another form of social arrangement. Formation of community entails issues of leadership within the community, the goals of a community, and the quality of community life together.

Leadership within the Community

Sociological studies of leadership in congregations distinguish between *authority* and *leadership*. Authority is legitimate power. Leadership is not synonymous with authority. There can be ministers who claim to have 'legitimate authority,' but lack all leadership. Leaders may have only 'intrinsic' or 'informal' authority, but lack any formal authority. Leadership, however, is primarily an *activity,* which a number of people within a congregation can exercise. There are, moreover, alternative models of leadership style outside of or within congregations. Some leaders see their key role as one of building consensus around mission, programs, and legitimate processes for decision-making and conflict resolution. They are like orchestra conductors who build up a widely shared and collegial or democratic ethos in the community.

Others see themselves as the ultimate decision makers or discerners for a congregation. Often what are called 'charismatic leaders' function in this way. Still other leaders see themselves mainly as experts in ministerial tasks. Calling and competence, and office and personal authority, are neither to be conflated nor seen as mutually exclusive. A pastor who exhibits religious authenticity gains trust and is granted personal authority. He or she is trusted as both being competent and exhibiting personal depth: "Being granted personal authority by a congregation will not be acknowledged in a formal ceremony, but when it is given, it is not unlike experiencing a second ordination" (Ammerman 1998, 172).

As an activity, leadership in a group involves several key tasks: it involves helping the congregation gain a realistic understanding of its particular situation and circumstances; it involves helping members to develop together a vision for their corporate life that is faithful to their best understanding of God and God's purposes for the congregation in the time and place where it is situated; and it involves helping the congregation to embody that vision in the congregation's corporate life, while attempting to address the various challenges or 'messes' that arise (Ammerman 1998, 173). Good leaders are trusted, empower others, share responsibilities by delegation, and consult widely. Communities are always about communication. Studying the communication processes within a local congregation will uncover its form of leadership for community: democratic or consensual, rule by experts, or rule by formal authorities alone.

Goals of the Community

Without a vision, the community falters. Mission, vision statements, or key images for a congregation are ways by which a congregation talks about its community and answers this question: who are we and how do we do things around here? Mission or vision statements can, of course, be mere window dressing or rhetorical exercises. But Jackson Carroll suggests that good vision statements for a congregation have the following traits:

1. The vision is faithful to the congregation's best understanding of its religious tradition. In the Christian tradition, this implies

faithfulness to God's purposes as found in scripture and in church traditions, as well as openness to the ongoing leading by God's spirit.

2. The vision statement is oriented to the future. Rather than only affirming who we are in the present, the vision provides a statement of a desired future for the congregation that its members are committed to bring into being.

3. The vision is appropriate for this congregation. It takes into account the congregation's history, its core commitments, its size and resources, its unique capacities and what its members most deeply care about. A congregation's vision for its future need not be bound by its past or present but neither can a congregation ignore them. Unless it builds significantly on its core values as found in the culture of the congregation, the vision is highly unlikely to be accepted.

4. The vision statement is realistic in terms of the congregation's social context. It should be based on the best possible information about present realities and likely demographic trends.

5. The vision statement contains both judgment and promise, good news and bad news. It makes judgments on some aspects of the past and present, including, where necessary, core values and practices, while envisioning a more desirable future for the congregation.

6. The vision is, as far as possible, *a shared vision* of the desirable future. (Carroll 1998, 183-184).

Various exercises have been devised to help a congregation formulate and shape its vision. One, called a congregational time-line, lines up on a chalkboard or on butcher paper three or four important parallel time lines. One line looks at the most important events or turning points in a congregation's own history—its succession of pastors, its crises, its building of a new parish hall or church, and its growth points. In a collective effort, these are then juxtaposed to corollary dates of the history of its surrounding local community, its denomination or diocese, and/or to national or global history.

This exercise helps to see the intersection of the life of the local congregation with other histories. Another exercise simply involves an intentional walking around the neighborhood of the congregation to get a sense of its context and ambience, the existence of other churches, and community organizations. An even more complicated exercise undertakes a careful study of the census data results for the congregation's sector of the city or county.

A final exercise asks about the process—if any—for the intake of new members. In a collectively focused conversation, new members recount their surprises or disappointments on being initiated, and established leaders try to tease out their implicit assumptions about 'the way we do things around here.' Each can become more reflective about the images in the congregation, about who we are and how we do things in the congregation. How welcoming is the congregation? How intentional is it about the intake of new members? What concrete images of community are new members asked to buy into?

The Quality of Community Life

Penny Edgell Becker, in her study of twenty-three congregations in the Chicago suburbs, devised a typology of how congregations answer those two questions: who are we as a community and how do we do things around here. These are the four types: (1) The congregation as a house of worship, (2) The congregation as a kind of family, (3) The congregation as a community of intimate ties and shared values, and (4) The congregation as a leader or animator in its denomination or neighborhood, or even city. Each of these four involves competing notions of community and leadership and, in turn, generates distinctive forms of conflicts within congregations. All four models, as types for religious congregations, put emphasis on both worship and religious education. The typologies were designed to reflect real, competing patterns found in Becker's sample. Denominational affiliation did not determine the type of model followed. Catholic parishes could be a house of worship, a family-type, a community of shared values, or a conscious leader.

When we think of a congregation as *primarily* a provider of religious goods and services to individuals—worship, religious education, well-crafted programs, rituals such as weddings and funerals—it is likely to be a House of Worship model. Such congregations typically specialize on the core tasks of worship and religious education. They seek an intimate and uplifting worship experience and good programs to train children in the doctrines and practices of the church: "These congregations make limited demands on member loyalty and time and assume a segmented form of attachment, where religious involvement remains relatively separate from other areas of members' lives. Decisions are made by clergy, paid staff or committees" (Becker 1999, 13).

In family-model congregations, the congregation seeks a place where worship, religious education, and the provision of close-knit and supportive relationships are core tasks. Members know and care about each other's lives: "Informal, personal connections and length of membership are more important bases of authority than are formal structures or positions, with the congregation being run by a small group of long-time lay leaders who are all good friends and belong to extended family networks" (Becker 1999, 13).

What Becker calls "community-model" congregations lay great stress on shared ties and values. In community congregations, it is important to members that policies and programs express the values and sentiments of members regarding internal and social issues. The core task, really, is to figure out how to interpret and apply shared values: "If a House of Worship is like a religious store and family congregations are like patriarchies, community congregations are like democracies, with more emphasis on formal and open decision- making routines that include all members" (Becker 1999, 14). Community type congregations value process over outcome. When they engage social issues "they are heavily guided by the passions and commitments of particular members and they are likely to act only when broader social issues impact on their local community or constituency" (Becker 1999, 14).

Finally, leader congregations differ from these community congregations in several ways. The values they express derive more directly from official tenets of their tradition or denomination and less from the members' own interpretations and life experiences. Secondly, they cultivate a more activist notion of witness (this could be evangelical witness rather than social justice witness), focusing more on touching and changing the world beyond the congregation than in living intimately shared values: "Providing members with intimate connections or a feeling of belonging are low priorities in this understanding, although here too some individuals can find close friends by seeking them out. These congregations are participative but they are more like branches of a social movement organization with a strong mission than like democracies, which have a more diffuse mission" (Becker 1999, 112).

While each type of congregation agreed that worship and religious education are important programmatic values, they varied on how much they valued the promotion of fellowship and intimacy in the congregation (these were more important for family and congregation-model types); how much value they placed on the congregation as an arena for sorting out social, religious, and political issues that congregants found important (this was most salient for community-type congregations, second most salient for leader congregations, and least important in family and House of Worship models), and how active they were in the wider community.

Pastoral leadership styles also differ across the four models of congregations: thus, "The role of the pastor in a community congregation is largely that of a professional hired to perform ritual and administrative tasks and to facilitate the process of congregational consensus-seeking. Pastors exert a formal and process oriented leadership but they tend not to put issues on the agenda or take substantive stands during conflict" (Becker 1999, 123). Ultimately, in such congregations, authority springs from the members and is rooted in the community as a whole. Pastors in leader or House of Worship congregations have more formal authority.

The pastor in a family congregation is either an outsider or a beloved member of the family. Outsider's authority in family congregations, no matter the polity of the congregation, even in hierarchical denominations, is severely limited by the knowledgeable long-time insider family members. In leader congregations the pastor is the prime religious authority and exercises a great deal of direct control on many decisions. Frequently, his is a charismatic leadership authority, in the sense Max Weber spoke of it: "In the house of worship congregation, the pastor's role is more determined by the formal polity structure of the denomination. In the Catholic parish, this means the pastor is heavily involved in administrative decisions, while in the United Methodist church this means that the lay Administrative Council is the most powerful decision-making body in all nonreligious matters" (Becker 1999, 176-177).

Becker's typology allowed her to even predict which types of congregations would have most overt conflicts (the congregational model) and which might shove them under the rug (House of Worship models). But when conflicts do arise in family or leader congregations, they can be very intense, leading to schisms or the withdrawal of large numbers of congregants. In community congregations (which report twice the number of conflicts as family congregations) conflict, however, tends to be understood as moral rather than personal. The overall style of dealing with conflict is through a participatory moral community where religious authority is diffuse: "Conflict is not feared but is viewed as positive and healthy up to a point" (Becker 1999, 117). Intimacy is a high value in family and community model congregations. Intuitively, we connect such intimacy with strong community. Yet research by sociologist Daniel Olson has shown that when a congregation has been settled, members tend to feel they have all the friends they have time and energy to deal with and, thus, have less incentive to seek out new recruits. They experience a kind of inward implosion rather than an outward missionary thrust (1987). Too much intimacy in communities can actually undercut evangelism and mission.

There is one spirit, but a diversity of gifts—and, presumably, a legitimate diversity of leadership styles, images of congregations as communities, and ways of formulating a local community's vision statement. Attention to all three facets, however, is central to the ministry of formation of community. One way practical theology can enhance the understanding of ministry of formation of community is by studying (or by enabling a self-study of) a congregation in terms of its operative leadership style, community image, and mission or vision statement. Each of these then can be probed in terms of its consonance with the tradition's understanding of ministry of formation of community. In self-studies, members of the congregation would do some comparisons of the strengths and weaknesses of family congregations, House of Worship, community models, and leader congregations. They could assess their own congregation's operative images of who we are and the way we do things around here. Returning to the history of the tradition as found in Cooke's *Ministry to Word and Sacrament* they could, then, try to give a more explicit theological account of how their own community model meshes with, is deformed from, or adds to or revises the tradition in some ways.

Ministry of the Word

Cooke makes evident how central the ministry of the word was to Jesus. Jesus is seen in the scriptures as a witness, a preacher/ teacher/ prophet. Christ's ministry can be seen, most basically, as a mystery of the self-communication of the word of God. In scripture and tradition, we see many forms of the ministry of the word: witnesses, prophets, teachers, and evangelists (Cooke 1976, 219-337).

Practical theology in congregational settings will attend to the preaching and catechesis in the parish. What is the quality of the preaching? Is it rooted in scripture, yet made applicable to the lived reality of the congregation? In an exercise of reception hermeneutics, practical theology will ask what members of the congregation actually hear when they listen to a homily? It will ask whether the understanding of the ministry of the word is broadened, besides preaching and teaching, to include a kind of ministry of the word in spiritual conversations (O'Malley 1983, 141).[64] One-on-one conversations, in spiritual direction and pastoral care, are also forms of the ministry of the word. How reflective are the practitioners of pastoral care in the parish about its connection to scripture? Most decidedly, faith-sharing small groups—proven to be so vital within larger congregations—are also a form of the ministry of the word. Princeton sociologist Robert Wuthnow, in an important study of small faith-sharing or bible groups in congregations, has suggested some themes for reflection on the ways such groups might narrow conceptions of God in such a way that God becomes, reductively, the *affirming* God of the group (1994, 352-353).[65] They privilege a God who is close. The intimate group context shapes how scripture gets appropriated. Wuthnow suggests that the word in such groups almost never highlights what Cooke refers to as the ministry to God's judgment (Cooke 1976, 405-520).

[64] The early Jesuits made much of spiritual conversation as a ministry of the word.
[65] See also Brennan, Patrick. 1999. *Re-Imagining The Parish: Base Communities, Adulthood and Family.* New York: Crossroad.

The word gets conveyed, of course, in many forms and images. Parish bulletins serve to focus it and raise up motifs for a congregation. Images and artifacts in the sanctuary of the church represent—as medieval writers suggested about paintings of scripture scenes—a visual word for the congregation. Both bulletins and artifacts/images in local parishes call for explicit reflection about what about God and our relationship to him they convey.

Most local communities (and many preachers) display a distinctive—and, sometimes quite selective—textuality, a sort of canon within the canon of scripture. The lectionary, of course, provides one partial corrective to this selectivity. Don Browning notes, for example, how one pastor in a congregation he studied, mainly drew on the law-gospel contrasts from the Pauline letters. Whatever the assigned pericopes from the lectionary, the law-gospel contrasts served, for this pastor, as the implicit key to the scriptures.

Speaking of the textuality of the same church Browning studied with a team of scholars, Walter Brueggeman, a member of the team, contends that this church—which came to choose to be a sanctuary church for Central American refugees in the 1980's—repeatedly used only a few biblical selections in congregation-wide discussions about the choice of sanctuary. Brueggeman also notes that there were distinct levels of textuality within the congregation. Wider groups appealed to texts about love of neighbor and the parable of the Good Samaritan—bland appeals, in a sense, to mercy and love which tended to construe the decision as more about charity than justice. Only one sermon was ever explicitly preached on the decision to choose to become a sanctuary church—after the decision was made! This sermon, by an associate pastor, appealed to Matthew 2:1-12, a passage which suggests foreigners recognized Jesus and which includes an allusion to the "civil disobedience" of the wise men who did not report back to Herod what they had seen. A religious education program within the congregation had sparked the wider discussions of choosing sanctuary. It focused on the difficult teaching of obedience to authority in Romans 13 and the call in the Sermon on the Mount to be willing to endure persecution for "righteousness" sake.'

This second level of textuality, within the congregation, used primarily by the inner group of leaders for the decision for sanctuary, deepened and extended the blander textuality in the neighbor-love and Good Samaritan passages: "It provided the real motivating power that led the rest of the congregation to its final courageous vote on sanctuary. It was this second set of texts that opened the possibility of real sacrificial discipleship—a hospitality and neighbor love that are willing to pay a price." (Browning 1991, 229; Brueggeman 1989, 48-69). Note that it did not primarily emerge from explicit preaching.

So, in congregational settings, practical theology might focus on the concrete textuality of the scriptures (and its adequacy and breadth) appealed to in order to justify congregational mission and vision statements and the validation of congregational models of who we are and how we do things around here. At important and key moments of congregational decision or transitions (e.g., building a new building, relocating, opening or closing a program, the transition of members on ministerial teams, and internal crises), what range of scriptural texts get called upon to give meaning or direction to the congregation's choice. The kind of exercise Brueggeman did on the *actual* textuality in a congregation exemplifies how practical theology can add to a more historical and systematic understanding of the ministry to God's word.

Ministry of Service

Cooke's treatment of ministry of service to God's people roots it in the image of Jesus the servant (cf. Philippians 2). The main emphases, he notes, in the history of the tradition have been the following aspects: (1) *Healing*—where the ministers are seen as a kind of physician of souls, following the metaphors used by Origin and Clement of Alexandria. There is a wide spectrum of activities which fit under the canopy of healing ministries: physical medicine, psychological therapy, spiritual direction, sacramental anointing, forgiveness of sins, and the reuniting of opposing social groups; (2) *Taking Care of the Needy*; (3) more generally, the *corporal works of mercy* (feeding, housing and clothing); and (4) *Hospitality*—e.g., in providing hostels for travelers. This latter theme is a strong emphasis in the letter of James and in the *Didache* (Cooke 1976, 343-401).

Again, a proliferating set of sociological studies have begun to focus on what congregations actually do in terms of service and what their limits are. From national surveys of congregations, we know that:

1. American congregations report that they sponsor at least one outreach service (only 1.6 percent report no such outreach service), either alone or in collaboration with another congregation/organization (Cnaan 2000; Orr 1994).

2. 17.1 percent of the congregations sponsor formal counseling programs, for marriage and family or more general psychological health. Much informal counseling takes place within congregations.

3. 29.8 percent of American congregations have a formal cash assistance program for the needy. 78 percent report that they engage in *ad hoc* help, when confronted with those in need of cash.

4. The majority of congregations serve as referral units, mediating between parishioners and formal networks and programs in the wider community for service delivery.

5. 27.9 percent of American congregations engage in health screening programs in their church. 25.1 percent are involved in HIV/AIDS programs of some sort (education, meal provision, and counseling programs). 30 percent sponsor blood donation drives. 50 percent have formal programs for the visitation of the sick of the parish. Only a small percentage of congregations have their own health or dental clinics, but a growing number are engaging in a parish nurse program. Little systematic study, however, has been done on the range, effectiveness, and theological justification of parish health or nurse programs. It is a challenge to practical theology to do this assessment.

6. Much less happens in congregations on explicit programs geared toward social change or movements for justice. The congregations tend to mention three particular things under this rubric: interfaith programs, voter registration, and education against racism. Little direct advocacy takes place at congregational levels. There is a widespread taboo against introducing controversial political issues—even ones with striking moral consequences—into the local congregation. So, little direct preaching on justice occurs from parish pulpits. As Robert Wuthnow claims, the local congregation may find that public debates about economic and civic matters inside the very heart of the church "can easily become polarized, taking

on an aura of antagonism that runs against the grain of religious teachings about fellowship and reconciliation" (1994, 268). There exists—as Gallup data repeatedly shows—a wide-spread and strong dislike in America of religious leaders playing too direct a role in political issues (Knickerbocker 2000, 8).

7. Many congregations that do not mount social service programs of their own, nonetheless, collaborate with other congregations and/or civic organizations for such provision. While only 7.2 percent of American congregations have their own homeless shelters or soup kitchens, 25 percent provide support for shelters, soup kitchens, or food pantries run by other groups.

8. Congregations also share space. 31.5 percent of American congregations host Boy or Girl Scout troops; 30 percent share their space for day-care center groups; 30 percent host twelve-step programs, such as Alcoholics Anonymous; 25.1 percent host police-community meetings; 29.1 percent share space for Habitat for Humanity programs; and 45.5 percent lease or loan their space to neighborhood groups and associations.

The majority of outreach programs (75 percent) service non-congregants. On average, American congregations outlay more than 15 percent of their budgets on outreach programs. Yet, there is some evidence that many congregations show reluctance to becoming involved in civic outreach that they themselves do not sponsor (Wuthnow 1997, 199). Congregations also show a tendency to form alliances more easily with other religious groups than with secular organizations. This limits the larger structural imagination and coordination needed to tackle large urban problems. Congregations frequently find themselves too small and limited to address even local and neighborhood problems, such as homelessness, ecological deterioration of a neighborhood, or police protection. In most cases their civic outreach tends toward immediate pay-offs: "Churches do not provide massive monetary relief, health care or housing to the poor. Churches avoid the doctrine of entitlements that undergirds public assistance programs. But churches meet short-term emergency needs among their own members, contribute to the needs of other people … and provide volunteer assistance that may be lacking from other agencies" (Wuthnow 1997, 192-193).

When the rubber meets the road, congregational studies in practical theology will inquire about the outreach or service programs that currently exist in a parish and on what theological rationale. They will want to know whether they only (or overwhelmingly) reach members of the parish or are more broadly conceived. How is service to non-congregants (even to non-believers or the non-churched) justified in a congregation? Carl Dudley and Sally Johnson have suggested that there is a distinct difference in congregational ethos between what they call 'servant' and 'prophet' churches (1993). Key here is the role played in each type in thinking about structures of justice/ injustice in society. How does the congregation conceive of alliances with 'secular' groups, or does it only enter into coalitions with other like-minded religious groups, and on what theological justification? Is the textuality for service in a congregation (as we saw in the study by Brueggeman) mainly one that points to service in charity, or do justice themes get explicit attention? Much evidence exists that even congregations that focus fairly uniquely on the commandment of neighbor-love to justify service, nevertheless construe neighbor love more broadly than do non-churchgoers (Gill 1999).

Cooke's themes of hospitality and conflict resolution in Christian settings also cry out for further work in practical theology. The study of hospitality in congregational settings has not been much mined, although a start has been made (Nixon 2002; Pohl 1999; Murray 1990). Perhaps because the Christian scriptures present such an idealized view of the loving community and of conflict resolution (cf. Matthew 18: 15-17), many congregations deal with conflicts by denial or passive aggression. As we have seen, the community model for a congregation is the one most forthright about expecting conflicts to emerge. Some preliminary work has begun on the study of conflicts and their resolution in congregational settings (Burgess 1998; Jones 2000; Zaccaria 1984; Hartman 1996). But because the issue of conflict within Christian communities is, generally, such an allergic one, the future agenda should privilege, on the one hand, theological reflection on the meaning of conflict in groups and, on the other, resources to secular wisdom about conflict resolution.[66]

---

[66] More secular accounts of conflict resolution in groups can be found in Mayer, Bernard. 2000. *The Dynamics of Conflict Resolution.* San Francisco: Jossey-Bass and Masters, Marcik and Robert Albright. 2001. *The Complete Guide to Conflict Resolution in the Workplace.* Washington, D.C.: AMACOM

Ministry to the Church's Sacramentality

In many ways, liturgics represents the branch of theology most attuned to Cooke's final facet of ministry, the ministry to the church's sacramentality. Cooke, a noted sacramental theologian, shows especial richness in the section of his book devoted to this topic (1976, 525-656). Any extended treatment of the theme of practical theology and the ministry to the church's sacramentality would be like bringing the proverbial coals to Newcastle. Yet, liturgics often operates without a close connection to congregational studies. The key question here might be how the whole community comes to find a way to celebrate not just the Christian mystery, the presence of the risen Christ to the believer in a kind of rich experience, but how to celebrate this mystery in ways that closely touch the lived history, life, and cycles of the local community (Ammerman 1998, 84-87). Most congregations are more successful in celebrating the cycles of the liturgical year or national feasts and anniversaries, such as Thanksgiving, than in finding ways to ritualize their own crises, growth periods, and transitions. Thus, for example, rites of passage can be devised for the community, not just the life-cycles of individuals. Few congregations devise rites for the reception of new members who have transferred in from other parishes. Few, except for a kind of 'thank-you liturgy,' have found deeper ritual ways to deal with transitions from the ministerial teams and committees of the parish: "Newness can break into the congregation's routine, requiring people to be more intentional than usual about what they do and why. The congregation, itself, may take the transitional time between pastors as a liminal time, for instance. It can be a time of self-study and reflection, not just of what pastoral skills are needed, but on what sort of congregation this is" (Ammerman 1998, 87).

I have tried to show how Cooke's work in *Ministry to Word and Sacrament* sheds light on practical theology and congregational studies and how they, in turn, might enrich the work he began there. I have made strong claims for the nexus between congregational studies and practical theology. But in the end, I suspect that any practical theology of congregations will need, again and again, to return to Cooke's rich retrieval of ministry to formation of community, ministry of the word, ministry to service, ministry to God's judgment, and ministry to sacramentality. For where any local church authentically is, these must be an integral part of its very constitution and meaning.

References

Becker, Penny Edgell. 1999. *Congregations in Conflict: Cultural Models of Local Religious Life*. New York: Cambridge University Press.

Browning, Don. 1991. *A Fundamental Practical Theology*. Minneapolis: Fortress Press.

Brueggeman, Walter. 1989. "Texuality in the Church." Nelle Slater, ed. 1989. *Tensions Between Citzenship and Discipleship*. New York: Pilgrim Press.

Burgess, John. 1998. *Why Scripture Matters: Reading the Bible in a Time of Church Conflict*. Louisville, Kentucky: Westminster/John Knox

Carroll, Jackson. 1991. *As One With Authority: Effective Leadership in Ministry*. Louisville, Columbia University Press.

Cnann, Ram and Stephanie Boddie. August 12, 2000. "Congregations for Society: Which Congregations are Serving Their Community?" Paper presented at the Association for the Sociology of Religion annual meetings.

Dolan, Jay. 1987. *The American Catholic Parish: A History from 1850 to the Present*. 2 vols. Mahwah, New Jersey: Paulist Press.

Dorsey, Gary. 1995. *Congregation: The Journey Back to Church*. New York: Viking Press.

Dudley, Carl. 1978. *Making the Small Church Effective*. Nashville: Abingdon.

Dudley, Carl. 1983. *Building Effective Ministry*. San Francisco: Harper and Row.

Dudley, Carl and Sally Johnson. 1993. *Energizing the Congregation: Images That Shape Your Church's Ministry*. Louisville, Kentucky: Westminster/John Knox.

Eisland, Nancy. 1998. *A Particular Place: Exurbanization and Religious Response in a Southern Town*. New Brunswick, New Jersey: Rutgers University Press.

Freedman, Samuel. 1984. *Upon This Rock: The Miracles of A Black Church*. New York: Harper Collins

Geertz, Clifford. 1973. *The Interpretation of Culture*. New York: Basic Books.

Groome, Thomas. 1991. *Sharing Faith*. San Francisco: Harper San Francisco.

Hartman, Keith. 1996. *Congregations in Conflict: The Battle Over Homosexuality*. New Brunswick, New Jersey: Rutgers University Press.

Hopewell, James. 1987. *Congregation: Stories and Structures*. Philadelphia: Fortress.

Hough, Joseph Jr. and Barbara Wheeler, eds. 1988. *Beyond Clericalism: The Congregation as a Focus for Theological Education*. Atlanta: Scholars' Press.

Jones, W. Paul. 2000. *Worlds Within a Congregation: Dealing with Theological Diversity*. Nashville: Abingdon Press.

Kelsey, David. 1992. *To Understand God Truly*. Louisville, Kentucky: Westminster/John Knox.

Knickerbocker, Brad. Sept. 1, 2000. "Why Line is Fading Between Politics and Piety." *The Christian Science Monitor*. 8

Konieczny, Mary and Mark Chaves. Sept. 2000. "Resources, Race and Female Headed Congregations in the United States." *The Journal for the Scientific Study of Religion*. 39, no. 3: 261-271.

Mette, Norbert. 1980. *Theorie der Praxis* Dusseldorf: Patmos Verlag.

Murray, Harry. 1990. *Do Not Neglect Hospitality: The Catholic Worker and the Homeless*. Philadelphia: Temple University Press.

Nixon, Paul. 2002. *Fling Open the Doors: Giving the Church Away to the Community*. Nashville: Abingdon.

O' Dea, Thomas. 1961. "Five Dilemmas in the Institutionalization of Religion." *The Journal for the Scientific Study of Religion*. Vol. 1: 30-39.

Olson, Daniel. 1987. *Networks of Religious Belonging in Five Baptist Congregations*. Phd. Dissertation, Dept. of Sociology, University of Chicago.

Orr, John, Donald Miller, Wade Clark Roof and J. Gordon Melton. 1994. *Politics of the Spirit: Religion and Multi-Ethnicity in Los Angeles*. Los Angeles: Center for Religion and Civic Culture at the University of Southern California.

Pohl, Christine. 1999. *Making Room: Recovering Hospitality as a Christian Tradition*. Grand Rapids, Mich.: W.B. Eerdmans.

Roozen, David, William McKinney, Jackson Carroll. 1983. *Varieties of Religious Presence: Mission in Public Life*. New York: Pilgrim Press.

Schleiermacher, Friedrich. 1966. *Basic Outline on the Study of Theology* Richmond, Va.: John Knox Press, 1966.

Schreiter, Robert. 1998. "Theology in the Congregation: Discovering and Doing" in Nancy Ammerman, et.al. 1998. *Studying Congregations: A New Handbook*. Nashville: Abingdon Press.

Warner, R. Stephen. 1988. *New Wine in Old Wineskins: Evangelicals and Liberals in a Small Town Church*. Berkeley: University of California Press.

Warner, R. Stephen. "The Place of the Congregation in the Contemporary American Religious Configuration" in James Wind and James Lewis, ed., *American Congregations*. vol. 2: 54-59.

Warner, R. Stephen and Judith Wittner, eds. 1998. *Gatherings in Diaspora: Religious Communities and the New Immigration*. Philadelpia: Temple University Press

Warren, Mark. 2001. Dry *Bones Rattling: Community Building to Revitalize American Democracy*. Princeton: Princeton University Press.

Wilkes, Paul. 1994. *And They Shall Be My People: An American Rabbi and His Congregation*. New York: Atlantic Monthly Press.

Wilkes, Paul. 2001. *Excellent Catholic Parishes*. Mahwah, New Jersey: Paulist Press.

Wills, Gary. 2000. *Papal Sin: Structures of Deceit*. New York: Doubleday.

Wind, James and James Lewis, eds. American Congregations; ed. 2 vols. Chicago: University of Chicago Press, 1994.

Wood, Richard. 2002. *Faith in Action*. Chicago: University of Chicago Press.

Wuthnow, Robert. 1994. *Sharing the Journey: Support Groups and America's New Quest for Community*. New York: The Free Press.

Wuthnow, Robert. 1997. *Crisis in the Churches*. New York: Oxford University Press.

Yang, Fengang and Helen Rose Ebaugh. 3 Sept. 2001. "Religion and Ethnicity Among the New Immigrants" in *The Journal for the Scientific Study of Religion*. 40, no. 3: 367-378.

Zaccaria, Joseph. 1984. *Facing Change: Strategies for Problem Solving in Congregations*. Minneapolis: Augsburg Publishing.

12 Newman's Cognitive Conversion to Anglo-Catholicism

Walter E. Conn

John Henry Newman (1801-90), in the most famous event of his life, converted from the Church of England to the Church of Rome in 1845. Three decades earlier (1816) he had experenced the most important event of his life—a profound personal conversion at age fifteen, moving him from the conventional Anglican Christianity inherited from his parents to a deeply meaningful Evangelical faith. Elsewhere I have argued that this first conversion of 1816 is best understood as a basic Christian moral conversion (Conn forthcoming; Conn 1986; Dulles 1997).[67] In this essay, I will show that these two conversions are linked by another conversion, a cognitive conversion which effected Newman's shift from an Evangelical to an Anglo-Catholic form of Christianity. I will trace the many influences on, and phases of, this cognitive conversion and religious shift through the 1820s, the third decade of Newman's life. Specifically, we will follow Newman as he moved from Evangelical, through Liberal, to High Church theology. In this development we will see a critical stage of Newman's lifelong search for truth in his fidelity to conscience, the radical drive for self-transcendence.

Cognitive conversion is a complex, multifaceted reality. We can specify it by making a basic distinction in knowing between content and structure. Content conversion in knowing is simply a significant

[67] Avery Dulles distinguishes three conversions in his "Newman: The Anatomy of a Conversion" (1997, 21-36).

change in *what* one knows, a change in one's views or beliefs, be they aesthetic, political, religious, or whatever. For example, before he discovered the true meaning of Christmas, Linus Van Pelt believed in Santa Claus; but no longer. Now, with the wisdom of age, he believes in the Great Pumpkin. In contrast, structural conversion is a transformation in *how* one knows. For example, Jean Piaget distinguishes between the concrete thinking typical of childhood and the abstract thinking first available in adolescence. Or we may consider how the responsibilities of adult experience make possible a shift from uncritical to critical thinking, from being dependent on authoritative others in one's knowing to standing independently on one's own cognitive feet. Fundamentally, cognitive conversion is a new, more accurate understanding of the nature of one's knowing, most radically in the realization that the criterion of truth is not external but within one's own drive for self-transcendence. In the following pages we will note signs of these various aspects of cognitive conversion (content and structure) as Newman advances from adolescence into early adulthood.

1. Heading off to Oxford

John Henry's five-month process of conversion to Evangelicalism at age fifteen was nearing its end when, on December 14, 1816, he went off to Oxford with his father and Reverend John Mullens, a family friend and curate of St. James, Piccadilly.[68] Mr. Mullens, an Oxford man, had taken an interest in John Henry's education, and was probably responsible for the last-minute decision to head for Oxford rather than the more scientific and Protestant Cambridge. Mullens' old college, Exeter, had no openings, so John Henry was enrolled at Trinity. Even there, rooms were scarce and it was June before John Henry was able to take up residence, just as the other students were leaving for the long summer vacation. By then he was sixteen, but still some two or three years younger than his classmates. Though he had spent the interval at home in Alton, he was not one to be idle, and had read through an impressive list of Greek and Latin literary works, as well as half of St. Mathew's Gospel in Greek.

[68] Biographical studies include: Blehl 2001; Gilley 1990; Ker 1988; Trevor 1962; Ward 1948. Autobiographical works include: Newman 1947, henceforth *Apo.* and Newman 1956, henceforth *AW*. The 1874 Memoir in *AW* is written in the third person.

Newman's first stay at Oxford was only three weeks—just long enough to count for a term in the lax atmosphere of the pre-reformed university, and just long enough also for the new student, despite his loneliness, to fall in love with the university and its beautiful country town. He bought a gown, and managed to obtain, by his last day, a reading list for the summer. The most important event of these first weeks was meeting John Bowden, a classmate who had been assigned by Newman's tutor to brief Newman on college customs and escort him to dinner on his first night. Bowden, though three years older than Newman, would become his inseparable college companion, and a loyal friend until Bowden's early death in 1844 (Ker 1988, 7).

Newman applied himself to his studies during his first full year, and he did so well that in the spring his tutor urged him to stand for the college scholarship, though he would be the youngest of the competitors. The exam, which was open to outsiders as well as Trinity men, included Greek and Latin authors, as well as mathematics and an English essay. On May 18th, Trinity Monday, it was announced that Newman had won the competition, and was the new Scholar of Trinity, with a tidy £60 a year for nine years. During that summer of 1818 Newman read some Gibbon, but mostly John Locke on knowledge, and, influenced by the role of the mind in deriving ideas from sense impressions, began to develop his own epistemology, with an emphasis on the personal and subjective dimensions (Gilley 1990, 31; Moleski 2000).

The 1818-19 school year found Newman and Bowden publishing an anti-Catholic romance in verse titled *St Bartholomew's Eve* and several issues of an anonymous periodical called *The Undergraduate*. The latter came to a quick end, however, when Newman was too embarrassed to continue it after his involvement became public. During the summer vacation Newman read more Gibbon, and took to imitating his style. He was enthusiastic about the romanticism of Scott's *Ivanhoe*, but also appreciated the realism and common sense of Crabbe's *Tales of the Hall*. And he continued writing his own verse. Maisie Ward, a great admirer of Newman's prose, finds him "tone-deaf to poetry," both as a versifier and as a reader (Ward 1948, 48).

By the next school year Newman and Bowden were deep into preparation for their final examinations, often spending twelve hours a day at their books. Newman, on the wake of his scholarship success, was thinking about a career in law, and became a member of Lincoln's Inn. As the year went by, he became more and more anxious about the final exam, worried that he was reading the wrong books, and concerned that he coveted academic success. The exam dread continued through the summer, while he was alone at Oxford, and into the next school year, as he even increased his reading. The exam week, at the end of November 1820, was a disaster. Though he passed, and earned his B. A., his and others' hopes that he would win high honors were crushed by a decidedly lackluster performance. His fear of failure was fulfilled, his nerves broke, and he went without honors in both math and classics (Ker 1988, 13-14; Gilley 1990, 36).

Despite the great disappointment, Newman remained steady in failure, and even seemed to gain in maturity and responsibility from it. In a letter to his sister Harriet, he reflected in his Evangelical mode on how his "disappointment was at once a chastisement for former offences, and a kind of preventive of future." As he had worried during the previous year, he was aware that, "among *many* other diseases of the mind, I am very vain, and the least success is apt to alter me,—witness my getting the Trinity Scholarship" (Blehl 2001, 30; Gilley 1990, 35). Academically, he had learned much from his hard work, in both matter and method, especially from his study of Aristotle's *Ethics*, with its focus on virtues and character, the nature of moral truth, and practical moral judgment.

2. Responding to a Vocation

Following the exam fiasco and Christmas holidays, Newman returned to Oxford in February 1821 in good spirits. With the exams behind him, and his Trinity Scholarship good for several more years, he was able to lighten up a bit academically, attending lectures on mineralogy, and expanding his reading in many directions: anatomy, chemistry, and geology; Hebrew, Arabic, and Persian; Plato, Cicero, and Hume. He also had more time now for his music: "Signor Giovanni Enrico Neandrini has finished his first composition," he announced in a March letter home (Ward 1948, 55).

But 1821 was also the year when, in Newman's own words, "he was more devoted to the evangelical creed and more strict in his religious duties than at any previous time." A dream he had in May tells us something about his religious imagination. In it, a spirit spoke to him of "the other world": "Among other things it said that it was absolutely impossible for the reason of man to understand the mystery (I think) of the Holy Trinity, and in vain to argue about it; but that every thing in another world was so *very, very plain*, that there was not the slightest difficulty about it." He stresses: "I cannot put into any sufficiently strong form of words the ideas which were conveyed to me. I thought I instantly fell on my knees, overcome with gratitude to God for so kind a message" (Tristram 1956, 80, 166-167).

During that summer Newman read Evangelical theology and compiled a large collection of scriptural passages, summarizing his beliefs on various themes. Conversion, in particular, puzzled him because his own experience of it did not square with the descriptions in the books. This was also the time when his belief in the Calvinist doctrine of predestination began to fade. Diary entries make it clear that this was a very difficult year in Newman's interior life: distraction and emotional dryness in prayer, sexual temptations, and accusations of pride, vanity, and arrogance fill the records of his self-examinations (Blehl 2001, 35; Ward 1948, 59).

When he returned to Oxford after the summer vacation he moved into out-of-college rooms at a coffeehouse. The family plan was to have his younger brother Francis share lodgings and study with him until Francis entered a college. Like John Henry, Francis had been influenced by Reverend Mayers during his school years at Ealing, and was at least as strong as John Henry in his Evangelical devotion. It was Francis, in fact, who, with his brother's support, had recently provoked a bad scene with their father by refusing to copy a letter for him on a Sunday. Newman soon took on a Trinity undergraduate as a private pupil at £100 a year. Unhappily, news came in November that his father's efforts in the brewery business had finally ended in bankruptcy. His father's spirit was crushed, and the family again had to uproot itself. Newman gave sensitive moral support, and more. With prospects of more private pupils, he offered to support Francis' education. And looking for other financial means to help his family, he also hit upon the idea of standing for a fellowship at the intellectually prestigious Oriel College. Given his exam disappointment, his friends at Trinity thought the idea dangerously unrealistic, simply courting another disaster. But Newman knew he was better than his last exam performance, and thought the attempt, even if unsuccessful, would at least be good practice for a future victory.

Early in January 1822 Newman, home for Christmas vacation, had a conversation with his father after a Sunday church service. Affectionately concerned about his son's religious attitudes and opinions, Mr. Newman took the occasion to caution John Henry in his common sense and very direct way. He had thought, for example, that his son's tone in a published letter to the editor of the *Christian Observer* was "more like the composition of an old man, than of a youth just entering life with energy and aspirations." Newman recorded the substance of his father's warning in his journal that evening, and included a slightly edited version of it in his Memoir five decades later. Because of its importance to Newman, as well as its prophetic insight, this advice of a loving father is worth repeating here. "Take care," he begins, "you are encouraging a morbid sensibility and irritability of mind, which may be very serious. Religion, when carried too far, induces a mental softness. No one's principles," he continues, "can be established at twenty." He then pointedly predicts: "Your opinions in two or three years will certainly, certainly change. I have seen many instances of the same kind. You are on dangerous ground. The temper you are encouraging may lead to something alarming. Weak minds are carried into superstition, and strong minds into infidelity;" and he concludes, "do not commit yourself, do nothing ultra" (Tristram 1956, 179, 82). Newman's journal indicates that he took his father's advice to heart.

A few days later, just at the end of Christmas vacation, Mr. Newman told John Henry that he should decide on a career. Although the father had envisioned his son in the law, he was satisfied enough with John Henry's choice of the church, a decision the son had already made. Newman, of course, was not just choosing a career, but responding to a vocation. As he set off for Oxford the next day, his father's last words were, again, "Do not show any ultraism in any thing" (Tristram 1956, 180).

On February 21, 1822, Newman writes in his journal: "My birthday. Today I am of age. It is an awful crisis. I say 'awful,' for it seems to leave me to myself, and I have been as yet used to depend on others."

He goes on: "May this be a point, from which I may date more decision and firmness in my profession of religion!" He concludes with a short prayer of self-offering: "I am now entering upon a new stage of life, Lord go with me: make me Thy true soldier" (Tristram 1956, 183). When writing to thank his mother for a birthday letter, Newman goes a little further: "I seem now more left to myself, and, when I reflect on my own weaknesses, I have cause to shudder." His mother, fearing depression, responded anxiously: "I see one great fault in your character, which alarms me very much, as I observe it increases upon you seriously . . . . Your fault is want of self confidence, and a dissatisfaction with yourself, that you cannot exceed the bounds of human nature" (qtd. in Blehl 2001, 43). Newman tried to reassure her that he was in good health, relaxing at many wine and music parties.

3. Imbibing Oriel Liberalism

The truth, however, was that, with the exam for the Oriel Fellowship approaching, Newman's emotions were anything but steady. His confidence waxed and waned almost daily, and by the exam week his journal consisted mostly of brief reports on his nerves. The Oriel exam put great weight on Latin composition, and the examiners were looking for sharp minds, not just accomplishment. Luckily, during his preparation Newman made a breakthrough on Latin style, discovering the secret of a truly Latin sentence structure; and, of course, he was blessed with acute intelligence. On this occasion both stood him in good stead, and despite a terrible case of nerves and wretched illness, he came from the back of the pack and triumphed over the academic stars of the university. On April 12th, the Friday of this Easter exam week, he was elected a Fellow of Oriel, fulfilling his greatest dream, but a dream he had fretted over mightily as it seemed a temptation to pride and vanity.

On that day, "of all days most memorable," Newman took his seat in the Oriel chapel and dined in the common room, sitting next to John Keble, the young Fellow commonly acknowledged as the university's most brilliant star. This day, he later recognized, was the great "turning point of his life." His election "raised him from obscurity and need to competency and reputation." Theologically, it placed him on "the high and broad platform of University society and intelligence," and exposed him to personal and intellectual influences which "gradually developed and formed" the "religious sentiments in his mind, which had been his blessing from the time he left school"—from the time, that is, of his first conversion (Tristram 1956, 63).

Newman's extreme shyness, now exacerbated by the fame of the Oriel common room's brilliance, along with his Calvinistic "isolation of thought and spiritual solitariness,"(Tristram 1956, 65-66) made the Fellows wonder if his election had been a blunder. Some of them enlisted Richard Whately, a former Fellow, to bring Newman out of himself. A great extrovert, of "generous and warm heart" (Newman 1947, 10), Whately was clearly the man for the job, succeeding, to a degree, in just a few summer months. The independence of mind and action that finally resulted from what Whately began was, of course, beyond anyone's expectation. Whately got Newman to assist with his work on logic, but it was mainly through conversation that he led Newman to "look about" himself and taught him to "think correctly" and to rely on himself (Tristram 1956, 68). As Newman put it in his *Apologia* (1864), he "opened my mind, and taught me to think and to use my reason"—he "not only taught me to think, but to think for myself" (Newman 1947, 10). Whately soon thought Newman was "the clearest-headed man he knew" (Tristram 1956, 68) and assured the Fellows that they had made no mistake. Still, Newman did not feel really at home at Oriel for quite a while, and remained something of a loner. In his *Apologia* he recalled a day when he was out walking by himself and met the provost, Dr. Copleston, who courteously bowed and quoted Cicero: "*Numquam minus solus, quàm cùm solus*" (Newman 1947, 14).[69] This quotation was not to become Newman's motto, but it might have; it fitted him more perfectly than even Copleston probably knew.

Newman did not rest on his Oriel laurels. He continued to live with Francis in lodgings for the next school year, tutored private pupils, worked hard on the classics, and, thanks to Whately's recommendation, wrote for the *Encyclopedia Metropolitana*. In April of 1823, Newman's probationary year ended successfully with his admission as an actual Fellow, and Edward Pusey, soon to be Newman's great friend and ally,

---

[69] From *De officiis*, III. 1: "Never less alone [lonely], than when alone [solitary]."

joined him as a new Oriel Fellow. In June, Newman began seriously considering how soon he should take holy orders. Toward that end, in November, Newman and Pusey began attending private lectures given by Charles Lloyd, the Regius Professor of Divinity, of the "high-and-dry" school of theology. While the scholarly Lloyd did not "leave a mark upon his [Evangelical] mind," (Tristram 1956, 71) his brusque manner in the give-and-take of the sessions further helped to draw Newman out of himself.

In May 1824 Newman decided to accept the position of curate at the Oxford working-class parish of St. Clement's, and he was therefore ordained deacon on June 13th. He marks the occasion in his journal: "It is over. I am thine, O Lord." With an elderly and incapacitated rector, Newman was soon engaged in intensive pastoral duties, in addition to his academic work. His preaching was appreciated, though some thought he was too severe. This was probably deliberate, as he believed that "Those who make comfort the great subject of their preaching seem to mistake the end of their ministry. *Holiness* is the great end. There must be a struggle and a trial here. Comfort is a cordial, but no one drinks cordials from morning to night" (Tristram 1956, 71, 172). One of his frequent sermon topics was sin. In "Sins against Conscience" (No. 101), he made his favorite, crucial point that conscience must be followed to reach truth.

Newman's new parish duties obligated him to spend the long summer vacation of 1824 in Oxford. This was the occasion for him to develop a close relationship with Oriel Fellow Edward Hawkins, likewise obligated by his duties as Vicar of the University Church, St. Mary's. This also was the beginning of two significant years during which Newman "underwent a great change in his religious opinions, a change brought about by very various influences" (Tristram 1956, 73).

Reviewing these influences in his Memoir, Newman mentions first the great Oriel common room, whose brilliant members were "as remarkable for the complexion of their theology and their union among themselves in it, as for their literary eminence." These Oriel Noetics were neither High Church nor Low Church, but a new school, characterized by "moderation and comprehension." If their enemies were the suspicious "old unspiritual high-and-dry" and the envious members of the smaller and less distinguished colleges, their friends were of the Evangelical party, grateful for the Oriel liberality of mind (Tristram 1956, 73).

Among these influential members, Hawkins was the most important for Newman at this juncture. During the long vacation he and Newman had the dining hall and common room to themselves, took walks together, and generally spent much time in each other's company, with the older Hawkins as mentor. He taught Newman to weigh his words, to be cautious in his statements, to make clear distinctions—all the mental techniques that formed Newman into a great controversialist (Newman 1947, 7). Hawkins also criticized Newman's Evangelical views, which, as Newman later admitted, he took for granted rather than held intelligently. Central here, of course, was the Evangelical teaching on the nature and primacy of personal, consciously experienced conversion as *the* grace-filled saving event in the life of the elect. For example, when Newman showed him his first sermon, Hawkins came down hard on its implied denial of baptismal regeneration. Hawkins told Newman that it is impossible to draw a line, as his sermon did, between "two classes, the one all darkness, the other all light," because "moral and religious excellence is a matter of degree. Men are not either saints or sinners; but they are not so good as they should be, and better than they might be,—more or less converted to God." Preachers, he said, "should follow the example of St Paul; *he* did not divide his brethren into two, the converted and unconverted, but he addressed them all as 'in Christ.'" Hawkins had this view from John Sumner's *Apostolical Preaching* (1815), which he gave to Newman. This book, according to Newman, was finally successful, "beyond any thing else, in routing out evangelical doctrines" from his creed (Tristram 1956, 77), and leading him to accept the doctrine of baptismal regeneration (Newman 1947, 8).

But this change did not come easily. In a journal entry for August 24, 1824 we see the pain in Newman's conscience as he struggled for the truth. "Sumner's book threatens to drive me either into Calvinism, or baptismal regeneration, and I wish to steer clear of both . . . . I am always slow in deciding a question; but last night I was so distressed and low about it, that . . . the thought even struck me I must leave the Church. I have been praying about it," he continues, and "I do not know what will be the end of it. I think I really desire the truth, and would embrace it wherever I found it." Five months later (January 13, 1825), he was still struggling, but with more clarity: "I think, I am not certain, I must give up the doctrine of imputed righteousness and that of regeneration as apart from baptism." Continuing, he explains, "It seems to me that the great stand is to be made, *not* against those who connect a spiritual change with baptism, but those who deny a spiritual change altogether. . . . All who confess the natural corruption of the heart, and the necessity of a change," he went on, "should unite against those who make it (regeneration) a mere opening of new prospects, when the old score of offences is wiped away, and a person is for the second time put, as it were, on his good behaviour." Among the reasons he lists favoring this view is that "it seems more agreeable to the analogy of God's works, that there should be no harsh line, but degrees of holiness indefinitely small." If the reference to analogy sounds Catholic, decades later, as a Roman Catholic, Newman reflects on the radicality of these ideas in his Memoir: "Here he had in fact got hold of the Catholic doctrine that forgiveness of sin is conveyed to us, not simply by imputation, but by the implanting of a habit of grace" (Tristram 1956, 202-204, 78).

This critical questioning of his Evangelical beliefs on the intellectual level was supported on the experiential level not only by his personal experience of conversion, which as he had discovered did not conform to the Evangelical model, but also by his pastoral work. Indeed, in his parish duties Newman "found as a fact" what Hawkins had told him—that "Calvinism was not a key to the phenomena of human nature, as they occur in the world." Evangelical teaching was "unreal," it "would not work in a parish." This empirical sense appears in his journal a few months later: "I may add to my . . . remarks on my change of sentiment as to Regeneration, that I have been principally or in a great measure led to this change by the fact that in my parochial duties I found many, who in most important points were inconsistent, but whom yet I could not say were altogether without grace. Most indeed were in that condition as if they had some spiritual feelings, but were weak and uncertain." So, with his own experience reinforcing Hawkins' advice, Newman, "before many months of his clerical life were over, had," as he puts it in his Memoir, "taken the first steps towards giving up the evangelical form of Christianity" (Tristram 1956, 79, 206, 78).

On September 29, 1824, Newman's father died at age fifty-nine. Newman had arrived home for his father's last few days, when "He seemed in great peace of mind," despite his financial ruin. Newman was now the man of the family. The death occasioned a journal musing: "When I die, shall I be followed to the grave by my children? my Mother said the other day she hoped to live to see me married, but *I* think I shall either die within a College walls, or a Missionary in a foreign land—no matter where, so that I die in Christ"(Tristram 1956, 202, 203). Little did he know how foreign a land Rome would be.

Hawkins was not the only important influence on Newman. After his election in October 1824 as junior treasurer of Oriel, which brought welcome additional income, Newman was appointed by Whately, now principal of Alban Hall, a small university residence, as his vice-principal (dean, tutor, bursar, etc.), in March 1825. This put him again in close contact with Whately, and exposed to his ideas, which had "a gradual, but deep effect" on his mind. In his *Apologia*, Newman puts Whately's influence this way: "What he did for me in point of religious opinion, was, first, to teach me the existence of the Church, as a substantive body or corporation; next to fix in me those anti-Erastian views of Church polity, which were [in the next decade to become] one of the most prominent features of the Tractarian movement." For Newman this principally meant the mutual independence of church and state; the church's right to retain its property; and the state's entitlement to the church's support (Newman 1947, 11-12; Tristram 1956, 69).

In 1825, Newman read Bishop Joseph Butler's *Analogy of Religion* (1736), with its "inculcation of a visible Church, the oracle of truth and a pattern of sanctity, of the duties of external religion, and of the historical character of Revelation." Two of Butler's points especially influenced him, and became fundamental principles of his thought, as he later explains in his *Apologia*: "First, the very idea of an analogy between the separate works of God leads to the conclusion that the system which is of less importance is economically or sacramentally connected with the more momentous system, and of this conclusion the theory, to which I was inclined as a boy, viz. the unreality of material phenomena, is an ultimate resolution." Then, to analogy Newman adds probability: "Secondly, Butler's doctrine that Probability is the guide of life, led me, at least under the teaching to which a few years later I was introduced, to the question of the logical cogency of Faith" (Newman 1947, 9). These ideas, he later thought, placed "his doctrinal views on a broad philosophical basis, with which an emotional religion could have little sympathy" (Tristram 1956, 78; Gilley 1990, 57; Trevor 1962, 59).

In the *Apologia,* Newman acknowledges two further influences from the Oriel common room. The Reverend William James taught him the doctrine of apostolical succession, though he was "impatient" with it at the time, and the former Roman Catholic priest Joseph Blanco White introduced him to "freer views on the subject of inspiration than were usual in the Church of England at the time" (Newman 1947, 9, 8). But it was Hawkins and Whately who had the greatest impact on Newman's thinking in these years, so we should return to them to complete this survey of Oriel influences. When Newman was an undergraduate he had heard Hawkins preach a university sermon on tradition, a sermon Whately had encouraged him to give. Now, as a Fellow himself, Newman read and studied the sermon very carefully, and was greatly impressed by its "*quasi*-Catholic doctrine of Tradition, as a main element in ascertaining and teaching the truths of Christianity" (Tristram 1956, 78). It asserts the basic point that "the sacred text was never intended to teach doctrine, but only to prove it, and that, if we would learn doctrine, we must have recourse to the formularies of the Church; for instance to the Catechism, and to the Creeds." This view, "most true in its outline, most fruitful in its consequences," opened a "large field of thought" for Newman (Newman 1947, 8-9).

Newman was ordained to the priesthood on the feast of Pentecost, May 29, 1825. His journal entry for that day reflected considerably less spiritual condescension toward his fellow ordinands than it had the previous year, when, in his narrowly Evangelical view as to who counted as a real Christian, he had harshly judged some to be "coming to the Bishop . . . without the Spirit of God" (Tristram 1956, 206). He now held the more generous presumption in favor of Christians being in the kingdom of grace by virtue of baptism. In Meriol Trevor's judgment, Newman had made the shift "from a subjective to an objective view of the scheme of salvation" by the time of his ordination (Trevor 1962, 59). In other words, Newman had by this time dropped the Evangelical insistence on the once-and-for-all subjective experience of conversion, with its assurance of salvation, and moved to a view of sanctification as more gradual and objectively linked to baptism.

In his 1874 Memoir Newman made it clear that, despite all the good it had done for him, Evangelicalism was never really right for him. Yes, it had converted him to a spiritual life, but the "peculiarities of evangelical religion had never been congenial to him," he writes, "though he had fancied he held them. Its emotional and feverish devotion and its tumultuous experiences were foreign to his nature, which indeed was ever conspicuously faulty in the opposite direction, as being in a way incapable, as if physically, of enthusiasm, however legitimate and guarded." He also cites his great attraction to the Greek and Latin classics and to the Fathers as another reason why "the ethical character of the Evangelical Religion could not lastingly be imprinted" on his mind (Tristram 1956, 82).[70] In short, though just what he needed at fifteen, Evangelicalism was not, in the final analysis, a good fit for Newman.

4. Checking the Drift toward Liberalism

But if Newman had escaped "the crags and precipices of Luther and Calvin" by the time he was ordained a priest, where was he to go? The likely refuge was the "flats" of a cold Arminian doctrine, at the time "the intellectual and ecclesiastical antagonist and alternative of the Evangelical creed" (Tristram 1956, 83). And, indeed, Newman, influenced by the Liberalism of the Oriel common room, headed in that direction. Typical of people in transitional phases, he had lost his firm cognitive bearings. Expanding the metaphor a bit, we may say that Newman had left a secure Evangelical port and now, sailing on a cloudy night without an intellectual compass, found himself seized by a strong Liberal current, named, from different perspectives, Rationalist or Latitudinarian. For example, in preparation for an encyclopedia article on miracles, he read Hume, and was particularly impressed by

---

[70] Newman deleted two paragraphs containing these quotations in the autograph.

the equally skeptical Conyers Middleton (Newman 1947, 12). In his correspondence with his youngest brother, Charles, now an atheist, Newman argues the then rather radical anti-literalist view that "the New Testament is not Christianity, but the *record* of Christianity" (qtd. in Gilley 1990, 57), and any problems in the books do not overthrow the faith they record. But he also argues that rejection of Christianity arises "from a fault of the *heart*, not of the *intellect*," that a "dislike of the *contents* of Scripture is at the bottom of unbelief" (qtd. in Ker 1988, 25). And in the *Apologia*, he turns this last argument against himself. "The truth is," he writes, "I was beginning to prefer intellectual excellence to moral; I was drifting in the direction of the Liberalism of the day. I was rudely awakened from my dream at the end of 1827 by two great blows—illness and bereavement" (Newman 1947, 13).

Everything seemed to be going well. Early in 1826 Newman had been appointed an Oriel tutor, the position he much desired. His *Metropolitana* articles had been well received. He preached his first university sermon, and began to be known. In 1827, he was appointed a public examiner for the B.A. degree. As he puts it in the *Apologia*, he had come out of his shell and "began to have influence" (Newman 1947, 14).

But, then, in late November 1827, exactly seven years after failing to gain honors in his own exams, everything fell to pieces as he was conducting his first public examination. Suddenly he found his "memory and mind gone," and could not continue (Tristram 1956, 212). Several external pressures had been aggravated, as seven years earlier, by extreme overwork and worry in his preparation for the exams. He was confused, unable to think, and his brain and eyes seemed twisted. After consulting a doctor and being leached on his temples, he left Oxford, finally joining his family in Brighton.

He had hardly recovered when, suddenly, while he was still at home just six weeks later, his greatly loved youngest sister, Mary, only nineteen, took ill at dinner and, after a night of violent spasms, died the next day, January 5, 1828. Newman was devastated. His journal entry thirteen weeks later calls Mary's death "the heaviest affliction with which the good hand of God has ever visited me" (Tristram 1956, 213). One major effect of Mary's death on Newman was a more intense intuition of an invisible, but more real, world hidden behind this world. He expresses this heightened supernatural *sense* in a letter to his sister Jemima a few months after Mary's death, relating how, as he rode through the green countryside, "Dear Mary seems embodied in every tree and hid behind every hill. What a veil and curtain this world of sense is! beautiful but still a veil" (qtd. in Blehl 2001, 80). To such intensely personal blows no merely intellectual response could be adequate. They shook Newman from his Liberalism, and set him on a new religious course, fortified, beyond rational logic and common sense, with the richly imaginative power of metaphor. As Whately and Hawkins had been his guides out of Evangelicalism, he would have new companions for the next part of his journey, principally, Edward Pusey, R. Hurrell Froude, and John Keble.[71]

5. Turning towards High Church Theology

Edward Pusey had been elected to an Oriel Fellowship in April 1823, one year after Newman. Both were scholarly and religious, and they bonded immediately, though Pusey had little sympathy for Newman's Evangelical views. They talked constantly about religion, and participated in Lloyd's theological sessions the following school year. Newman's journal entries reflect a growing appreciation of Pusey's depth of character, despite their theological differences. His entry for December 16, 1824 indicates Pusey's theological influence: "I am lodged in the same house with Pusey, and we have had many talks on the subject of religion, I arguing for imputed righteousness, he against it, I inclining to separate regeneration from baptism, he doubting its separation &c." This was less than a month before Newman writes (January 13, 1825), as already noted: "I think, I am not certain, I must give up the doctrine of imputed righteousness and that of regeneration as apart from baptism." A year later (February 21, 1826), he wrote: "I am almost convinced against predestination and election in the Calvinistic sense, that is, I see no proof of them in Scripture." He immediately adds an intriguing comment: "Pusey accused me the

---

[71] For an assessment of the Oriel influence, especially on Newman's understanding of the relationship between faith and reason, see Merrigan, Terrence. 1986. "Newman's Oriel Experience: Its Significance for His Life and Thought," *Bijdragen, tijdschrift voor filosofie en theologie* 47: 192-211.

other day of becoming more High Church" (Tristram 1956, 203, 208). Pusey himself was soon off to Göttingen and Berlin to study German theology, but their important relationship continued. On his return in 1827, he brought Newman a collection of the Fathers.

In March of 1826, R. Hurrell Froude had been elected a Fellow of Oriel. Newman immediately found him "one of the acutest and clearest and deepest men in the memory of man" (qtd. in Ker 1988, 27), and they eventually became the greatest of friends. Froude's father was a traditional High Church archdeacon, and Froude himself was an uncompromising High Churchman, more enchanted with the medieval church than with the Reformers (Ward 1948, 147). When they first met, Froude was put off by what was left of Newman's Evangelical views as well as by the Liberalism Newman was then flirting with. But Froude would soon deal with what he saw as Newman's heresies. Though Froude's personality was complex, with a definite dark side (Gilley 1990, 59), Newman, in the *Apologia*, rhapsodizes about his gentle, playful, graceful character, and praises him as "a man of high genius," overflowing with original ideas, possessed of an "intellect as critical and logical as it was speculative and bold." While Froude had "no turn for theology as such," Newman describes him as "an Englishman to the backbone in his severe adherence to the real and the concrete," but with "a keen insight into abstract truth" (Newman 1947, 21, 22). Newman was clearly impressed.

Almost four decades later, in his *Apologia*, Newman summarizes Froude's influence on him: "He taught me to look with admiration towards the Church of Rome, and in the same degree to dislike the Reformation. He fixed deep in me the idea of devotion to the Blessed Virgin, and he led me gradually to believe in the Real Presence" (Newman 1947, 23). All of this was combined with a high regard for tradition and a scorn for the idea of scripture alone. This influence was spread over a decade, till Froude's early death in 1836, and it is difficult to say exactly how much of it was present in the late 1820s. But Newman did invoke Froude's authority as early as March 1828 as he argued "for lowering the intellectual powers into hand-maids of our moral nature," intellect being subordinate to something more fundamental in us. "Each mind," he writes, "pursues its own course and is actuated in that course by tenthousand indescribable incommunicable feelings and imaginings. It would be comparatively easy to enumerate the various external impulses which determine the capricious motions of a floating feather or web, . . so mysterious are the paths of thought" (qtd. in Gilley 1990, 70). Also from 1828, Newman relates a key event, which he quotes from Froude's *Remains*: "Do you know the story of the murderer who had done one good thing in his life? Well, if I was ever asked what good deed I had ever done, I should say that I had brought Keble and Newman to understand each other" (Newman 1947, 16). This brings us to the other great personal influence on Newman—John Keble.

Newman had first met Keble in the Oriel common room the day Newman was elected Fellow in 1822. Newman was tongue-tied on that occasion. Keble was not then in residence, so Newman saw little of him. In retrospect, Newman thought that Keble was "shy" of him for years because of Newman's Evangelical and Liberal perspectives (Newman 1947, 16). In 1828, a new provost needed to be elected at Oriel; Hawkins and Keble were the candidates. Newman favored his mentor Hawkins, who was, in fact, successful. But the election campaign was the occasion for Froude to sing the praises of his former teacher Keble, and Newman "became conscious for the first time of his own congeniality of mind with Keble" (Tristram 1956, 91). With Hawkins now provost, Newman succeeded him as Vicar of the University Church, St. Mary the Virgin, on March 14, 1828.

Keble's collection of sacred verse, *The Christian Year*, had appeared in 1827. As Newman looks back at the volume's impact on him, he writes that he could not pretend to analyze "the effect of religious teachings so deep, so pure, so beautiful." He does emphasize, however, that it reinforced "the two main intellectual truths" that he had learned from Butler, now creatively recast by his "new master": the sacramental system (analogy) and probability. The first, the sacramental idea in the large sense, is "the doctrine that material phenomena are both the types and the instruments of real things unseen." The second is the claim that in matters religious, "it is not merely probability which makes us intellectually certain, but probability as it is put to account by faith and love . . . which give to probability a force which it has not in itself." As much as he agreed with this "beautiful and religious" view of probability, Newman was dissatisfied because it was not logical enough, "it did not go to the root of the difficulty." He would later try to improve it in various works, including, of course, his *Essay in Aid of a Grammar of Assent* (1870). In his *Apologia*, he capsulizes his basic argument this way: "that that absolute certitude which we were able to possess, whether as to the truths of natural theology, or as to the fact of a revelation, was the result of an *assemblage* of concurring and converging probabilities, and that, both according to the constitution of the human mind and the will of its Maker" (Newman 1947, 16-18).

After his first conversion in 1816, Newman had become "enamoured" of the great Early Christian writers, especially Augustine and Ambrose, learned from extracts in Milner's *History*. However, this early interest waned over the next decade to the point "of a certain disdain for Antiquity," which "showed itself in some flippant language against the Fathers" in his contribution to the *Encyclopedia Metropolitana*. As he now "moved out of the shadow" of Liberalism, that interest revived, and in the summer of 1828 he started reading the Fathers chronologically, beginning with Ignatius and Justin. Before long he was developing the idea "that Antiquity was the true exponent of the doctrines of Christianity and the basis of the Church of England." He was particularly attracted to the Alexandrians. Later he writes: "Some portions of their teaching, magnificent in themselves, came like music to my inner ear, as if the response to ideas, which, with little external to encourage them, I had cherished so long." These teachings were "based on the mystical or sacramental principle," which he understands "to mean that the exterior world, physical and historical, was but the manifestation to our senses of realities greater than itself." He extended this idea both to the entire history of salvation and to such specific topics as angels and other preternatural creatures (Newman 1947, 6, 12, 23-26).

Despite Newman's affection and respect for Hawkins, and his enthusiastic support of his candidacy for provost, two events—important in Newman's development—damaged their relationship soon after Hawkins became provost. First, they split on the question of Robert Peel's re-election to Parliament, brought on by the issue of Catholic emancipation. Second, they disagreed on the nature of an Oriel tutorship, with Newman favoring maximum attention to the most promising students. As a result, Newman was given no new students. Newman's great hopes for Oriel under Hawkins thus ended in deep disappointment. Only in retrospect would Newman realize that this end of his tutorship (1832) made possible the next great phase of his life—the Tractarian Movement of the 1830s. But that is another story.

6. Cognitive Conversion?

What was going on in Newman's knowing during this dozen years? Did he experience a cognitive conversion as he moved from Evangelical to Liberal to High Church theology? We can begin an answer by recalling the distinction between content (what) and structure (how).

First, in terms of *content*, it is clear that Newman underwent a major change in his views or beliefs during these years. We have noted how he was influenced by Whately (and Butler) on his understanding of church, by Hawkins on tradition, and by James on apostolical succession and White on inspiration. Perhaps the most important doctrinal change during this period was in Newman's shift, influenced by Hawkins (Sumner) and Pusey, from regarding a personal experience of conversion as necessary for salvation to an acceptance of baptismal regeneration. Though more difficult to pin down exactly in terms of time, we also noted the general influence of Froude's preference of Rome over the Reformation. There were other important changes in *what* Newman thought: for example, the crucial epistemological views of Butler and Keble on analogy and probability, and the lessons from Locke and Aristotle on the nature of knowledge and morality. Though surely matters of content, these are better understood as changes in the *how* of Newman's knowing, to which we now turn.

When we consider change in the *structural* shape of Newman's knowing, there are several aspects to examine. In these concluding paragraphs we will attend to structural transformation from the following angles: subjective/objective; independent judgment; empirical/ideal; and emotional/rational.

Newman's recognition of the *subjective*, personal dimension of knowing, learned from his study of Locke, was nicely complemented by Butler and Keble's stress on probability and by Aristotle's understanding of moral judgment, both of which involve the grasp of meaning in concrete situations through personal insight. At the same time, his thinking, as Trevor points out in relation to baptism, was becoming more *objective*. Though his theology was not systematic in the ordinary sense, he was becoming more systematic in his thinking. Greater subjectivity results in greater objectivity.

The key issue of *independent judgment* is also complex with Newman. Although he explains that Whately taught him to think for himself, it is clear that personal influences remained very important for him—not only Whately and Hawkins, but also Pusey, Froude, and Keble. Indeed, the latter trio influenced him away from the views (and eventually even the friendship) of the first pair. Newman's critical independence of mind was growing, but it was still far from complete at this point. As in other aspects of his knowing, there was a decided ambivalence here.

Newman's undergraduate study of Aristotle and Locke made a definite and central impact on the *empirical/ideal* aspect. Both authors contributed much to Newman's appreciation of the empirical dimension of knowing. This empirical emphasis was an important counterbalance to a cognitive idealism that had dominated his childhood. In his *Apologia,* Newman includes some childhood memories he had recorded as a young man (1820). He recalls that he was "very superstitious," and that his "imagination ran on unknown influences, on magical powers, and talismans," adding: "I thought life might be a dream, or I an Angel, and all this world a deception, my fellow-angels by a playful device concealing themselves from me, and deceiving me with the semblance of a material world." Newman also recalls in his *Apologia* that the belief in final perseverance involved in his first conversion at age fifteen had directed his mind along the lines of his childhood fantasies: "in isolating me from the objects which surrounded me, in confirming me in my mistrust of the reality of material phenomena, and making me rest in the thought of two and two only absolute and luminously self-evident beings, myself and my Creator." (Newman 1947, 1-2, 4). Despite the later empirical influence, this idealistic dimension remained, and surfaced clearly, as we noted, in Newman's reaction to his sister Mary's death in 1828. The intuition of an invisible world, more real than the visible, was a definite aspect of *how* he knew—his alleged English Platonism (Merrigan 1991, 23-29).

With this tension between the empirical and the ideal, it is easy to appreciate how the analogical (sacramental) views of Butler and Keble appealed so strongly to Newman, as they allowed him the possibility of integrating these two basic tendencies of his knowing.

In the next decade Newman would develop his famous *Via Media* argument justifying Anglo-Catholicism in relation to the extremes of Romanism and Protestantism. But here, in the 1820s, he anticipated the structure of this ecclesiological *Via Media* in an important epistemological *via media*. After years of struggling with the cognitive extremes of *emotional* Evangelical religion on the one hand, and Liberal *Rationalism* on the other, he finally found a satisfying *via media* in the patristic use of images, symbols, and analogy. This is the same insight that resolved his empirical/ideal tension. Thus, in one insight he solved his two key epistemological dilemmas. Confirming his basic childhood intuition of a really real invisible world of the supernatural, this epistemological *via media*, unlike the later *Via Media*, was a middle way he would follow for the rest of his life.

At the end of the 1820s it was not clear where this new way would take him, but it is now clear that Newman had made a definite turn in both the content and structure of his knowing, a significant cognitive conversion. Because his understanding of probability needed greater nuance, because his independence of mind was less than firm, and because his resolution of the tension between the empirical and the ideal was more imaginative than critical, still tied to the invisible world of his childhood fantasies in a supernatural realism, Newman's cognitive conversion of the 1820s, though real, was less than completely adequate. But the most important point is certain: the moral commitment of Newman's first conversion at age fifteen was definitively expanded into a radical search for truth through this cognitive transformation in his twenties. His conscience had found true north; there remained the excruciating labor of charting and following his journey's course.[72]

---

[72] For Thomas Merton's use of this true north image in his autobiography, see my *Christian Conversion*, 174-76.

References

Blehl, Vincent Ferrer. 2001. *Pilgrim Journey: John Henry Newman 1801-1845*. New York: Paulist Press.

Dessain, Charles Stephen, *et al. The Letters and Diaries of John Henry Newman*. 1978-99 (Vols. 1-8) Oxford: Clarendon Press. 1961-72. (Vols. 11-22) London: Nelson. 1973-77 (Vols. 23-31) Oxford: Clarendon Press.

Conn, Walter E. 1986. *Christian Conversion*. New York: Paulist Press.

————. forthcoming 2004. "Young Man Newman: The First Conversion," in James Keating, ed., *Christian Living: Fundamental Issues and New Directions in Moral Theology*. New York: Paulist Press.

Dulles, Avery. 1997. "Newman: The Anatomy of a Conversion," in Ian Ker, ed., *Newman and Conversion*. Notre Dame, IN: University of Notre Dame Press: 21-36.

Gilley, Sheridan. 1990. *Newman and his Age*. London: Darton, Longman and Todd.

Ker, Ian. 1988. *John Henry Newman: A Biography*. New York: Oxford University Press.

Moleski, Martin X. 2000. *Personal Catholicism: The Theological Epistemologies of John Henry Newman and Michael Polanyi*. Washington, DC: Catholic University of America Press.

Merrigan, Terrence. 1991. *Clear Heads and Holy Hearts: The Religious and Theological Ideal of John Henry Newman*, Louvain Theological & Pastoral Monographs, 7. Louvain: Peeters Press.

Newman, John Henry Cardinal. 1947. *Apologia pro Vita Sua*, ed. Charles Frederick Harrold. New York: Longmans, Green.

————. 1962. *John Henry Newman: Autobiographical Writings*, ed. Henry Tristram. New York: Sheed & Ward, 1956.

Trevor, Meriol. 1962. *Newman: The Pillar of the Cloud*. London: Macmillan.

Ward, Maisie. 1948. *Young Mr. Newman*. New York: Sheed & Ward.

13 The Sacramentality of Friendship and Its Implications for Ministry

Barbara J. Fleischer & Gerald M. Fagin, S.J.

After sharing many years of friendship and wonderful table fellowship with Bernard Cooke and his wife, Pauline, it seems very natural to us to turn to the prominent role that friendship and human love play in Bernard's exposition of the sacramentality of Christian life. Bernard has taught us much about the meaning of friendship and his theology of friendship offers rich fare for reflection. In this essay, we will discuss some of the characteristics of human love and friendship, Jesus' Abba experience, God as friendship, and finally the connections among friendship, community, and praxis.

The Sacramentality of Human Love and Friendship

In his writings and teaching, Bernard Cooke consistently affirms the experiential dimension of Christian sacraments as a primary key to their transformative power. Fundamentally, sacraments are human experiences that transform our perspectives, meaning, and action as we experience God's Word communicated to and for us. As moments of encounter with the saving power of Jesus in his life, death, and resurrection, sacraments challenge and deepen the root metaphors out of which Christians live their lives. What it means to be human, to live in community and in relationships, and to act in the world with love and integrity take shape through our sacramental engagement with God's Word to us. And because God's self-communication is not confined to sacred spaces and times, all human experiences hold the potential of becoming a locus for revealing the Transcendent and for communicating God's love and Word for us. This larger sacramentality of life itself forms the broader context within which thicker moments of Christian sacramental celebrations take place.

In his focus on the sacramentality of human experience, Bernard Cooke points to the revelatory power of human love and friendship as peak experiences that can disclose who God is for us and who we as Christian community are called to be in the midst of our friendship with God and sharing in God's Spirit. In *Sacraments and Sacramentality* he writes, "It is the reality of human relationships, above all that of true friendship, that is the basic experience of humans which reveals the God known by Jesus as 'Abba' to be a loving God" (1994, vi). Thus, his exposition of Christian sacraments begins not with baptism and sacraments of initiation but rather with "Human Friendship: the Basic Sacrament" (78). Bernard affirms that our human experience of love provides the best window and experiential path for understanding the reality of God. "If we experience the love and care that others have for us, beginning with an infant's experience of parental love, and experience our own loving concern for others, this can give us some analogue for thinking how the ultimate might personally relate to us" (84). Moreover, the experience of human love is not, for Bernard Cooke, solely an analogue for understanding a God who is infinitely different or other than human. Loving relationships themselves become a "word" of God and "in this word God is made present to us, revealing divine selfhood through the sacramentality of our human experience of one another" (83). We come to know the God of Love by loving and by being loved.

The key to sacramentality, for Bernard Cooke, is a "hermeneutic of experience" that uses our daily and peak experiences to help us understand, interpret, and appreciate the experiences and life of Jesus of Nazareth, particularly, as Bernard has highlighted for us, what we can glean about Jesus' experience of his Abba and the ways in which that experience shaped his relational life with others. Experiences of friendship provide a particularly rich lens through which to view and enter into the love Jesus experienced in his Abba and shared with his community.

Human Love as Window to
Jesus' Experience of His Abba

The human experience of love and friendship offers many avenues for understanding the God whom Jesus reveals, the One described as Love itself (1 John 4:8). As Bernard Cooke points out, in the experience of being loved we learn that we are significant to another who cares about our well-being (1994, 78). We learn that we are loveable and in that knowledge grow in personhood and self-awareness. We enjoy the gifts of laughter and sharing, and we experience an abundance of life beyond solitary existence. Friendship also expands our appreciation and understanding of Love through our own befriending and caring for others. As our capacity for love and fidelity expands, we grow in appreciation of what divine fidelity and *hesed* must be. As I experience unconditional caring for another, I learn more of what divine forgiveness and self-gift might be like. By analogy, I can appreciate that God's love and forgiveness must be so much greater than my most selfless and compassionate acts. But even in the absence or betrayal of broken friendships, we can learn from our longings and desires, our hopes for understanding and reconciliation, our search for patterns of care and equality. The desires of our hearts themselves can disclose to us what love is and what it is not.

While each person's own experience of friendship and human love provides a very human path for imagining and entering into an experience of God's infinite love for each of us, as Dick Westley points out in *Redemptive Intimacy*, "it is communally funded experience that should shape our theology" (1981, 8). Our task in theological reflection includes gathering up experiences from a wide variety of regions and perspectives to find commonalities and emerging consensus. With respect to the sacramentality of human love and friendship, it is important to explore what these experiences of intimacy mean to people with a variety of backgrounds. As we collect many examples of mature human love, we can discover what is most essential and characteristic in the best of what we call love in human experience. We can further use this wider range of experiences to shape our own "hermeneutic of experience" to gain clearer insight into the Abba and communal relationships that Jesus is calling us to enter and experience. And we can use this wisdom to guide our responses to the human and wider planetary needs we face in our contemporary world.

One path for collecting a variety of experiences of human love and growthful relationships is to review some of the experiences of twentieth century psychologists and therapists who, as students of human maturity and capacity for sustained loving relationships, offer us their wisdom and insights from hundreds of encounters with persons revealing their deepest heart desires and relational journeys. This collection, of course, offers only one small glimpse into communally funded experiences of human love and friendship, but it does offer us reflections from a wider range of personal experiences. Insights from the field of psychology highlight what has been experienced, at least in contemporary Western culture, as most significant in relationships that lead to healing, growth, and maturity in the human person. These key dimensions of human love, when resonant with Jesus' experience of his Abba and his mission, provide us with greater clarity about both the Abba Jesus reveals and the dimensions of human love and friendship that need to be fostered in our Christian ministries. Our theological reflection will then put those insights on what seems to be the most growth enhancing dimensions of human relationships in conversation with the very insightful study that Bernard Cooke offers us on the Abba experience of Jesus. In this twofold reflection on the human experience of love and Jesus' experience of the Transcendent, we hope to draw deeper insights into what it might mean to know, love, and live in God as Jesus did. Our theological reflection will then move to considering what implications these insights hold for spirituality, Christian ministry, and communal praxis.

The Centrality of Trust and Acceptance

Carl Rogers, after a lifetime of "deep therapeutic relationships with an ever-widening range of clients" (1961, 14) drew several simple but profound insights from both his personal experiences in those relationships and from various studies on fostering growth in human maturity and relational capacity. He found repeatedly that human persons grow and blossom personally when they can become engaged in a relationship that engenders *trust* and where there is an assured sense of safety and acceptance in the relationship that enables the person to reveal who they are while still receiving "unconditional positive regard" (47). Trustworthiness and acceptance on the part of the therapist, teacher, or friend are key elements that lead to the unfolding of mature personhood. Therapists and others who are genuine and "real" in their responses, avoiding all forms of manipulation and disingenuous communication, who are warmly accepting and non-judgmental, and who show an empathic desire to understand the person's feelings, perceptions, and actions from a deeply magnanimous perspective enable a person to engage in a freeing exploration that leads to growth. Gradually, the person gains confidence to unlock fears, drop adaptive masks, and grow in self-awareness, expressiveness, and the capacity to relate lovingly with others (36-38).

Developmental psychologist Erik Erikson states that basic trust is the "cornerstone of a vital personality" (1968, 97). Without this foundational sense of trust that is normally developed in early childhood through a relationship with nurturing parents, persons move toward "severe estrangement" from others and have extreme difficulty forming friendships or intimate relationships. Persons who have experienced emotional scars from less than ideal human relationships, however, can grow and mature when they finally encounter a more healthy and mature loving relationship. A person in a therapeutic or healing relationship can grow and change as rejected aspects of his or her inner world come to awareness and are explored without inducing rejection on the part of the friend-listener or therapist. As areas of personal experience that once evoked self-hatred or shame are reintegrated, the person's relational capacity and maturity develops. The person is then able "to recognize and face up to the deep contradictions" which she or he discovers in exploring the meaning of experiences and perceptions (109). The formation of a healthy relationship appears to be the primary crucible for growth and maturity. Rogers cites research that shows that regardless of the theoretical approach of the therapist, successful therapy is associated with a strong mutual respect and liking between therapist and client (44). Through the unwavering fidelity of a listening companion, the person learns to befriend self.

More recent studies on the importance of trustworthy, accepting relationships show that the ability to share deeply on an emotional level relates significantly not only to psychological but also to physical health. Scores of studies have shown that people who do not express their important emotional events have higher levels of depression, anxiety, and health problems (Pennebaker 1997, 25). Studies on the physiological correlates of self-disclosure show immediate changes in brain wave patterns, with drops in blood pressure, heart rate, and improvements in immune system functioning following the disclosure of emotionally charged memories (56). Researcher James Pennebaker notes that "central to true self-disclosure is an overriding sense of trust" (110) and that trust is often dependent on an assured sense of safety and acceptance in the relationship (111).

Insights from the Experience of Loving

Psychoanalyst Erich Fromm calls the desire for interpersonal union the most powerful of human forces. He notes, however, that several approaches to this union, while sometimes characterized as love, lead more to fusion or to escape from intimacy. Among the love substitutes he names are regression to infantile dependency, impersonal or transitory sexual unions, flight to addictions of various types, conformity to social expectations, and sublimation into work or creative activities (1956, 9-15). In contrast, he speaks of mature human love as an experience of giving that is powerfully rewarding in and of itself. In giving, he writes, "I experience myself as overflowing, spending, alive, hence as joyous" (19). The ability to love requires a giving orientation as well as a growth in character beyond narcissism and the desire to exploit others or hoard (22-23). More positively, Fromm asserts, love requires four key elements: *respect, knowledge, responsibility and caring.*

Respect, Fromm points out, is a derivative of *respicere*, to look at or behold. In respecting another I behold the person in his or her uniqueness. Respect is the ability to see the other's path as distinct from my own—to see the person as a subject, not an object. For Fromm, respect means "the concern that the other person should grow and unfold as he [or she] is" (1956, 23). Respect, seeing the person, is naturally intertwined with knowledge—understanding the person deeply through the many layers of emotions and experiences that I am privileged to learn. This knowledge is held in reverence, free from any exploitative desire to use it for dominance. Knowing a person involves not only learning the story of his or her life but also perceiving empathetically the meanings and experiences in the person's life that have been prominent and emotionally significant.

In love, says Fromm, a person is also responsive to the needs, expressed or unexpressed, of the other. Responsibility means the ability to respond, and it comes from within, from one's deep sense of caring, rather than from duty imposed from external sources (1956, 23). Fromm's emphasis on caring and concern as the overriding activity of love provides perspective to the other elements and keeps them in interdependent balance. Love, says Fromm, is "the active concern for the life and the growth of that which we love" (22). Thus, it is not exploitative or domineering and seeks the ultimate growth and welfare of the beloved. For Fromm, love is an art that builds upon maturity but also requires patience and practice. As we grow in our capacity and depth of love, we learn "by heart" what love and faithfulness to another entail.

Therapist Gerald May distinguishes between "falling in love" and "being in love." Falling in love happens and often feels choiceless. A sudden moment of recognition and flowing connection opens; a new dimension of reality emerges. This experience is but a threshold, says May, "it is the place where love invites us into itself" (1991, 27). Abiding love requires choices - a daily, even momentary, yes to continue choosing love. Being in love, in contrast to falling in love, "is a willing yielding into love's presence" (28). It requires an active awareness of both the other and of my responsive choices. For May, our ability to love is grace.

> Grace is love happening, love in action, and I have seen so much grace in the midst of so much brokenness in myself and others that I know we are all in love. We are in love, within love, as fish are in the sea and clouds are in the sky. It surrounds us, penetrates and perfuses us. In a very real sense, we are made of love. Love creates us, and we create love (1991, 7).

Contemporary descriptions of therapeutic and healing relationships speak of the importance of unconditional acceptance of the person and the development of relationships of trust as basic to fostering the growth and maturity of persons and their capacity for friendship and community. Where elements of dominance, exploitation, rejection, or disdain enter in, human growth becomes inhibited, or in some cases, reversed. If these are the conditions for wholeness and transformation on a human plane, they also point to a Transcendent that draws forth our maturity and growth without dominance or punishing rejection. They point to a Transcendent Love that exceeds even the best of human love that fosters the development of full personhood. They lead us, too, to question any images of God that run directly contrary to those growth-fostering relational qualities in personal relationships or in the wider society. God's love is at least as growth enhancing as the best of human love. The reign of God depicts not only the quality of a society in which love reigns as ultimate value, it stands as a generative contrast against societies that diminish genuine human and natural world connection in the service of corporate greed or exploitative gain.

Connections to Sacramentality

If human experiences are to engage us sacramentally, they must lead us into a twofold connection: on one level we fully experience our environment, relationships, human emotions, intuitions, actions, responses, and imaginings in our daily life and secondly, we connect our understandings of those experiences with the larger Christian story, rooted in the life and paschal mystery of Jesus of Nazareth. It is in nourishing our understanding of who Jesus is, how Jesus experienced his Abba, how his Abba experience shaped Jesus' ministry and relationships to others, and how our own intimacy with Abba can grow and form all of our other encounters and actions that human friendship truly becomes sacramental in a Christian sense. When seen in the light of Jesus' Abba experience, friendship and human love open up widely beyond complacence with a small circle of friends to the development of community, praxis, and socially transformative action.

Jesus' Experience of His Abba

Bernard Cooke refers to Jesus' Abba experience as Jesus' awareness of God's special and unique love for him and his own experience of "Abba's supreme loveableness" (1992, 11). While we can only glean glimpses of what this experience must have been for Jesus from the historical memories of him recorded and edited by the various gospel communities, these portraits of Jesus provide profound insights into the totality and power of this experience for his life and ministry. As Bernard Cooke points out:

> That this [experience] is basic to Jesus' self-identification seems hard to dispute. While other elements of that self-identity, such as being the eschatological prophet or being the son of Man, may have become more cognitively formulated in Jesus' consciousness…the experience of loving and being loved by his Abba seems to have transfused the entirety of Jesus' life experience (1992, 11).

Bernard Cooke points out that Jesus, as Jewish male, would naturally use the language and metaphors of his culture to speak of the divine. Unquestionably, his culture was one of strong patriarchy, and language pointing to divine presence was "thoroughly masculine" (1992, 50). God in the language of Jesus' Jewish culture was definitely "he." Within that framework of first century Palestine, the gospel portraits of Jesus relating to his "Abba" convey perhaps one of the most intimate masculine images available in that culture for portraying a loving, personal, and special encounter with the God of Israel. The gospel depictions of Jesus' encounter with his Abba speak of the uniqueness of his experience and the profound depth of his relationship.

Jesus embodies the *Shema,* loving his Abba with his whole heart, soul, and strength (Deut. 6:11), and the Abba he reveals addresses him as beloved, *agapetos*. His life, becomes revelatory, a Word, expressing not only the utter beauty and compassion of his Abba but drawing others into the quality and Spirit of their relationship. His ministry is an invitation to live in the spirit of love so completely that the reign of Love becomes a reality. The *Shema* he reveals is intimately woven with its relational effect, all-embracing love of neighbor (Luke 10:27) as each one grows in the experience of being beloved by the Abba who is all of "ours."

The gospels describe Jesus' experience of the Transcendent by highlighting his naming of Abba and by pointing to a relationship that is both intimate and immediate, says Bernard Cooke (1992, 12). Jesus' experience of the Transcendent was of *someone* supremely loving and loveable. Bernard explores two gospel scenes that are particularly illustrative of how the gospel stories convey this intimacy between Jesus and his Abba. The first, the account of Jesus' baptism at the Jordan River, while highly theologized, nonetheless describes Jesus as the beloved one in whom his Abba *delights* (1992, 12-15). Abba not only "accepts" Jesus completely, his Abba delights in him. The narratives clearly portray Jesus' experience of ultimacy as someone, his Abba, outpouring special love for him and addressing him as "beloved." The presence of the Spirit imaged as a dove, descending yet able to take flight upward, speaks of the love experienced by Jesus and returned to his Abba. Empowered by this love, God's Spirit shared intimately with him, Jesus then moves to the desert in the gospel narratives where he shows the strength both to resist and to confront evil in all its forms and temptations. From there the power of God's love moves Jesus into his public ministry.

The second gospel scene that Bernard Cooke highlights is the deeply anguished portrait of Jesus communicating with his Abba in the garden of Gethsemane. In the intimacy of this prayerful encounter, along with Jesus' resolute acceptance of the cross that followed we find, "the supreme witness to Jesus' trust in his Abba" (1992, 16). The gospel narratives of Jesus' night of turmoil in the garden show him questioning and agonizing on the eve of his unbearable suffering and death yet drawing strength and resolve from his yes to his love for Abba. To deny that he experienced Abba's love and acted from that experience in his ministry or to reject his public actions that were so integral to that experience would probably have spared his earthly life, but such a denial of Abba's love would have betrayed his most life-giving encounter. While recoiling from the imminent implications of his fidelity to Abba, Jesus could not deny the truth of his relationship. His decision for "obedience" was a decision to affirm publicly his love for and experience of special love from his Abba, regardless of the human consequences. His Spirit was Abba's and he would surrender it in complete trust. Ultimately, his life was in the hands of his Abba who is infinitely trustworthy.

The Abba whom Jesus reveals is the same God of Israel who acts in history and calls Israel to loving covenant (e.g., Hosea). Yet, as Bernard points out, there were significant incongruities between the Abba Jesus knew and the portrait of the God of Israel presented by many of the religious leaders and people of his society (1992, 19-20).

Jesus challenged any image of a god who demanded appeasement for sin by animal sacrifice or who expected purity and separation of those deemed sinful or unclean from those who saw themselves as followers of the Law. Jesus ate and drank with sinners, touched the "unclean," included the irreligious in his table fellowship, and insisted that God's love was as foolishly extravagant as that of the father portrayed in the story of the prodigal son. Loving community is where the experience and love of God breaks through and nothing—no concern for what to eat or drink or for what others may think or even for former boundaries of enmity—takes precedence over creating and cherishing the bonds of faithful and caring communion. The divine is not seeking wrathful vengeance or fear-ridden dominance. God, as depicted in the actions, parables, and healings of Jesus initiates reconciliation and seeks that which is lost. In his actions and teaching Jesus is parabolic, overturning inadequate images of God and reversing expectations. Rather than vengeful judge or exclusive protector of Israel, Abba is universally compassionate, forgiving, embracing, and extravagantly generous. The realization, acceptance and yielding, loving response to this Ultimate Love create the reign of God in human community. Where love is, there God is ever found.

Jesus' ministry was fundamentally one of revealing the Abba he experienced as "our" Abba (Mt. 6:10) and calling others into that same experience. Those who are open to this new revelation, this word revealed in the person of Jesus, share in that same Spirit that empowered Jesus' healing and teaching. The Spirit of God impels those who enter into "the mind of Christ" to heal, to challenge structures that separate and condemn, and to create bonds of community where none exist. In community, those who share in this Spirit become "body of Christ" and continue to bring about this awareness and experience of Abba's love in history. The love of Abba is also extended beyond the human community to all of creation and care for the earth (Romans 8:19-23).

Jesus reveals a new kind of relationship and community born in an encounter with a God who engenders trust and brings about wholeness. The preponderance of healing stories in the gospel narratives point to a Spirit of God that is restorative and creative on physical, spiritual, and social dimensions. Those once excluded as unclean, rather than being discarded, are made whole and reintegrated into community. The blind, physically and spiritually, see the truth of God's *hesed*.

The Abba Jesus reveals is One who delights in us and invites us to discover our belovedness. With respect to trust, Jesus' Abba is shown by the gospels to be the One upon whom we can be radically dependent with our very existence. The life, death, and especially resurrection of Jesus reveal the utter trustworthiness of his Abba and the profoundly trusting relationship that Jesus exemplifies for us. Likewise, we are called to be those whom others can trust with their deepest stories and life questions, without judgment or condemnation (Luke 6:36-38).

The sacramentality of mature human love, as we are coming to understand it through our communally funded experiences, helps us both to understand Jesus' Abba experience as depicted in the gospels and to enter into that loving experience itself. Human love and friendship are basic sacraments because they participate in the reality of a God who is Love (1 Jn. 4:8) and because they help us learn to trust the loving embrace of the Transcendent as larger than all of our anxiety producing concerns. Such a sacramental experience is transformative of all of our relationships, both human and planetary. Moreover, what we can learn and experience as a human community with respect to the best of human love helps us sift through false images of domineering gods to find the true Abba that Jesus reveals as calling us into a new reality, the reign of God.

God Is Friendship

On another level, Jesus' Abba experience is rooted in the very life and nature of God. If we turn to the trinitarian theology that emerged in the fourth and fifth centuries and was more fully developed in the Middle Ages, we discover an attempt to articulate the mystery of God's inner life. In classical trinitarian theology, the life of God is a life of communication and love. Using the patriarchal imagery of the time, the Father's knowledge of self gives birth to the Word, the perfect expression of God's Self. The Father and the Son love each other and that love of relationship is the Holy Spirit. Whatever imagery we may call upon, the important insight is that God is a series of relationships of knowing and loving that constitute the inner life of God. These relationships have been called persons as a way of honoring the distinctions yet the unity within God. These relations are not relations of hierarchy and subordination but ones of radical equality. To say that God is eternal relations of knowing and loving is to say analogously that God is friendship. Communication, love and equality are at the heart of friendship and the very life of God is imaged as mutual knowing and loving. The persons of the Trinity love each other in equality, mutuality and reciprocity. The Trinity is a community of equals constituted by mutual relationships.

In a patriarchal society, one of the most powerful ways to image love is the love between a Father and Son. A contemporary understanding of love and friendship offers a new language for describing the deeply relational life of God, the language of love and friendship. In the search for a more inclusive yet relational language for speaking about God, perhaps friend, befriended and befriending could offer at times an alternative to the traditional language of Father, Son, and Spirit. The life of God is a life of friendship that implies dynamic relationships of equality.

But if we describe God in the imagery of friendship, then Jesus' Abba experience can also be described as an experience of God as love and friendship. If God is friendship, then Abba's love for Jesus is a love of friendship and the gift of the Spirit given at Jesus' baptism can be imaged as the gift of friendship. God as Friend names Jesus as Beloved Friend, as one who shares profoundly the life of God.

Jesus invites us to share his Abba experience by calling us to be friends. "I do not call you servants any longer. . .but I have called you friends. . ." (Jn. 15:15). The amazing revelation given in John's Gospel in Jesus' discourse on the night before he died is that we are called to be friends of Jesus and friends of God. This gives a richer meaning to the words of Jesus, "As Abba has loved me, so I have loved you. Abide in my love." (Jn. 15: 9) Abba's love for Jesus is a love of friendship and Jesus in turn loves us as friends. Jesus shares with us the very Abba love he has received. In Jesus, we become friends of God. We experience God as friendship.

Jesus' invitation to friendship and not servitude is dramatized in the description of the Last Supper in John's Gospel when Jesus acts out this new relationship by washing his disciples' feet. Sandra Schneiders in her commentary on John's Gospel views this text as "a human expression that functions as a mediation of meaning."(1999, 162) The meaning the text mediates "is not behind it, hidden in the shroud of the past when the text was composed, but ahead of it in the possibilities of human and Christian existence that it projects for the reader." (162) The text reveals to us the deepest meaning of love and service in the Kingdom of God. Schneiders interprets the footwashing as "a prophetic action that will reveal the true meaning of Jesus' loving his own unto the end."(167) Too often Jesus' washing of the disciples' feet is reduced to a simple act of humility that challenges all disciples to a humble stance of service of others, but, as Schneiders points out, the dramatic interchange between Jesus and Peter makes it clear that much more is at stake. Something much more profound is being acted out in Jesus' simple gesture. Accepting Jesus' offer of humble service is accepting a new view of human relationships and ultimately of salvation. Jesus' action sets a new standard for Christian service and Christian community.

Footwashing is an act of serving. As presented in John's Gospel, Jesus defines his salvific work by means of this gesture. Jesus' ultimate act of service and love will be laying down his life for us. "No one has greater love than this, to lay down one's life for one's friends" (Jn. 15: 13). Here the act of footwashing is a prophetic action that symbolizes the ultimate act of self-giving, his passion and death.

Schneiders highlights the deeper meaning of the footwashing by describing three different models of service. "In the first model service denotes what one person (the server) must do for another (the served) because of some right or power that the latter is understood to possess."(1999, 170). In this model, service is understood within the structures of domination and inequality. This is the service given by a slave to a master. In the second model of service, one person does something freely for another because of the other person's needs. Though at first glance this model seems loving and disinterested, it still implies an inequality and even dominance because one person is acting out of a certain superiority to the other. One person possesses something the other needs and cannot provide for themselves. For instance, a rich person may generously give resources to a poor person. The third model of service is friendship, the only human relationship based on equality. "Service rendered between friends is never exacted and creates no debts, demands no return but evokes reciprocity."(172) Service between friends is pure self-gift. This third model of service clarifies Jesus' salvific work. Jesus' ultimate self-gift of offering his life for our salvation was not "in John's perspective, the master's redemption of unworthy slaves but an act of friendship."(172) Jesus gave his life for his friends.

In light of this reflection on service and friendship, Schneiders takes us back to the scene of the footwashing. What Jesus performed was not a simple act of humility to be imitated by others. Rather Jesus was acting out the Gospel call to abolish all inequality and domination based on superiority and to establish a new social order rooted in friendship and love that expresses itself in mutual service.

> By washing his disciples' feet Jesus overcame by love the inequality that existed by nature between himself and those whom he had chosen as friends. He established an intimacy with them that superseded his superiority and signaled their access to everything that he had received from his Father (see 15:15), even to the glory that he had been given as Son (see 17:22) (Schneiders 1999, 173).

This radical meaning of Jesus' gesture explains why Peter so vehemently resisted the footwashing. He was threatened by such a fundamental restructuring of society and its authority. In John's perspective, the community of disciples is characterized by the love of friendship that Jesus acts out in washing the disciples' feet. Service in this community will not be an expression of domination or superiority but rather an expression of mutual friendship among equals. This becomes clear when Jesus challenges the disciples to do for one another what he has done for them—wash one another's feet.

It seems that this interpretation of the footwashing gives content to Jesus' words in Chapter 14 of John, "Love one another as I have loved you." If Jesus loves us as friends, as equals without any claimed superiority or posture of domination, we are to love one another in the same way. We are to be friends of one another and express that friendship in mutual loving service. True friendship always leads to service because the friend is always interested in the good of the other. Jesus modeled for us that total self-gift in his death and resurrection and he invites us to love one another with the same total and selfless love. The call to live the Christian life is a call to live in friendship in a community of disciples. Friendship is at the heart of Christian life and ministry.

This reflection highlights the central image of the love of friendship that begins in God and ends in the sacrament of human friendship. We can image God as friendship, the mutual love among the three persons. Likewise, Jesus' Abba experience is an experience of friendship, of Abba's love of him as the Beloved. Jesus loves us with the same love of friendship with which Abba loves him and Jesus exhorts us to love one another as he has loved us. Thus, we are to be friends to one another as Jesus is to us and God is to Jesus. Human friendship with God and with one another is the way we live and share in the life of God. And if we are to participate in some way in God's life, we must live in friendship and love as a community of friends. By its connection to the inner life of God, we can affirm again that human friendship is the basic sacrament of God's love manifested in Jesus.

At the heart of all this is God's desire to share friendship with us. This desire is manifested in God sending Jesus to reconcile us to God, to restore the broken relationship between God and us. God's desire for friendship is manifested again in the gift of the Spirit, the very love that exists within God. The Spirit is the expression of God's love and friendship. This same Spirit binds us to one another and makes us one in friendship. In John's Gospel, Jesus' great prayer in Chapter 17 is a prayer for unity. Jesus is portrayed as expressing his desire that we may be one as he and Abba are one. He and Abba are, of course, united by the love of the Holy Spirit, and the Spirit is the friendship between them. It is that same Spirit of God poured into our hearts as the love of God that will accomplish this unity in us and create a community of friends.

Friendship, Community, and Praxis

Some may argue that emphasizing friendship over other aspects of human experience will lead to an enclave mentality or an overly pietistic or privatized sense of who God is for us (or me). Others may see friendship as a primary metaphor for Christian life as too tame for a community that should be impelled to challenge social structures and act boldly on behalf of social justice. Given the context of American individualism, notions of friendship can easily slip into a mode of selective and exclusive relationships, and so interpretive dangers are present. However, to call human love and friendship sacramental means that they point to and participate in a larger reality affirmed by Christian faith.

Erich Fromm points out that love that is directed to one "object" or person while excluding care for all others and creation itself is not love but rather a "symbiotic attachment, or an enlarged egotism" (1956, 39). Fromm asserts that love is an "orientation of character which determines the relatedness of a person to the world as a whole" (38). Echoing the insights of Martin Buber in *I and Thou*, he writes: "If I truly love one person I love all persons, I love the world, I love life. If I can say to somebody else, 'I love you,' I must be able to say, 'I love in you everybody, I love through you the world, I love in you also myself'" (1956, 39).

While human finitude and limits of time may place boundaries on how many deeply nurtured relationships a person may develop, a person who is maturely loving maintains the capacity and orientation for loving relationships by nurturing qualities of magnanimity, under-standing, openness, trustworthiness, and avoidance of dominance in all its forms. Love involves intention, activity, and a growing capacity to embrace the other.

While each person has many choice points to nurture a loving, non-dominative response to another or not, the norms and patterns of culture can either foster or impede the orientations of persons toward trusting, open relationships. Fromm points out that societies based upon highly competitive interchanges and commodity markets press their members into utilitarian and disposable orientations in their relationships. Consumer-based societies require and foster the devel-opment of persons who have highly malleable tastes that can easily be enticed through advertising. Fromm chillingly describes such societies as spawning cultures in which persons are alienated from themselves, from each other, and from nature (1956, 72). The person in contem-porary industrialized societies becomes a "commodity" and

> experiences his [or her] life forces as an investment which must bring…the maximum profit obtainable under existing market

conditions. Human relations are essentially those of alienated automatons, each basing his [or her] security on staying close to the herd, and not being different in thought, feeling or action. While everybody tries to be as close as possible to the rest, everybody remains utterly alone, pervaded by the deep sense of insecurity, anxiety and guilt which always results when human separateness cannot be overcome (72).

Fromm goes on to point out that the consumer society offers several ways of dulling its members' consciousness of their aloneness and desires for true and loving connection with human community and the natural world. The first is by routine and bureaucratic repetitive work (quite often, overwork) that "helps people to remain unaware of their most fundamental human desires, of the longing for transcendence and unity" (1956, 73). If the pattern of work does not fully silence this human longing, says Fromm, the "the passive consumption of sounds and sights offered by the amusement industry" and "the satisfaction of buying ever new things, and soon exchanging them for others" offers further palliative assistance (73). The consumer, individualist society militates strongly against the formation of strong bonds of friendship and solidarity.

A Relational Anthropology

The reign of God that Jesus ushers in offers a stark contrast to the consumerist society that Fromm depicts as squashing the capacity for generative and genuinely caring, loving relationships. Theologian Roberto Goizueta contrasts the premises of competitive individualism, wherein each person creates his or her own selfhood through choices and self-determination, with a relational anthropology that sees each person as constituted by the community and relationships through which he or she develops (1995, 77). Community, in cultures that glorify individualism, sometimes connotes a shackling or limiting of human freedom. The rugged individual can strike out on his or her own, regardless of what others may think or feel, and create a life "my way." In such a mindset, individuality and community may be considered mutually exclusive. Goizueta, however, drawing upon both Latin American culture and the story of Our Lady of Guadelupe, points out that true community involves free subjects in "intersubjective relationships" (75). Authentic community is the crucible for the experience of trust and nurturance of one's unique gifts and individuality. Authentic communities thus foster the development of "free and unique human persons" (75) and enable the giftedness of each person to flourish.

> Indeed, the true test of an authentic relationship or community is one whose participants are, like Juan Diego, free to disobey, to criticize, and to be different. Just as community is a prerequisite for individual freedom, so too is individual freedom a prerequisite for community. This, however, is not the ahistorical 'freedom' of the autonomous, unsituated individual; it is, instead, a personal freedom which already presupposes ... relationality, situatedness, and community... (Goizueta 1995, 76).

In such a community, human persons can learn to trust and reveal themselves, the capacity for deep human love is nurtured, and mature human love and friendship can thrive. Moreover, the rich relational life of the community can give rise to liberative praxis, because in caring for one another and the many webs of relationships that connect members through intertwining multi-community links, the concern of one becomes the concern of all. Christian praxis arises from these tangible, caring connections.

This focus on the connection between praxis and friendship recalls C.S. Lewis' observation that "Lovers are normally face to face, absorbed in each other; friends, side by side, absorbed in some common interest" (1960, 91). Sallie McFague, in her reflection on God as friend, defines friendship as "a free, reciprocal trustful bonding of persons committed to a common mission. (171). She relates this to friendship with Jesus and our responsibility for the world: "To be friends of Jesus, in this sense, means to stand with him and with all others united by and committed to the common vision embodied in the shared meal extended to the outsider. . .It means being willing, as an adult, to join in mutual responsibility with God and others for the well-being of this world" (175).

Poiesis and Praxis

Poiesis in Aristotelian thought is a kind of activity that separates the "visioning" and planning from the doing. It involves technique and making things in the future. I can envision a chair, for example, then set about with proper tools and technique to make it. In praxis the doing and the knowing are intimately intertwined. A jazz pianist improvises. The music and knowing of the music arises in the activity of playing. In conversation, too, exact outcomes cannot be specified in advance if the dialogue is a truly spontaneous encounter. Such is the nature of praxis. Goizueta critiques a Marxist notion of "praxis" as actually being more akin to poiesis, of envisioning an ideal future apart from the realities that are affecting the community's interconnections in this time and place. Such a basis for social transformation ignores the relational needs of the present moment and subsumes them into an activity aimed at some future goal. Moreover, persons who do not fit the idealized image of the future can be discounted or even "eliminated" for the sake of the final goal.

To reduce human action to social transformation is to reduce it to productive activity, which is to reduce it to technique; and to reduce human action to technique is to reduce the human person to but a passive object, a mere instrument of production (Goizueta 1995, 84).

By contrast, in Latin American liberation communities and theologies, praxis on behalf of social justice arises from authentic fellowship and solidarity. Liberation is not found at the end of a struggle, the future product of social transformation efforts. Liberation is largely found in the process of acting together in community and thus strengthening and forging stronger connections of solidarity, respect, and caring as the journey toward a new society unfolds.

Reflecting on his experience with Hispanic communities of faith, well engaged in struggles of social justice, Goizueta observes that public action and empowerment arose naturally out of the relationships and concerns of the community. Action on behalf of justice in these communities is not an appendage to their inner, relational life. It arises from their very friendships and solidarity in the midst of suffering caused by larger structures.

Conclusion

We have tried in this essay to reflect in the light of psychology and theology on Bernard Cooke's insight that friendship is the basic sacrament that reveals God's love to us. We hope these various approaches to friendship will highlight the richness of this theme in his writings. Psychology has taught us that friendship is characterized by trust and acceptance, as well as by respect, knowledge, responsibility and caring. Each of these elements of genuine human love and friendship has named for us qualities of God's love. Human friendship truly is a sacrament of God's love for us.

We have reflected on Bernard Cooke's connection between human friendship and Jesus' experience of Abba. Human friendship offers a window into a deeper understanding and appreciation of Jesus' experience of God as Abba. If we image God as friendship and Jesus' Abba experience as an experience of friendship, then we are able to grasp more deeply Jesus' invitation to us to be his friends and friends to one another.

Finally it is clear that we are called to live the life of God by being in a community of friends and servants to one another. Friendship becomes a model for ministry. Ministry is not an experience in domination or simply a fulfillment of others' needs, but a mutual sharing among friends of the gifts of God. We recognize as well that Christian friendship is not a call to turn inward or to focus on a select few. Rather it is a mandate for social transformation and the relational reality out of which transformative praxis arises.

In his writings, Bernard Cooke has focused our attention on human friendship as a central paradigm for appreciating more deeply the meaning and experience of sacramentality. We would suggest that this paradigm can also open for us a richer understanding of God's inner life, Jesus' experience of Abba, Christian community and Christian ministry. All of these are themes Bernard has explored with insight and wisdom throughout his long years of theological reflection.

References

Cooke, Bernard. *God's Beloved: Jesus' Experience of the Transcendent.* Philadelphia: Trinity Press International, 1992.

Cooke, Bernard. *Sacraments and Sacramentality.* Mystic, CT: Twenty-Third, 1994.

Erikson, Erik H. *Identity, Youth, and Crisis.* New York: W.W. Norton, 1968.

Fromm, Erich. *The Art of Loving*. New York: Bantam, 1956.

Goizueta, Roberto S. *Caminemos con Jesús*. Maryknoll, NY: Orbis, 1995.

Lewis, C. S. *The Four Loves*. New York: Harcourt Brace, 1960.

May, Gerald. *The Awakened Heart*. San Francisco: HarperSanFrancisco, 1991.

McFague, Sallie. *Models of God: Theology for an Ecological, Nuclear Age*. Philadelphia: Fortress, 1987.

Pennebaker, James. *Opening Up*. New York: Guilford, 1997.

Rogers, Carl. *On Becoming a Person*. Boston: Houghton Mifflin, 1961.

Schneiders, Sandra. *Written that You May Believe*. New York: Crossroad, 1999.

Westley, Dick. *Redemptive Intimacy*. Mystic, CT: Twenty-Third, 1981.

14 Prayer and Pedagogy: Some Reflections

Lawrence S. Cunningham

Teach your mouth to say what is in your heart.
Abba Poemen

Introduction

More than anything else Bernard Cooke was and is a teacher who even in his *soi disant* retirement fills a classroom on occasion and also extends himself spiritually in the classroom through the many scholar-teachers who were once his pupils. I was not his student but have always been both an admirer and a consumer of the fruits of his teaching that one finds in his published works. Who can even think about sacramental theology or the theology of ministry without reference to his many books and monographs?

As an act of homage, then, these reflections derive from the experience of one teacher who wishes to share them with another teacher. Chaucer once said of his model scholar (in the prologue to *The Canterbury Tales*) "gladly would he learn and gladly teach." It is in that spirit that these reflections are written, namely, as a teacher who wishes also to learn. They are less inspired by Cooke's work on sacraments and ministry (about which I am too inexpert to comment) than as a tribute to his contributions as a teacher of theology.

A Pedagogical Experiment

In the year 2001 the Department of Theology at the University of Notre Dame, in consultation with the office of Campus Ministry, decided to offer a series of one-credit courses in the evening for any students who wished to enrich their knowledge and/or experience in the practice of their faith. This decision came from anecdotal evidence gathered by the staff of campus ministry that students wanted more than what was offered through the two semesters of required theology courses that all undergraduates take as part of their general education.

A number of faculty members in the Department of Theology offered to teach such courses, with the first set of five being advertised for the fall term of 2001. The classes were limited to thirty students, who met on six evenings for a couple of hours. To the pleasant surprise of all who were part of the experiment, the classes were fully subscribed and, further, we discovered that many of those who enrolled were seniors. Our collective hunch was that the preponderance of seniors meant that they wanted something to take with them for the future.

My own contribution to this enterprise was to offer a course simply entitled "Prayer." The course attracted over thirty students in the fall and the same number again in the spring term. The course was structured in this fashion: we would meet each Sunday evening for six weeks. Class lecture and discussion would run roughly an hour and a half. We would then go to the basilica of the Sacred Heart on campus and complete our evening by participation in Sunday night Vespers, which uses the cathedral style of vespers beginning with the lamp lighting (*lucernarium*) and ending with the traditional singing of the Magnificat, intercessions, blessing, a Latin hymn in honor of Our Lady and the kiss of peace. Participation in Vespers afforded me the opportunity to speak about liturgical prayer, the place of the Psalter in the life of the church, and other aspects of communal worship. The service also allowed for a wonderful array of texts, both biblical and non-biblical, to explore. My own focus was a set of reflections on the psalms and canticles in particular.

The course presupposed that the students would have read the fourth part of the *Catechism of the Catholic Church* on prayer for general background, but we would focus more generally on the nature of prayer, the kinds of prayer, and liturgical prayer. Each evening we would begin with a gloss on some pericope from scripture. In addition, students would be asked to bring to class a contemporary paraphrase of one of the psalms. At the final meeting the students brought a short reflection paper on any aspect of prayer that they wished to explore beyond what we read or spoke of in class.

My purpose in recounting this pedagogical background is not to advertise or detail the course (it is very much in the process of being invented since it will again be offered in the following academic terms) but to bring some reflections to bear on the kinds of questions and issues raised by the students who participated. It has never been my custom to delve into the personal faith life of students, but it is inevitable that they would betray what is on their minds (and hearts) as we attempted to focus this course according to their needs.

Students revealed these concerns in a variety of ways. Before the class began they got an e-mail asking them to bring a short paper outlining the kinds of things that they wanted to discuss. In the course of doing the psalm paraphrases they revealed—often in painful and touching ways—what was closest to their own lives. When they turned in a final short reflection paper other matters came to light. It is on the basis of that anecdotally gathered information that these reflections developed.

Rather than narrate those concerns let me stipulate a series of points developed for them as a kind of global response to what they raised and, in the process, gloss those points. Those "points" are an attempt to provide a wide angle on the question of prayer, to provide some kind of frame within which my students (as well as myself) can be encouraged to cultivate a life of prayer.

Stipulations about Prayer

First, it seems to me not useful at the offset either to define prayer too narrowly or to subdivide prayer into its various kinds. Inspired by some words of Roderick Strange, my point of entry into the subject of prayer is simply to speak of *the willingness to pray*: "If we want to come close to God—or, even if we wish we did, which at times of discouragement may be as much as we can imagine—then that desire itself is prayer." (Strange 2001, 13).

The classical formulation that encourages us to embark on a life of prayer with confidence is the Pauline assertion that "the Spirit helps us in our weakness; for we do not know how to pray as we ought; but that very Spirit intercedes with sighs too deep for words (Rom 8:26)." Commenting on this passage, Joseph Fitzmyer tells us that the Spirit is, according to Paul, "the source of all genuine prayer." He adds: "Such assistance is not limited to the prayer of petition, but would include all manner of communing with God ... above all, recognition of God as Father (Rom 8:15) and Jesus as Lord (I Cor 12:3b)." (Fitzmyer 1995, 141-42). In other words: turning to God in prayer is always under the assistance of the Holy Spirit and, further, if we pray to the Father in the manner Jesus tells us to pray, we also pray in the Spirit. Hence, prayer is, in the Christian reading of things, irreducibly trinitarian.

The corollary of the above point is this: there is no such thing as "bad" prayer or "ineffectual" prayer since every attempt to pray, or even the will to pray, is a gesture beyond the confines of the self to the Other who is the object of that act or the desire to make such an act.

In that sense, secondly, every gesture of prayer is, simultaneously, an act of faith. Thus, when Saint Augustine titles his work the *Confessions*, he gives to that title a multi-layered sense of confessing directly to God (Whom he addresses in the opening pages of Book One) in prayer and, also, confessing his faith as well as his sinfulness. That complex act of acknowledging his creatureliness (which is to say, his sinfulness) and his praise of God gets recapitulated in the powerful opening chapters of Book X. Prayer is always a cry for faith as well as an openness and searching before God which at times is articulate and other times inchoate, stammering, and clouded by doubt.

Thirdly, then, is the matter of language. Prayer may be expressed by joining in the language of the cloud of witnesses (Heb 12:1) who have sanctioned the language of prayer in liturgical usage or immemorial custom or in the language that we address to God in our own fashion. We may pray with the prayers that Jesus prayed (the psalms) or the prayers addressed to Jesus in the Gospels. The language of prayer always points to something beyond the language even when the language is familiar—too familiar?—or strange to our ears. At times, as the mystics assure us, our prayer is beyond language; it becomes pure presence, pure silence, pure simplicity. Nonetheless, I did want to pay special attention to the most common expressions of informal prayer since those expressions were the ones with which the students had the greatest familiarity and further, hallowed as they were by immemorial use, might be a fit subject for serious retrieval.

Stipulations Considered

The broad context within which I speak about prayer to my students, then, is simple: prayer is an act of faith by which we turn from ourselves to God as an openness to God in an act of faith. We do that in various forms of language (or without even using words), which may be formal or spontaneous. Within that framework our discussion can ramify out in expected directions (how do we know that God listens? Why is it so hard to focus on prayer? etc.) as well as in startlingly unexpected ones (one student asked, "Is it ok to simply be in the overwhelming presence of God which I experience most frequently outside of church and, if so, should I still try to go to Mass which bores me?").

The broader problem when reflecting on the willingness to pray—and it is a broad cultural problem more than a religious one—involves the very milieu within which our young people live. Everything in contemporary culture conspires against the cultivation of that fundamental interior silence or that attitude of stillness that is crucial to prayer. Students live with headphones wrapped over their skulls; they walk with cell phones as an appendage to their ears; they read from within the limited square of a computer screen; music is frequently not listened to but becomes the ambience within which they also find stimulation from lights (and worse) in a concert setting. Beyond such aural stimulation is the added epistemic bombardment from the world of images especially images from the mass media, which are both ubiquitous and rapid.

The observable data noted above are not meant to be read as a critique from an old geezer who deplores the electronic world within which the contemporary world of our youth operates; it is merely an observation of what is, in fact, the case. As over against that fact one must ask: is it possible to do honor to the demand of the psalmist: "Be still and know that I am God" (Ps 46:10)? Is there any way in which we can nurture, to borrow a very old word, a contemplative spirit which is both a pre-condition for, and the fruit of, authentic prayer?

One potential starting point in recovering the minimum re-collection required to be present to God is to observe what Saint Gregory of Nazianzen once called the "remembrance of God." In his first theological oration he observes (and this is surely a remonstrance for us theologians!) that it is not the continual remembrance of God that he would hinder but "only the talking about God," which is not wrong in itself, but "only when unseasonable" (*NPNF vol. 7*, 286). The moral I would draw from his warning is this: do not talk a lot about prayer but simply pray. The very act of praying creates, in the act itself, a pause in the continuum of the quotidian. If we do that—if we pray—what will happen? Strange, quoting another spiritual writer, states apodictically that God "will take possession of us" (Strange 2001, 15).

But, it may be urged, how do we remember God in our busy lives? A simple beginning would be to frame our day by putting ourselves under the protection of God in the morning and in the evening with a punctuation of that presence by expressing gratitude for our food when we eat. This beginning may seem "simple" but, in fact, its practice compels each day to say that our "day" comes from God just as our sustenance does.

Beneath this simple practice are the seeds that, if allowed to be nurtured, develop into what Brother Lawrence of the Resurrection describes as living in the presence of God; what De Caussade calls the "sacrament of the present moment"; what Thomas Merton, variously calls, "awareness of the reality of the Source"; "spiritual wonder"; "spiritual vision"; etc. (Merton 1961, 1-2). In other words, to be open to God over us as the day opens and closes is both to speak out in faith and listen in response to what God speaks to us in life, activity, and sustenance albeit at quite brief but strategic moments in the day. If such a remembrance is done reflectively in the use of our words it takes on the character of something quite profound. Hans Urs von Balthasar says it starkly: "This looking to God is contemplation … . The more the soul finds God, the more it forgets itself and yet finds itself in God. It is an unwavering 'gaze' where 'looking' is always 'hearing'" (Von Balthasar 196, 20).

Is this really too much to assert? Will these simple acts of every day piety bear the weight of my claims? Can we argue in seriousness that saying morning and night prayers and table blessings is a path to, or even the realization of, contemplation?

Please note what is not being argued. There is no suggestion here that one can bracket the ordinary sacramental life of the church, participation in the liturgy, the prayerful use of the scriptures, or forms of community prayer (liturgical or non-liturgical), or the ordinary exercises of piety or devotion. Further, the examples of daily devotions are meant to be exactly that: exemplary not prescriptive. What is being suggested is simply this: if we put ourselves in relationship to God by remembering God in the ordinary course of life, we are both making an act of faith and, simultaneously, speaking/listening to God in some inchoately articulate fashion. Hence, my use of the regular exercise of these particular daily prayers is merely a launching pad to indicate what might be a starting point in the life of prayer.

While a person can certainly express these short daily acts in the language of the tradition, one suggestion I often make to students is to create very short prayers for these occasions after the model of the Roman collects for Mass. The collect has a basic structure that follows this pattern: an address directly to God with a clause describing some attribute of God, followed by a petition and the reason for the petition, and a conclusion (Jones 1992, 225). I also recommend that these brief prayers be opened and closed with the sign of the cross.

There are two reasons why this form is a useful one. First, as has often been noted, the Roman collects are brief and articulate. Second, the use of a personal collect allows a person to create a useful vocabulary of prayer. Hence, in the morning we might say something like this: "Oh God, who brings us another day, bless my work that it may be always one under your watchful eye. I pray in the Name of Christ, the Giver of Your Spirit. Amen." Similar prayers that incorporate the traditional motifs of gratitude, a plea for forgiveness, and so on are easily incorporated into such brief collects.

My further suggestion is that these prayers or the standard prayer formulas be always framed by the sign of the cross. That practice, alluded to as early as the time of Tertullian, is a bodily gesture - a sacramental - which is a gestural act of faith. It was Romano Guardini who urged this gesture as a profound practice of faith. "Make," he once wrote, "a large unhurried sign, forehead to breast, shoulder to shoulder, consciously feeling how it includes the whole of us, our thoughts, our attitudes, our body and soul, every part of us at once, how it consecrates and sanctifies us" (Guardini 1956, 13). The key words are "consciously" and "feeling." What the great German thinker urged, of course, is that gesture be thickened by reflection when doing one of the more primordial Christian acts.

Breaking into the Ordinary

The above suggestions may seem, at first glance, banal in their offering something as elementary as beginning with prayers usually taught to toddlers. There are, however, behind such elementary practices, suppositions that are potentially profound, and it is those suppositions that I wish to urge upon my students. Among them are these:

First, every prayer is a conscious breaking into the quotidian. To orient the self away from the ordinary is a way of saying that the ordinary is not all that there is. Hence, the beginning of the day with prayer or the moment of gratitude before eating interrupts the plane of the routine and the reflexive. In that sense all prayer is a kind of re-location or re-orientation of the flow of life. One might say that, understood as operating in a minor key, it is a form of conversion in the sense that the act of prayer turns us to God and, in that turning, turns us away (aversion) from the ordinary. The paradox, of course, is that in that complex of turning towards and turning from we sanctify the quotidian by punctuating it with recognition and gratitude.

The small gestures of daily prayer are a microcosm of the great liturgical cycle of the church which stipulates praise (lauds) for God as the day begins and thanksgiving to God as the lamps are lit and the day ends (vespers). In an imperfect sense, then, daily prayers have a quasi- liturgical character to them.

Second, the habit of breaking into the ordinary gives rise under grace to a way of attention that in itself is the cultivation of the contemplative way of being. Among the many advances made in demystifying the contemplative life by recent writers is the strong conviction that the development of a contemplative way of living is not for the few but for all. Thomas Merton insists that this contemplative gift comes to us in the openness by which we live: "Hence contemplation is more than a consideration of abstract truths about God, more than affective meditation on the things we believe. It is awakening, enlightenment, and the amazing intuitive grasp by which love gains certitude of God's creative and dynamic intervention in *our daily life*" (Merton 1961, 5; my emphasis).

My conviction is that if people are encouraged to become reflective about prayer, at whatever level prayer begins, they will cultivate a kind of awareness that is inchoately contemplative. The regular discipline of prayer, even at the rudimentary level I have suggested, is a way to energize that awareness or watchfulness which is, as Roderick Strange insists, "not simply vision, a matter of clear sight. It is a cast of mind, a way of looking" (Strange 2001, 4).

The cultivation of such awareness spills over, in time, to a new way of considering sacramental signs, liturgical proclamations, reception of the Eucharist, as well as the way we see others. It has always struck me as important that in the Byzantine liturgy the deacon cries out "Wisdom! Let us attend!" as if there were a conviction that mere presence at the liturgy is no guarantee that the congregation would be alert to the proclamation of God's Word. This new plane of attention must either be commanded or brought into clearer focus.

Awareness and Others

Every attempt to pray must not be thought of as a turn to "my" sanctity or "my" possession of God. All prayer, even that described as "private" prayer is irreducibly social. To remind ourselves of that datum is to remind ourselves that prayer is not "spirituality" in the flaccid sense that it is often understood as in New Age circles. After all, when Jesus taught us to pray he told us to say *Our* Father and when the church calls us to pray, the liturgy says "Let *us* pray."

On the social character of prayer a number of points can be made which may be mentioned briefly:

(1) When we use prayer formulas we are using a language that has been hallowed by the tradition and, as such, these prayer formulas, often derived from scripture, are the common memory of the followers of Christ through time and space.

(2) It is useful to pray as a member of the communion of saints.

Making that article of faith explicit helps us to understand that not only do we pray in union with the angels, Mary, and the other saints, but with all who have gone before us who have been marked with the sign of faith. Hence, our prayer is also the prayer of all the deceased members of our extended family.

(3) To pray for the needs of the world—for the poor, the sick, for those who thirst for justice, for the dying, etc.—is to remember them. If prayer is remembrance of God, it is also remembrance of the world.

(4) As I have argued elsewhere (Cunningham and Egan 1996, 59-62), the life of prayer and progress in it may be likened to a widening circle in which we begin in our particular place and in our particular circumstances. As we become more aware of our world, we widen our circle to the immediate needs of our place and time, but constantly attempt to widen our horizon to be concerned with the larger world. This kind of prayer is radically *catholic* prayer in the sense that it seeks to be more universal and embracing. That kind of prayer is an application of the ecological imperative to "act locally but think globally."

Praying in this fashion demands that we make a beginning and allow the Spirit to widen and deepen our hearts and minds. If we do that as a singular effort we will soon be drawn into a more profound communion with God and with others. As a very wise spiritual writer once observed, "You are never likely to be able to pray everywhere and all the time unless you first learn to pray somewhere some of the time" (Llewelyn 1985, 20).

A Modest Conclusion

This brief essay has been partly a description of a little course I teach, partly a reflection on issues raised by the students in that course, and partly what the Catholic Workers call "clarification of thought." On rereading parts of it I sense some of the incoherence in my own thinking brought about mainly by my desire to be honest with my students on a topic over which I cannot claim mastery (who dares describe him or herself as a "master" of prayer?), but about which there is an inbuilt urgency if we resist the idea that theology is just one more academic field. The old monastic author, Evagrius of Pontus, once wrote that the one who prays is a true theologian; the true theologian is only the one who prays. If we wish to discourse about God we must also speak to God. That understanding of the place of theology in a university would not gain majority status at the convention of the American Academy of Religion and might even find critics within the community of the Catholic Theological Society of America.

It also strikes me that as one wrestles with particular issues about prayer, other fundamental issues of theology inevitably intrude themselves into the conversation. To speak of prayer inevitably brings one to speak of how God is "pictured" or not "pictured"; how language becomes adequate or not adequate to speak about God or to God, thus raising the fundamental question about the most elementary understanding of theology itself. Similarly, does faith precede prayer or does prayer lead to faith—an issue raised by Augustine on the first page of the *Confessions*— or, more plausibly, is the gesture of prayer in itself an act of faith or the desire to make that act?

The kinds of questions like those mentioned above have led me to the conviction that in a longer, more academic course on prayer it would be to the classic treatises on prayer, like those in the Cistercian or Carmelite tradition, that one would naturally turn, since those treatises rooted in experience also anchored themselves in the perennial wisdom of the theological tradition, bringing together what has been sadly riven apart so often today, namely, the synthesis of reflection and praise, which is what constituted theology for so long in the church. What Karl Rahner once wrote about prayer can be understood to also describe, at its root, what all theology attempts to do, which is to enter into dialogue with the God who first spoke to us: "prayer exists, and in it God becomes our You, the One addressed of whom we have a fundamental expectation that He can answer, that He has addressed his word to us even before we begin to speak, that our address to God is therefore an answering address. Prayer like that exists" (Rahner 1983, 86).

References

Cunningham/Egan. 1996. *Christian Spirituality: Themes from the Tradition*. New York: Paulist.

Fitzmyer, Joseph. 1995. *Spiritual Exercises Based on Paul's Letter to the Romans*. New York: Paulist.

Gregory Nazianzen. [1995 reprint]. "First Theological Oration." *Nicene and Post-Nicene Fathers*. Second Series. Volume vii. Peabody, MA: Hendrickson.

Guardini, Romano. 1956. *Sacred Signs*. Saint Louis, Pio Decimo.

Jones, C., ed. 1992. *The Study of the Liturgy*. rev. edition. New York: Oxford University Press.

Llewelyn, Robert. 1985. *Prayer and Contemplation*. Fairacres (Oxford): SLG Press.

Merton, Thomas. 1961. *New Seeds of Contemplation*. New York: New Directions.

Strange, Roderick. 2001. *Living Catholicism*. New York: Paulist

Rahner, Karl. 1983. *The Practice of Faith*. New York: Crossroad.

Von Balthasar, Hans Urs. 1956. *Prayer*. New York: Sheed and Ward.

15 Dancing Together:
Families as Symbols of the Trinity

Joann Heaney-Hunter, Ph.D.

Introduction

In his article "The Open Table," Denis Edwards states, "the concept of the family as domestic church can be seen in its real depth in the context of the theology of the Trinity"(Edwards 1995, 327-329). In the same article, he asserts, "the family is the icon of the Trinity, the image of God's interpersonal life"(1995, 327-329). These are intriguing statements, which lead to further questions such as: *How* can the Trinity provide the context for family life, and *how* does the family serve as its icon? In this essay, I will attempt to answer these questions using the following methodology: I will first sketch some historical and contemporary perspectives on the Trinity, paying particular attention to Catherine Mowry LaCugna's definition of *perichoresis*[73] in her work *God for Us*. I will then apply these perspectives to a discussion of family life. In particular, I will focus on the image of trinitarian *perichoresis* and show how contemporary families can serve as symbols of it. My conclusions will discuss some implications of seeing the family as a unity of persons, dancing together to enrich the world.

---

[73] *Perichoresis* means being-in-one another.

Perspectives on the Trinity

In her work *God for Us*, Catherine Mowry LaCugna argues that while in recent years, the theology of the Trinity "has been relegated to the margins"(1991, Foreword), an understanding of it is central to our belief as Christians. Her thesis is that the doctrine of the Trinity is central to theology because it is the "affirmation of God's intimate communion with us through Jesus Christ in the Holy Spirit (1991, Foreword). Moreover, according to LaCugna, the theology of the Trinity is not simply an esoteric concept studied and researched by a few scholars. Because it is so central to Christian faith, it is practical and has consequences for all Christian life, including, I believe, family life. An exploration of the Trinity, then, can shed light on what it means to live as a family of faith in this complex world.

One way that theologians structure discussion of the Trinity is by distinguishing between "economic Trinity" and "immanent Trinity." This distinction represents two aspects of the life and work of God. "Economic Trinity" refers most specifically to the loving interaction of God with the world (LaCugna 1991, 211). The primary meaning of "immanent Trinity" is the "relationships of Father, Son, and Spirit to each other, considered apart from God's activity in the world" (LaCugna 1991, 212). As Rahner puts it: "the immanent Trinity is the 'intradivine' self-communication, while the economic Trinity is the historical manifestation of that eternal self-communication in the missions of Jesus Christ in the Spirit"(LaCugna 1991, 212). This distinction, however, represents thought that has its foundation in the scholastic theology of Thomas Aquinas, and does not necessarily reflect earlier church perspectives on the Trinity and its life.

As with so many Christian teachings, definitions of and perspectives on the Trinity have evolved over the centuries of Christianity (Boof 1988; Deddo 1999; Downey 2000; Johnson 1992; Rahner 1967; Segundo 1974). In the earliest years of the church, trinitarian formulas were used (particularly in baptism), but not explained. As in so many other areas of theology, reflection on the meaning of the formulas was reserved for a later time. One example of a trinitarian statement without explanation is found in the baptismal formula of Matthew 28. John Meier points out that while one might be surprised by the trinitarian formula in the gospel, it undoubtedly reflects the practice of the local Christian community. Moreover, he states that as a person in Matthew's community is baptized, washed, plunged, "into the name" of the Trinity, he or she is immersed in the bonds of "family love which bind together not only Father, Son and Spirit, but also the members of the church, the family of God. Matthew thus conceives of baptism as incorporation into the life of God and the Church" (Meier 1981, 372). Matthew's baptismal formula represents the beginning of an understanding of Trinity as love reaching out beyond itself to others. According to Matthew, faith in the triune God requires not only awareness, but concrete action in the community.

John's gospel presents a somewhat expanded picture of the dynamic relationship of the triune God in the verses of the final discourse.[74] According to the author of the fourth gospel, persons in God relate as a communion, and share their life not only within that communion but also beyond it to the entire world (McPolin 1979, 197-204; Segovia 1991, 95-96). For example, John 14:11–15 demonstrates that the union of Father and Son is so intimate that "to contemplate Jesus with the eyes of faith is to see the Father, for they live together in intimate communion" (McPolin 1979, 198). Furthermore, Jesus' confidence that his prayer to the Father will bring forth the Spirit further emphasizes the connection. This Spirit of God, according to John, will be a helper and counselor for all Jesus' followers (McPolin 1979, 200-201). Throughout the final discourse, one can see the dynamism of God relating as a community of persons, which overflows to all so that they might have life (LaCugna 1991, 243). Again, the union of three persons does not exist solely for itself, but for the good of the world—the unity of persons moves beyond itself to embrace all.

In the next four centuries of Christianity, understanding of the nature of the Trinity underwent refinement and development. The controversies about the nature of Christ and the Holy Spirit sparked a reflective process on the existence and workings of the triune God. Early theologians not only explained the concept of Trinity, they articulated their views of how it functions in the world. As Michael

---

[74] In the final discourse, however, readers get an explanation of *how* the Father, Son and Spirit work together in perfect communion.

Downey points out, early Christian reflection focused on God's work in and through Jesus Christ and the Spirit. It explored "what God had done in history through the sending of the Son and the gift of the life-giving Spirit, proclaimed and handed on in the scriptures and in the living traditions of Christian communities (Downey 2000, 50).

Leaders in this process were the Cappadocians in Greek theological tradition, and Augustine in Latin. The Cappadocians were instrumental in developing and preaching the idea that God exists as three *hypostases* (persons) in one *ousia* (nature). To explain this reality, they use the language of personhood and relation.[75] In the Latin theological tradition, Augustine writes at length about the nature of the triune God. In his extensive work *On the Trinity*, he emphasizes the *unity* of God, and asserts that the work of God is always the work of the three-in-one.[76] These thinkers expressed the importance of the persons in God relating to each other as well as to the world.

In the eighth century, John Damascene further emphasized the dynamic character of each person of God, as well as the interrelationship of the persons in the Trinity, by using the term *perichoresis* (Damascene, 1.8). In other words, he declared that to be a divine person by nature means to be in relationship. *Perichoresis* has been described in a number of ways - one image is that of the dance - which brings to mind coming together and moving apart in a fluid motion that includes mutual giving and receiving among members of an ensemble or between partners. Anyone who has tried to dance in an ensemble knows that it takes a concerted group effort to succeed. All the individuals in the ensemble must use their gifts to work together toward a common goal. Moreover, when one person is missing from the ensemble, the entire dance suffers. *Perichoresis,* therefore, highlights qualities of inclusion and community, and provides a beautiful metaphor for the persons in God and for God in relationship with human beings (Kastner 1983, 131-133).

As the church moved through the Middle Ages, however, theological reflection on the *inner life* of the Trinity was emphasized to the detri-

---

[75] See Basil of Caesarea, *Letter 243.4,* Gregory of Nazianzus, *Oration 18.16* and *Oration 43.33*, and Gregory of Nyssa, *On the Holy Trinity, and Of the Godhead of the Holy Spirit.*

[76] See, for example, Augustine, *On the Trinity, 6.10,* and *9.*

ment of thought about the Trinity's movement *outward* to the world. Rahner points out that Thomas Aquinas is the first great theologian to truly separate the economic from the immanent Trinity, and to place almost exclusive emphasis on the intradivine life of God. He states that Thomas' treatise on the Trinity locks itself in "splendid isolation, with the ensuing danger that the religious mind finds it devoid of interest. As a result the treatise becomes quite philosophical and abstract and refers hardly at all to salvation history" (Rahner 1970, 16-17).[77] Thus, from the time of Thomas Aquinas forward, the Trinity was perceived as distant from the world. More emphasis was placed on philosophical reflection about the inner life of God than about the workings of God in the world. This shift in focus and emphasis has influenced the way that contemporary Christianity perceives the Trinity.

Contemporary theology of the Trinity has worked to reconnect the inner life and outward movement of the Trinity. Scholars such as LaCugna link the two by pointing out that it is the intimacy of the persons *in* God that enables them to move outward toward all creation. This integrated view of trinitarian life and action will serve as the foundation of my reflections on the family. It draws on LaCugna's idea that "trinitarian theology is par excellence a theology of relationship: God to us, we to God, we to each other. The doctrine of the Trinity affirms that the essence of God is relational, other-ward, that God exists as diverse persons united in a communion of freedom, love, and knowledge" (LaCugna 1991, 243).

The Family as Symbol of the Trinity

The *perichoretic* union of the Trinity provides the family with a context for its own existence. The unity of families, regardless of their structure, serves as an anchor for its life. With this solid foundation, families have the potential to move beyond themselves and others in a joyful dance of moving outward to the world. With the Trinity as a model of unity and outreach, families are challenged to relate to each other and share their gifts in a troubled world, and by doing so, are called to manifest the life of God within them.

---

[77] See also Thomas Aquinas, *Summa Theologica, First Part, questions 27-43.*

Particularly in the uncertain times we face in society and in the Church, exploring a trinitarian vision of family life becomes especially relevant. Faithful families today need a solid foundation on which to build, as well as concrete strategies for carrying out the process of building. I believe that the image of Trinity as a union of persons embracing each other in a bond of love and moving beyond themselves in a gesture of reaching out to the world, provides an idealistic yet attainable goal for families today. The remainder of this essay will explore the ways that families can embody, or symbolically represent, the *perichoresis* of the Trinity. Each family, regardless of its structure, has the potential to become an expression of the dynamic life of God that moves beyond itself in a stance that is both self-reflective and missionary. Moreover, just as the Trinity serves as a model for family life, I believe that the family can serve as a symbol of the Trinity itself.

Families and the Embrace of the Trinity

The first element of *perichoresis* is the embrace of the partners or members of the ensemble – an expression of its unity. This image provides a lens through which one can perceive the inner life of the family. What can the embrace of the Trinity tell us about the ways that families work together, support each other, and develop as communities? While it is certainly not the case all the time, at its best, in daily life, the family builds itself up, works at developing intimacy, embraces one another, and dances together in a *perichoretic* union reminiscent of the Trinity. In a family, members are drawn close with flexible bonds that encourage individuality and interdependence within the support of family unity. Just as in the expression of Trinity we call "immanent," the family develops as an intimately related community, with the potential to be open to people and experiences, and to be united as a model of unconditional commitment.

At the heart of a Christian family community is the paschal mystery, where families concretely experience on a daily basis the events of Christ's death and resurrection. We see a clear reference to this in Romans 6:4: "Through baptism into his death we were buried with him so that, just as Christ was raised from the dead by the glory of the Father, we too might live a new life." This experience of Christ, raised from the dead by God, and filled with the Spirit, provides a foundation for creating the family as a symbol of trinitarian *perichoresis*. Because a faithful family has experienced and named death and resurrection in its own life, it is better able to witness this experience within the family and beyond it. To say that a family "participates in the paschal mystery," assumes that it shares a common purpose rooted in faith—to embrace each other and reach out to others.

What are some of the ways that family communities participate in this saving work of God? In the challenge to strive for unity, interdependence, and growth; in the call to communicate well; in the need to be honest and open; and in numerous other ways, family members die and rise daily. Just as Christ died - we are called to die - and just as death was not the final answer for Christ, it is not the final answer for us. In the experience of daily life, families encounter "little deaths." For example, they may endure unfulfilled dreams or promises, sorrow, and broken commitments. Specifically, family members frequently are called to let go—to die—to an aspect of life that they knew as individuals, so that the family relationship or community can grow. For some, this means dying to self-centeredness so that others might flourish. It may mean the death of absolute freedom and the movement to the freedom of a life rooted in commitment and covenant.

One concrete example of death and resurrection that resonates with many families is the experience of raising children. Parents often describe the need to let go of their control, their expectations, and their own needs, so that their children might develop strong roots and beautiful wings. Another way that families experience death and resurrection is by coping with issues of a multigenerational family, such as the illness or death of an elderly relative or child, which are painful and wrenching regardless of any expressed belief in the resurrection. As believing families encounter these daily small deaths and the final death, they trust that there will be new life for all because Christ has been raised from the dead.

All families at one time or another experience suffering. Families who serve as symbols of the trinitarian life may make this suffering redemptive through the firm conviction that suffering will ultimately end in glory. While families must be vigilant at working to end wrongful suffering, they can derive meaning from the cross of Christ and the promise of God that death does not have the final word.

Families also embody the dynamic unity of the Trinity by recognizing their own unity in daily life. In a world that so often pulls people apart, what are the events and people that lead families to the "embrace" of *perichoresis*? Families today may have difficulty identifying such events - but even the busiest families should be able to recall times and people that have brought them together - shared meals, family gatherings, births, graduations, reunions, deaths, and a host of other occurrences that have the potential to be times of grace. Moreover, unifying events need not be extraordinary. For example, time spent together in conversation (over coffee, in a car, while completing chores) can provide unexpected opportunities for unity. The simple, ordinary activities of daily life may be vehicles for creating unity and fostering opportunities for embodying the life of the Trinity.

An essential yet difficult way for families to express trinitarian unity is to manifest the radical dignity and equality of all persons (John Paul II *Familiaris Consortio*, nos. 22-24; *Evangelium Vitae*, no. 99; Gaillardetz 2002, 47-60). This may be more problematic at some stages of life than at others. When children are small, for example, it may be easy to view them as children of God, and affirm their dignity as such. Rebellious teenagers, on the other hand, may challenge that easy affirmation. Just as the persons of the Trinity carry out a variety of roles and functions, however, family members with different gifts and talents do the same. Because both husbands and wives are created in the image and likeness of God, for example, they possess equal dignity, even if their roles in the relationship are different (John Paul II *FC*, nos. 18 and 20). Since all family members, including the most vulnerable or the most difficult in the family, are created in God's image, they must be respected and supported. While some segments of popular culture may be quick to dispose of those who appear to be weak, a vision of families grounded in the unity of the Trinity promotes moral responsibility and care for the vulnerable in their midst. In particular, the elderly and the young, including the unborn, should be cherished and supported by all (John Paul II *FC*, nos. 26-27). The notion that families are called to build a community of equality is at the heart of its trinitarian perspective. Whatever their concrete situation, families are challenged to build community by recognizing the life of God within each member. By doing so, they serve as concrete symbols of the inner life of God—a God in a dynamic relationship of loving unity.

Just as the Trinity can be an image of unity for the family, the family can serve as a symbol (albeit an imperfect one) of trinitarian life. The family enhances its ability to become the symbol of the interpersonal relationship of God by becoming more aware of and acting on the presence of God at the center of its life. Families recognize their sanctity, not because of what they do, but because of who they are - a unity of persons called to reveal God's life within it. The essence of the family - its unity - serves as a sacrament, a tangible expression of God's life in the midst of the world. Family activities and work, while not *making* a family holy, can further express God's activity to others. Caring for the vulnerable, becoming involved in the local community, taking stands on political issues, and many other facets of daily life have the potential to put flesh and bones on God's saving activity in the world.[78] Families reveal the Trinity through their commitment to live as communities that embody God's life, and perhaps most especially, that embody Christ's paschal mystery.

The concept that families can embody God's inner unity presents a challenge and a hope. It is challenging because families who follow this path cannot simply fall back on pious words and multiple church activities, but must LIVE God's loving care and concern on a daily basis. They do this by infusing the ordinary activities of life with God's love. Communicating with each other, enhancing relationships with spouses and children, making time for events such as a shared meal or vacation, or modeling compassion in the home can be concrete expressions of trinitarian unity within the family.

Families and the Outward Movement of the Trinity

The second element of *perichoresis* is turning outward in a gesture of outreach to others. Two ways that families serve as symbols of this second element of *perichoresis* are by reaching out to others as sacraments of God's life and by evangelizing through the witness of their lives.

[78] NCCB Committee on Marriage and the Family. 1988. *A Family Perspective in Church and Society,* Washington D.C., USCC.

Families as Sacraments in the World

Families serve as sacraments in a number of ways.[79] For example, in daily life, they can be concrete expressions of the call to serve church and world; moreover, through loving thanksgiving and sharing of themselves, they can serve as eucharistic communities. In this essay, I have chosen to focus on another way that families can concretely manifest the life of God—by seeing themselves as reconciling communities. Throughout salvation history, God has continually called people to be reconciled, to set relationships right, and to embrace fully God's outpouring of abundant, unconditional love (2 Samuel 12:1-13, Isaiah 43:1-8, Joel 2:12-17). A significant part of Jesus' ministry focused on reconciling people with themselves, with others, and with God (Mark 2:1-2, Mark 5, 25-34, Luke 7, 36-50, John 8: 1-11, John 14:25-28).

In daily life, individuals and families are called to radical conversion and a ministry of forgiveness. True reconciliation does not mean simply seeking peace at any price; it means recognizing that we have been forgiven, accepting those who have injured us, and translating intellectual conversion into concrete action (Upton 1999, 61; Coffey 2001, 32-78). At the risk of understatement, this can be a difficult task. God's gracious action in human life, however, makes it possible. Since the dynamic embrace of God exists within the hearts and actions of faithful families, they have the ability to enter into the ministry of reconciliation—to reach out their hands to forgive others, and to ask humbly for forgiveness themselves. While most people are very good, all those who try to live as faithful sacraments of God's life are called to a process of conversion on a daily basis (Vacek 20002, www.americamagazine.org).

Concretely, families can practice reconciliation in the midst of ordinary life. Parents can provide examples of reconciliation to their children by demonstrating that they forgive each other and let go of

---

[79] For a more extended treatment of this concept, see my articles, "Domestic Church: Guiding beliefs and daily practices," and "Living the Baptismal Commitment in Sacramental Marriage, both in William Roberts and Michael Lawler. 1996. *Christian Marriage: Theological and Pastoral Perspectives.* Collegeville: The Liturgical Press.

their anger. A profound witness of reconciliation for children occurs when parents can apologize to them. Throughout the family life cycle, persons engage in a process of reconciliation within the home, as well as beyond it. Families are called to be communities of reconciliation--sacraments of the forgiving power of God's love in the world. They accomplish this task in the midst of daily life, with the sure help of God, and consistent prayer.

Families as Evangelizers

Families working to live as symbols of trinitarian life must embrace a way of life that reaches out to spread the good news of God's life to the wider community (John Paul II 1981, 17-64). This, essentially, is the task of evangelization. I believe that families engage in this dimension of the second element of *perichoresis* by evangelizing to those around them. Perhaps the best definition of evangelization can be found in *Evangelii Nuntiandi*, where Paul VI declares that it means "bringing the Good News to all humanity, and through its influence transforming it from within and making it new" (Paul VI, no. 19).[80] Evangelization does not simply mean adding numbers to the faithful, but making the Gospel relevant to people so as to influence their value systems, points of interest, and ways of thinking and living (Paul VI, no. 19). To do this, believers must allow the life of God to penetrate to the deepest places of their lives and their cultures. This notion of evangelization is echoed in scholarship which recognizes the importance of transformation of minds and hearts (Brennan 1995; Oliver 1997).

Just as the early Christians moved beyond the fear of the locked upper room to preach the Gospel (John 20: 19-23), today, Christians in general and Christian families in particular hear the call to proclaim the Gospel to the world. As symbols of God's life within them, families are called to let their light shine rather than hiding it under a bushel basket (Matthew 5: 15-16). The task of evangelization is necessarily a prophetic and a missionary task, demanding that Christian families preach the good news through word and example.

---

[80] He further describes evangelization as: "proclaiming the Gospel of Christ through testimony and the witness of an authentic Christian life."

How have the official writings of the church described the ministry of evangelization in recent history? The documents of Vatican II, especially *Lumen Gentium, Gaudium et Spes,* and *Apostolicam Actuositatem,* provide the contemporary framework for discussion. Further elaboration on the role of evangelization and the people of the church comes from Paul VI's *Evangelii Nuntiandi* and John Paul II's *Christifidelis Laici.* In all of these documents, as well as documents from the U.S. bishops, there is a sense that a key task of all Christians is to evangelize.

How does the process of evangelization take place? A survey of the above documents provides a starting point. For example, *Apostolicam Actuositatem* clearly asserts that all of the baptized play a critical role as *ministers of* evangelization rather than simply *recipients* of an evangelizing ministry (no. 11). This idea is pivotal for the entire discussion. Following *Apostolicam,* the privilege and responsibility for evangelization flow not from sacramental ordination, but from baptism. Through baptism, all receive the grace necessary to proclaim the gospel. While not all accept this gift, baptized Christians have the potential to proclaim Christ as the disciples did after they were filled with the Holy Spirit (Acts 2:1-12). Furthermore, through baptism, Christians have the potential to serve the entire church. This may take place in the context of the ecclesiastical community, but it may also happen through service to the world—in other words, evangelization can occur in the secular realm as powerfully and truly as it does in an ecclesiastical setting.

The theme that the baptized are called to be evangelizers is echoed in *Evangelii Nuntiandi,* which presents a coherent blueprint for evangelization efforts. How does one evangelize? The answer is clear: witness the gospel through example:

> Let us suppose that [Christians] radiate in an altogether simple and unaffected way their faith in values that go beyond current values, and their hope in something that is not seen and that one would not dare to imagine. Through this wordless witness these Christians stir up irresistible questions in the hearts of those who see how they live: Why are they like this? Why do they live in this way? What or who is it that inspires them? Why are they in our midst? Such a witness is already a silent proclamation of the good

news and a very powerful and effective one. Here we have an initial
act of evangelization (Paul VI 1981, no. 21).

The living proclamation of the gospel makes evangelization a
particularly concrete activity. Christians are not simply called to *talk
about* what they believe, they are challenged to translate that belief
into action—the movement from theory to praxis. In essence, those
who evangelize make the life of God real in the world.

As one considers the task of evangelization, it is necessary to consider the *content* of the message, which is trinitarian at its core. The
first key component of the message is that God is love (Paul VI 1981,
no. 25). Given the circumstances of today's world, this is a message
that desperately needs to be proclaimed. When one considers the
recent events of the world and the church (particularly the tragedies
of September 11 and the sex scandals that have rocked the Roman
Catholic Church), declaring that God is love is something that we
cannot take for granted. The second element of the gospel message is
that Jesus Christ is the definitive expression of God in the world. For
Christians, Jesus is the primordial sacrament, the ultimate expression
of God in our midst. Over the last two millennia, the message that
Jesus is the Son of God has penetrated and shaped a considerable por-
tion of world history. A third component of the evangelizing message
is that the Spirit, God's graciousness itself, acts in the world today,
leading people to live, not just talk about God's message. Clearly, we
have become God's sons and daughters through the loving outreach
of a triune God, and not through human activity (Romans 5: 1-19).
This message must be transforming and life changing, involving the
conversion of individuals and the radical change of structures (Brennan 1995, 37).

In daily life, families proclaim this message through word and example
(Blum 1992, 164). Daily, they *tell* others what faith in Jesus Christ
means, and *show* what it means through the witness of their lives.[81]
To sum up, then, evangelization is witnessing the life of God in the
context of the community. Its message is central to the call of all the
baptized, for baptized persons are all called to bear witness to the good
news of transformation that comes through belief in God, acting in
the world. Through evangelization, families have the opportunity to

demonstrate the outward movement of the Trinity in the world—the second dimension of *perichoresis*.

The next question one must ask is this: *how* do diverse families in today's busy world carry out this crucial task? Evangelization in families involves a three-fold task of individual reflection, interaction with other family members, and movement toward and within the community of faith. The individual of faith may extend beyond him or herself and share that faith with others in the immediate family unit, however it is structured. This faith sharing spills over to include extended families and others in the immediate circle. The circle widens to build bridges of faith moved by action with others outside the small network. This building, in turn, creates clusters of faith within the community. These clusters of faithful families have the potential to transform large communities that can be moved to further evangelization.

The first element in evangelization, therefore, is the movement of an individual toward faith. God touches the mind and heart of an individual and leads that person to an experience of faith and conversion. The process ideally begins at baptism, and is nurtured in a faithful and loving family and larger community of faith. God can touch an individual in many ways: through a liminal experience such as a marriage, the birth of a child, or the death of a spouse; through the words or the deeds of another person; or through the intellectual conversion that can happen after being confronted with a passage from scripture or other significant text. Whatever the experience, God touches the heart of an individual, and calls that person to move to a new place in life.

For most people, further evangelization takes place in the context of relationship. Old or young, male or female, sexually active or celibate, most people experience the life of God through others. Moreover,

---

[81] A concept that is beyond the scope of this essay, but is nonetheless very relevant, is the sort of training that should be required of those called to the ministry of evangelization. Blum points to the importance of education for evangelization, and reports that some persons are called to be professional evangelizers. These persons support those in relational evangelization efforts, and provide a level of support that comes from education and experience. Blum. "The Need for Evangelization Training," 164-165.

for better or for worse, most persons find that initial experiences of evangelization take place in the context of a family—a family of origin, a family which has grown from a loving marriage, a family that was formed through other ties. These families, while never perfect, manifest the community of God that reaches out to the world. At their best, evangelizing families are open to the life of God through their loving service to neighbor. This is intimately connected to the call of the Christian family to be witnesses to the gospel message and to reveal the Trinity in the world.

Families serve as symbols of trinitarian outreach through loving service to others. Through service, families can create a climate that advances a consistent ethic of life, a radical care and concern for all life from the moment of conception to the moment of death. In simple ways such as lending a hand to someone in need, involving all family members in plans for charitable giving, being aware of the needs of families in the local community, and supporting efforts to help preserve them, families can demonstrate rather than simply talk about care and concern for all life. This service may take other forms as well. On a structural level, it may mean fighting against the causes of poverty among people, especially the vulnerable in our midst (John Paul II *EV*, no. 10). It may mean asserting the right to adequate housing, employment, and other basic economic and social requirements. It may demand engaging in serious critique of the political process. It may mean taking a stand for life, even when it is unpopular or inconvenient. The issues of today can be a fertile ground for family discussion and action. Families must consider their values as they engage in the process of evangelizing children and others beyond the immediate circle. They need not be heroic or extraordinary, but they must encourage in both adults and children an atmosphere of respect for all life in the family and beyond it.

Families that serve as symbols of God's loving activity share their talents and blessings with and for the local and global community (John Paul II *FC*, nos. 42-44). Church social teaching and Vatican II documents such as *Gaudium et Spes* remind us that part of the task of the Christian life in general, and family life in particular is to build a better world.[82] Evangelizing families reveal the Trinity by serving as a "city on a hill, a light for the world" (Matthew 5: 1-16). They recognize the needs of others in the community, and work to build just structures for all people: "Far from being closed in on itself, the family is by nature and vocation open to other families and to society and undertakes its social role." (Cahill 2000, 85; McGinnis, 181-203).

Assisting families with the task of embodying the life of the Trinity may seem to be a daunting task. It is therefore necessary to ask *how* to support families as they engage in this lifetime challenge. To accomplish the goal, local faith communities must continually be on the lookout for ways to assist families as they follow their call to be sacraments of God and icons of God's loving outreach. Family–community partnerships must recognize the inevitable stresses of families today, and must encourage a climate of faith-building in nuclear and extended families. Families formed as sacraments of trinitarian life will then have the potential to help others discover and embody the life of God within them.

In order to develop formation that addresses families' readiness to manifest trinitarian life, it will be necessary to engage in widespread efforts to work with adult members of communities. Through outstanding preaching, music, and community life, and consistent, organized invitations to engage in adult faith development, religious educators and pastors have the opportunity to enhance adults' awareness of God's gracious presence in their lives. Formation such as this will succeed when it is pastorally sound and highly sensitive to the diversity of adult Christians today and is respectful of the many commitments facing the typical adult. Surveying a community about its needs and interests may help create a climate of excitement about adult formation.

Local communities also must intensify efforts to assist children in making the connections between God's life and family life (Ratcliff 1992, 119-142; *Sharing the Light of Faith*, no. 229; Chesto 1995, 6-12; Marthaler 1973, 163). While efforts to build faith among children are already thriving in many communities, there is still much work to be done (Dunlop 1997, 19-22). I suggest some concrete steps for local church leaders: (1) Conduct studies of current catechetical materials to see if they help parents educate their children about God's life in the

---

[82] See, for example, *Gaudium et Spes,* nos. 53-93.

midst of the family;[83] (2) At all levels of religious education, and not just at the time of sacramental preparation, parents should be invited and welcomed, and helped to make concrete connections between the classroom and the life of God in the home. For example, preparation for First Eucharist should incorporate the idea of *eucharistia* or thanksgiving in the context of the family meal. Perhaps, given the rarity of shared meals in some families, focus could be placed on special meals such as Thanksgiving, birthdays, or other family celebrations (Hays 1979); (3) At Sunday celebrations, efforts should be made to include children and provide sound, appropriate liturgical experiences for them. Children should know that they are welcomed and cherished, rather than tolerated or pushed aside. Their place is in the midst of the community, not on the periphery of it.

Third, we must be vigilant in our efforts to keep adolescents and young adults aware of the continuing invitation to growth in faith development.[84] Adolescents and young adults are at the point in life where they are making many personal choices, accepting responsibility for their beliefs and their behavior, and thinking critically about issues such as faith and its connection to life (Hyde 1991, 119-161; *Sharing the Light of Faith*, nos. 227-228; Carotta, 238-239). These developmental issues, as well as other factors such as the conclusion of formal religious education for many young people, can lead to a separation from community and even family expressions of faith. Will these individuals be the next leaders of our Christian communities and the faith communities of their homes—or will they walk away from the church entirely? As Robert Ludwig has noted, young adults today are more concerned with living their beliefs than participating in rituals. They want to be involved in service, in worthy causes, in activities that will enhance and promote the betterment of the human condition (Ludwig 1996, 16-28).

---

[83] See Leif Kehrwald on the importance of "bridger activities" in "A Family Sensitivity in Parish Ministry," 167-180. An example of a religious education series that includes resources for parents is the *This is Our Faith* series, published by Silver Burdett and Ginn.

[84] One approach is "Theology on Tap." For a description, see "God and Beer in the Summertime," *National Catholic Reporter* (August 30, 2002) @www.natcath.com/ncr.

Leaders in youth and campus ministry declare that young people have expressed some very negative attitudes about the church institution as they struggle with the decision to maintain connections with it or sever them. According to Ludwig:

> The dominant perception of Catholicism among young people today is an institution in decline and growing old, its members controlled by an addictive guilt and deep patterns of codependency and without much genuine interest in either "the profound" or service to those in need. The enthusiasm of a changing church, retrieving its ancient dynamism and reclaiming its mission to the world…has largely been eclipsed by an image of a desperate power struggle pitting the Vatican against the common sense of the clergy and the people alike, a struggle in which what is truly essential is being lost and forgotten (Ludwig 1996, 26, 31).[85]

Nonetheless, these young adults are spiritually hungry, and seek to live what they believe - a perfect formula for helping them to recognize themselves as sacraments of God's life and messengers of the good news.

It is urgent that the church community presents an authentic and believable vision of life that will invite and challenge young people to grow (Ludwig 1996, 26), a difficult task in these times where official Church credibility is strained to the limits. Young people are hungering for spiritual guidance and leadership, but will not be satisfied by half-hearted efforts that simply say nice things about God and the church. They seek prophetic witness from their families and their communities, and try to find ways to *be* prophetic in their own lives. Church communities, both family and local, must examine themselves carefully and respond continuously to the needs of the young in their midst.

Communities must be aware of the many resources designed to assist family growth as symbols of God's life. They must also consider how vibrant family faith communities can serve as resources for the entire church. Families who have become more deeply aware of their vocation as evangelizing, sacramental communities may be available to share their gifts with the wider community, and church leadership may grow in appreciation of the family's unique contribution to the life of the church. In the 21st century, church communities and families will continue to engage in true partnership in the name of God. Through these partnerships, families will have numerous opportunities to embody the dance of God—both its embrace and its outpouring of love.

Conclusions

I conclude this essay with two questions: Can we say that the family serves as a concrete embodiment of the life of the Trinity? If so, how do faith leaders help them articulate and live this reality?

I believe that on a daily basis, families embody the Trinity in their lives in numerous ways, but have not necessarily named it as such. One task of theological reflection, therefore, is to articulate the ways that diverse families can name as well as manifest the dance of the Trinity. Day after day, families participate in the triune God's gracious activity by living the death and resurrection of Christ, building community in the home, and searching for sanctity in ordinary life. They need to increase their awareness of the rich values and traditions that form the bedrock of faith in the home and in the wider community. Accomplishing this goal can take place in ordinary family lives, and should be supported by loving and vibrant local church communities.

The second question addresses the ways that church leaders assist families in understanding themselves as symbols of the Trinity. I believe that faith formation in the midst of a prayerful community will assist families as they engage in the prophetic witness that their baptism demands. This formation should take place throughout the lives of families, and can serve as a source of support and nourishment as they grow in awareness of their roles as prophetic centers of faith.

Families have the potential to be powerful witnesses of trinitarian *perichoresis*. It will be a challenge and a blessing for the entire community to tap the wellspring of family life and draw from its abundant resources. With nourishment and support, families can continue to become what they are—concrete symbols of God's joyous dance of life and love.

References

Aquinas, Thomas. *Summa Theologica, First Part, questions 27-43.*

Basil of Caesarea, *Letter* 243.4, Gregory of Nazianzus, *Oration* 18.16 and *Oration* 43.33

Blum, Susan. 1992. "The Need for Evangelization Training," in *The New Catholic Evangelization*, Kenneth Boyack, C.S.P., ed. Mahwah: Paulist Press.

Boff, Leonardo. 1988. *Trinity and Society.* New York: Orbis Books.

Brennan, Patrick. 1995. *Reimagining Evangelization.* New York: Crossroad Publishing.

Cahill, Lisa Sowle. 2000. *Family: A Christian Social Perspective.* Minneapolis: Fortress Press.

Chesto, Kathleen O'Connell. June 1995. "Faith is Best Served Family Style," *U.S. Catholic* 60: 6-12.

Coffey, David M. 2001. *The Sacrament of Reconciliation (Lex Orandi Series).* Collegeville: The Liturgical Press.

Deddo, Gary W. 1999. *Karl Barth's Theology of Relations trinitarian, Christological, and Human: Towards an Ethic of the Family.* New York: Peter Lang.

Downey, Michael. 2000. *Altogether Gift: A trinitarian Spirituality.* New York: Orbis Books.

Dunlop, Jan. March 1997. "Kids Who Become Catholic," *St. Anthony Messenger* 104: 19-22.

Edwards, Dennis. July 1995. "The Open Table: Theological Reflections on Family," *Australasian Catholic Record* LXX, 11:327-339.)

Gaillardetz, Richard. 2002. *A Daring Promise.* New York: Crossroad.

Gregory of Nyssa, *On the Holy Trinity*, and *Of the Godhead of the Holy Spirit.*

Hays, Edward. 1979. *Prayers for the Domestic Church.* Kansas: Forest of Peace Books.

"God and Beer in the Summertime," August 30, 2002. *National Catholic Reporter* www.natcath.com/ncr.

Hunt, Michael. 1993. *College Catholics.* Mahwah: Paulist Press.

Hyde, Kenneth E. 1991. "Adolescents and Religion," in *Handbook of Youth Ministry*, Donald Ratcliff and James A. Davies, eds. Birmingham: R.E.P. Books: 119-161.

Johnson, Elizabeth. 1992. *She Who Is.* New York: Crossroad.

John Paul II, *Familiaris Consortio*, nos. 22-24, and *Evangelium Vitae*, no. 99. Washington D.C.: USCC.

Kastner, Patricia Wilson. 1983. *Faith, Feminism and the Christ.* Philadelphia: Fortress Press.

LaCugna, Catherine. 1991. *God For Us.* San Francisco: HarperCollins.

Ludwig, Robert. 1996. *Reconstructing Catholicism for a New Generation,* (New York: Crossroad Publishing:16-28.

Marthaler, Berard. 1973. *Catechetics in Context.* Indiana: Our Sunday Visitor.

McGinnis, James and Kathleen. "Building Families of Faith and Outreach," in *Using a Family Perspective In Catholic Social Justice and Family Ministries,* 181-203.

McPolin, James. 1979. *John.* Wilmington: Michael Glazier.

Meier, John. 1981. *Matthew.* Wilmington: Michael Glazier.

NCCB Committee on Marriage and the Family. 1988. *A Family Perspective in Church and Society,* Washington D.C., USCC.

Oliver, Robert. 1997. *The Vocation of the Laity to Evangelization: An Ecclesiological Inquiry into the Synod on the Laity (1987), Christifideles laici. (1989), Documents of the NCCB 1.,(1987-1996)*. Rome: Editrice Pontificia Universita Gregoriana.

Paul VI. *Evanglelii Nuntiandi*. No. 19.

Rahner, Karl. 1967. *The Trinity*. New York: Crossroad Herder.

Rahner, Karl. 1970. *The Trinity*. New York: Herder & Herder.

Ratcliff, Donald. 1992. "Social Contexts of Children's Ministry," in *Handbook of Children's Religious Education*, Donald Ratcliff, ed. Birmingham: R.E.P. Books: 119-142.

Segovia, Fernando F. 1991. *The Farewell of the Word: The Johannine Call to Abide*. Minneapolis: Fortress Press

Segundo, Juan Luis. 1974. *Our Idea of God*. New York: Orbis Books.

Sharing the Light of Faith, National Catechectical Directory for Catholics of the United States, 1979. Washington, D.C.: United States Catholic Conference, Nos. 227-229..

Upton, Julia 1999. *A Time for Embracing: Reclaiming Reconciliation*. Collegeville: Liturgical Press.

Vacek, Edward. February 25, 2002. "Do 'Good People' Need Confession?" *America* 186 @www.americamagazine.org.

16 The Family as Church of the Home: An Approach to a Contemporary Sacramental Familial Spirituality

William P. Roberts

"The family is, so to speak, the domestic Church," proclaim the bishops at the Second Vatican Council (*Lumen Gentium* #11). It is a "church in miniature," says Pope John Paul II (*Familiaris Consortio* #49). "You are the Church in your home," write the United States Bishops in their pastoral message to families on the occasion of the 1994 International Year of the Family (*Follow the Way of Love* 1994, 8ff).

Not too long ago I was recalling these quotations in a talk to an adult audience. When I was finished, hands went up around the room. "Please don't insult the family by calling it a church," a gentleman in the back shouted. "Church, to me, means outdated laws and fancy-robed hierarchs prancing around. We surely don't need any of that in the family." "How can you call family a church," an elderly lady queried, "with all the divorce, and spousal and child abuse that are taking place everywhere, along with the general breakdown of the family." Finally, a young woman arose and sadly noted, "I think it's terribly hypocritical for the bishops to call family a church when they prohibit any woman, and any man who starts a family from sharing in the full ministry of the church."

These are very real objections. Despite them, I think the value in ascribing to the family the notion "church of the home," or its synonym "domestic church" is that it opens the way for a very applicable spirituality of family life. One does not have to leave the family and enter a monastery to follow Christ. It is not despite the intimate relationships created by marriage and parenting that we become holy, but precisely in terms of them. Comments, however, like those quoted in the previous paragraph can be helpful because they remind us that not everything in the church lives up to Christ's inspiration, and that not everything in family is worthy of either the word "family" or the word "church." We must choose to *become* church. We must choose to *become* family. The family must choose to *become* the church of the home. None of these are givens. They only happen to the degree in which we freely respond to the call to live our lives and form our families in the image and likeness of Christ.

In this essay we probe what is involved in answering this call. How can families today truly become churches of the home? How do they become sacraments of Christ's presence to the world? What does it mean for the family to live an authentic Christian spirituality?

Since families come in a variety of forms, this topic is not as simple as it may seem at first sight. Hence, after considering how the Christian family, broadly understood, can be church of the home, we will look at the unique aspects of several of the forms in which the family is found today. These include families headed by a first time married couple, the hurting family, the single parent family, the blended family, and the three generation family. Before any of this is done, however, some clarification regarding the meaning of "church" is in order.

The word "church" stirs up diverse images in different people. To some it is the building where they worship. Others associate it with the pope and the bishops. To others it is an abstract institution. In this essay, when we apply the word church to the family, we are using the term in the sense spoken of in chapter two of *Lumen Gentium*, the church as the *people of God*.

Since the term church as people of God could be understood in various senses, let us further specify that we are using it to signify the community of the baptized, the community of those explicitly called to be followers of Jesus Christ and to share in Christ's ongoing mission to reach out in a healing way to all humankind. The question, then, to be addressed here is how the Christian family can truly live and grow as a Christian church, a community of baptized disciples of Christ.

There are many aspects involved in being this kind of a community. In applying the notion of church to family we are focusing on four of these. The church is a sacrament (*Sacrosanctum Concilium* #26). Through baptism all are called to participate in the death and resurrection of Christ (Romans 6:3, ff.). The church is a eucharistic community. The church is a community whose members are all called to the perfection of holiness (*Lumen Gentium* ch. 5).

1. The Christian Family as Church of the Home
A. The Church and Family as Sacrament

Christ is the sacrament of the encounter with God, as Dominican theologian Edward Schillebeeckx said over three decades ago in a book by that title. "No one has ever seen God; it is the only Son, who is close to the Father's heart, who has made him known" (John 1:18).

As risen, however, Christ is invisible to our mortal eyes. What makes him known on the earth today is the visible community of those who explicitly acknowledge him as Lord and Savior, not only through their verbal testimony, but, most importantly, through the witness of their Christlike behavior. It is in this sense that we can talk of the Church as a sacrament, a visible sign of Christ. Christ's voice is heard in the world today through the voice and lives of faith-filled Christians. Christ's healing is experienced through our reaching out in healing touch to others. Christ's love is manifest through the love and sacrifice of those who show care and concern. None of this happens automatically. It only takes place in as much as the community of Christians chooses to proclaim and incorporate in their actions and relationships the word of Christ, to extend its hands in curing the ills of humankind, and to allow its love to conquer the hatred that plagues the world. When the Christian community does this, it not only reveals the kind of healing, compassionate love that God and God's Word, Jesus Christ have for us; it makes their love visibly present to us. God and Christ are here and now loving us and enriching us through and in the love we show to one another. Our love is the embodiment of their love.

The Christian family is in a privileged position to be a sacrament of God's love, of Christ's love. Its members are already bound together by love, sexual intimacy, and blood. Their faith in Christ gives further insight, inspiration and direction to that love that is already rooted in these natural ties. The experience of the unparalleled intimacy of marriage and parenting can give sign of, and make present in a unique way the unimaginable intimacy with which God and Christ love each one of us.

B. Participating in Christ's Death and Resurrection

"We were indeed buried with him through baptism into death, so that, just as Christ was raised from the dead by the glory of the Father, we too might live in newness of life" (Romans 6:4, NAB).

Being immersed in the waters of baptism is a sign of death to sinfulness. Emerging from the waters symbolizes the new life of Christ with which we are now empowered.

The church, the community of the baptized, is called to live out in an ongoing way this participation in the dying and rising of Christ. But what does this mean? The New Testament sheds further light. It challenges Christians to "put away the old self of your former way of life, corrupted through deceitful desires, and be renewed in the spirit of your minds, and put on the new self, created in God's way in righteousness and holiness of truth" (Ephesians 4:22-24, NAB). In doing so, "You have stripped off your old behaviour with your old self, and you have put on a new self which will progress towards true knowledge the more it is renewed in the image of its Creator" (Colossians 3:10). "So for anyone who is in Christ, there is a new creation: the old order is gone and a new being is there to see" (2 Corinthians 5:17).

As a baptized member of the church one participates in the death and resurrection of Christ by dying gradually and daily to deceit and lying, greed and exploitation, self-centeredness and insensitivity, prejudice and grudges, disrespect and violence. In so dying we convert more fully to the Christlife of honesty and generosity, love and compassion, justice and peacemaking.

The creation of a healthy, intimate family is deeply dependent on the ability and willingness of its members to undergo countless dyings and risings (Roberts 1988, *Marriage*, ch. 5). First, there are all the kinds of deaths and new dimensions of life built into the diverse passages that are intrinsic to the human journey: from babyhood to toddlerhood, from childhood to adolescence, from young adulthood to midlife, from the working years to retirement, and then to old age. The scene is complicated when two or three (or more) generations are involved in the family structure, all of whom may be going through diverse passages at the same time. How do we deal with these transitions? Do we allow the people close to us to grow, or do we cling to attitudes and behaviors of the past that are no longer suitable to the new stage of a person's life and of our relationship, thereby hindering personal development? Are we willing to die to the fears and concerns that can stand in the way of our letting go and of our permitting new life to emerge?

Second, there are the dyings required in order to establish intimacy in our relationships. One must die to the fear of being rejected in order to expose oneself and share one's thoughts and feelings. Building intimacy requires putting oneself out for another, surrendering some of one's time, one's privacy, one's convenience, in order to be with and for the other. It is necessary to give up some of one's independence in order for others to be able to depend on our constancy and our reliability.

Third, the slow and gradual dying to sexism, is necessary if each member is to be treated as a person with equal human dignity and human rights. Only by getting rid of gender stereotypes can a just and fair distribution of family responsibilities and domestic chores be achieved. Patriarchal structures must be put aside, in order that a true partnership between wife and husband as coheads of the family be realized.

Finally, since no family is perfect, an important key to improving the quality and happiness of family life is the ability to criticize and confront in a constructive way the faults and disorders that block growth in bondedness (Roberts 1988, *Partners*, 48-51). These can range from bothersome habits (eg, the constantly loud chewing of gum, or leaving dirty dishes in the sink) to personally destructive behavior (overdrinking, inordinate gambling, drug abuse) to the violation of other family members' rights (invasion of privacy, violent outbursts).

The personal empowerment necessary to look another eyeball to eyeball involves its own kinds of dyings and risings. One has first to overcome the cowardliness that prevents us from taking the risk of offending, and perhaps alienating someone we love. This is especially true if that person tends to have the characteristics of a bully, or is very dominating or vindictive. Another barrier to conquer is apathy. "What can I do about this anyway?" It is often easier to tolerate injustice and "keep the peace," than to "take the bull by the horns" and cause a great stir. However, it is only by disrupting the facade of tranquility that true domestic peace can be created. A third obstacle to honest and constructive confrontation is the tendency to let our anger run away with us and lead us to overstatement, unfair charges, and abusive language and actions. Unless we refrain from such inclinations toward self-defeating overkill, we will not reap the fruits of meaningful, effective criticism.

C. The Church and Family as Eucharistic Community

At the Eucharist Christ gives us his Body-Person in the most visible and sacramental way. In the sharing of the Bread and the Wine Christ tells us to take and eat, take and drink, and enjoins us to "do this in remembrance of me " (Luke 22:19).

The Christian community manifests itself as church in a most visible way when it gathers to celebrate the Eucharist. It unites itself with Christ in his offering. It opens itself to receive Christ's present gift of his Body-Person. It goes forth, sent to "go in peace to love and serve the Lord." Its members do this by being the Eucharistic Body of Christ for others: giving their bread and their wine, their life and their cup of blessing, their gift of personal presence to those who need them.

Christian families are called to be small eucharistic communities. They live out their liturgical celebration of Eucharist by being in their daily lives Eucharist, Body of Christ, for one another. In unique ways they give of their own bodies to and for each other. Married couples commit themselves to be for one another in the totality of their lives: to be comfort and strength in their sorrows and struggles, celebration and affirmation in their joys and successes, encouragement and hope in their failures and disappointments. This bodily presence and commitment to each other throughout the ordinary routine of daily life is confirmed in a special way in the sharing of food at their common table, and the giving of their bodies in sexual intimacy. These special sharings empower them to become more deeply present to each other in all the other moments that constitute married life (See Roberts, *Marriage*, ch. 6).

In families where there are offspring the very conceiving, bearing, and birthing of children involve in a profound way the sharing of the parents' lives on behalf of a new life, a new body, a new human person. This nurturing of life continues in all the forms of physical, psychological and spiritual enrichment parents provide through the years of maturing and beyond.

Families live out the spirit of Eucharist whenever they extend their body-persons to one another: when they use their energy to provide each other with food and clothing, and a clean and comfortable environment; when they hug and kiss, and express compassion and concern; when they take time to listen and to be a companion; when they give each other their helping hand, their shoulder to cry on, their eyes full of understanding and love. "This is my body given for you." Families live out the spirit of Eucharist when they go beyond their four walls and work at a soup kitchen, give clothing and toys to the homeless center, donate blood at the local blood bank. "This is my blood (my life) poured out for you."

D. Called to Holiness as a Community of Christ's Followers

Breaking with the pre-Vatican II pattern of thinking that reserved the call to perfection to religious, priests and bishops, the Second Vatican Council reminds us that all the members of the church, whether cleric or lay, married or single, are called to the fullness of holiness.

> The Lord Jesus, divine teacher and model of all perfection, preached holiness of life, which he both initiates and brings to perfection, to each and every one of his disciples no matter what their condition of life: "You, therefore, must be perfect, as your heavenly Father is perfect" (Mt. 5:4-8). For he sent the holy (sic) Spirit to all to move them interiorly to love God with their whole heart, with their whole soul, with their whole understanding and with their whole strength (see Mk 12:30), and to love one another as Christ loved them … (*Lumen* Gentium #40, Flannery).

"It is therefore quite clear," the bishops further state, "that all Christians in whatever state or walk in life are called to the fullness of christian (sic) life and to the perfection of charity … " (Ibid.). This holiness that they speak of is not pie in the sky or isolated from daily living. Rather, it leads to "a more human way of living" on the journey through our present earthly pilgrimage (Ibid.).

Like the entire ecclesial community, the family, church of the home, is called to the fullness of holiness. "Married couples and Christian parents should follow their own proper path to holiness by faithful love, sustaining one another in grace throughout the entire length of their lives." (*Lumen Gentium* # 41). For our purposes here we focus on three aspects of the holiness to which Christian families are called. This holiness is founded on trinitarian faith, it is manifested in Christlike love, and it is imbued with Christ's universal salvific concern.

First, this holiness is trinitarian. It is based on the belief that God is Father/Mother, the ultimate Author of our life who dwells at the heart of our being. God loves us and nurtures us in ways that infinitely transcend the maternal/paternal categories. The challenge to Christian family holiness is to come to grips with whether or not we really believe that God is One who loves us so much. Or are we still caught up with a distant God perceived as lawgiver, judge, and worst of all, warrior? To which God do we as a family pray? To which God do we respond?

If we really accept God as our Father/Mother, then we see each other as God's daughters and sons, our equals in dignity and human worth. Then it becomes ever more clear that what we do to "the least of these" we do to God. The intimate love with which God regards us becomes a model and an inspiration for the intimate, familial love we strive to have for each other.

This trinitarian holiness is also founded on our acceptance of Jesus as the Christ, the Divine Word of God enfleshed as a human like us in all things except sin. Accordingly, we relate to Him as the most visible manifestation of who God is for us, and as the One who leads us to the God whom He calls "Abba." We receive His Word into the depths of our being and integrate His Life into our own. We put on the mind of the Lord Jesus, and treat each other as He does, and live by His values of truthfulness and generosity, peacemaking and justice, simplicity of living and trust, gentleness and kindness.

Trinitarian holiness also involves our being open in the roots of our being to the Holy Spirit who is sent forth from the Father and Christ. We recognize that each family member has received the gift of the Spirit through Baptism and, hence, is a "temple of the Holy Spirit." We respect the unique manner in which the Spirit works in each other. We appreciate the fact that one of the ways the Spirit can speak to us is through those who have deep love and concern for us. Together we strive to allow the Spirit to transform our "heart of stone" into a "heart of flesh" (See Ezekiel 36:26).

Second, this holiness to which all Christian families are called is marked by Christlike love. One of the best descriptions of this love is provided by Paul.

> Love is always patient and kind; love is never jealous; love is not boastful or conceited, it is never rude and never seeks its own advantage, it does not take offence or store up grievances. Love does not rejoice at wrongdoing, but finds its joy in the truth. It is always ready to make allowances, to trust, to hope and to endure whatever comes (I Corinthians 13:4-7).

Even when persons are the best of friends, living together in close contact day by day can at times be a test of nerves. In the family, love demands that we make allowances for the uniqueness, the differences, and the limitations of one another. Patience enables us to put up gracefully with what we cannot change in another, and to choose a gentle way in communicating what can be changed. The patient person does not let things build up inside, but in a controlled and constructive manner expresses annoyances before they get out of hand.

To be kind, Webster tells us, is to be affectionate, friendly, agreeable; it is to possess a sympathetic and pleasant nature. It can be easy to let our bad moods be the driving force behind the way we present ourselves to others. But with a little effort we can let the smile conquer the frown, and convert the cloud in someone's life into a sunny ray.

Someone once asked how Paul can say love is never "jealous" when God is referred to in the Old Testament as a "jealous God" (for example, Exodus 20:5, 34:14). The answer resides in distinguishing different kinds of jealousy. In our monotheistic religion the covenant between God and us demands fidelity to a unique love and worship that is due to this God alone and not to be shared with other "gods." In a monogamous marriage there is a unique depth of intimacy between wife and husband that is not to be shared with another. This uniqueness is to be jealously guarded. In other family relationships there are diverse levels of demands unique to those relationships. The kind of jealousy that authentic love excludes is a wrong kind of possessiveness, an unreasonable suspicion of infidelity, a hostile rivalry, an envy of the accomplishments of another (see Roberts, *Partners*, 44-45).

Love is not boastful or conceited. The first meaning that the dictionary gives for boasting is that it speaks of or asserts with *excessive* pride. One of the meanings given for conceit is that it is *excessive* appreciation of one's own worth or virtue. The word "excessive" is of utmost importance here. Contemporary psychology makes clear that in order to see the good in another one must be able to see the good in oneself (Harris 1967). In order to take the risk to love you and possibly be rejected, I need to feel secure within myself. To love another, one must first love oneself, as indicated in Jesus' command to love your neighbor *as yourself* (Matthew 22:39). Authentic love is rooted in humility, that is, an honest assessment of one's value, goodness and talents, along with an awareness of one's faults and limitations, and one's need of others. This balanced view of oneself enables a person to have the self-confidence necessary to reach out to others, and at the same time accept and appreciate the worth and strengths of the other, without being threatened by another's superior gifts.

One of the liabilities of living at the hectic pace of our workaholic culture is that people can get so caught up with the priority of their own agenda and the busyness of their lives that they don't even have time for the common courtesies. Accordingly, Paul's insistence that love is never rude and never seeks its own advantage may have special application to our society today. For families to grow in unity and bondedness it is necessary not only to avoid the harsh word and the boorish action, but also to take the time and energy to be sensitive to the feelings of others and to extend the common signs of politeness: the kind word, the gentle gesture, the thoughtful deed.

Love does not take offence or store up grievances. This does not mean we can't be offended, or angry. It means we do not retaliate, nor let our resentment and hostility build up. We do not give each other the silent treatment. We confront, repent, forgive, and get on with our lives.

There is no room in family love for taking pleasure in the wrongdoings of another, for laughing when another falls, for rejoicing when someone fails. The signs of love are rather seen in empathy, compassion, and the desire to lead the other to wholeness.

Holiness: it is so profound, and yet so simple. God is love, and each family is called to manifest the presence of God through the love they show. "Where charity and love prevail, there God is ever found."

Third, the holiness mandated of the Christian family is imbued with Christ's universal salvific concern. The gift of God's grace is given to every individual and every family not only for their own benefit, but also to benefit and enrich others. Like the whole church, each family of the baptized is called to share in Christ's ongoing mission of bringing the fullness of life to all. The first step in this sharing is to try to enter into Christ's mind and heart in regard to others. What is his love, his concern, his dream for them? Several areas of this universal salvific mission will be the focus of our attention here: our own family members, the wider community of families, the marginalized, peoples of other races and diverse religious persuasions, and the cosmos itself.

Within the range of "healthy" family, the greatest concern for our well-being comes from immediate family members: our spouses and children, our parents and siblings. This reality brings out an important aspect of the sacramentality of the family. The unique concern that we experience for the well-being of one another is a visible sign of the infinitely greater desire that Christ has for our self-fulfillment. From another perspective, Christ enriches and transforms us in the distinctive dimensions of our being through the profoundly intimate ways in which family members manifest their concern for us. It is precisely as a spouse, a parent, a daughter/son, a sibling that we have the singular opportunity and responsibility to be in a special way a vital "channel," a living sacrament through whom Christ's healing and transforming grace can touch the depths of our spirit and our lives. No family is an isolated unit. It exists within the wider human community of families. The kind of family we choose to become, has impact on this broader network of family life. When we allow Christ's redemptive presence to influence the way we relate within our own family, all family is somehow touched for the better. Through our peacemaking we counteract domestic violence. By our respect for the equal human dignity of each family member we diminish authoritarian familial structures, be they in the patriarchal or matriarchal mode. By creating deep bonds of relatedness among our own family members, we work toward reversing the breakdown of family life. Because of our love, the familial community becomes a more nurturing, life-giving environment.

Christ's salvific concern embraces the totality of the human person, physically, emotionally, spiritually. So, our sharing in his mission involves addressing all human needs. In Matthew's Gospel the Last Judgement centers around our response and our failure to respond.

> Come, you whom my Father has blessed, take as your heritage the kingdom prepared for you since the foundation of the world. For I was hungry and you gave me food, I was thirsty and you gave me drink, I was a stranger and you made me welcome, lacking clothes and you clothed me, sick and you visited me, in prison and you came to see me (Matthew 25:33-36).

As family members, we spend a great deal of our time and energy fulfilling this mandate within our own home. We are also called to go beyond our walls and be concerned about the dire poverty, hunger, and homelessness that plagues our neighborhoods, our cities, our nations. Having come to see the face of Christ in the members of our family, we are challenged to see Christ in the faces of the starving children in Africa, of the oppressed in the war-torn Mideast, of those dying with AIDS and other diseases in hospital wards throughout the world. Our strength as a family depends not only on how well we care for our own, but also on the extent and quality of our outreach to those dwelling on the margins of human society.

The Christian family is called to participate in Christ's love and concern for people of all races and religious persuasions. The first responsibility in this regard is to eliminate the prejudices that reside deep within the human bloodstream.

> … in that image (i.e., of the Creator) there is no room for distinction between Greek and Jew, between circumcised and uncircumcised, or between barbarian and Scythian, slave and free. There is only Christ: he is everything and he is in everything (Colossians 3:11, parenthesis mine).

This theme is reiterated by the Bishops at Vatican II.

> All women and men are endowed with a rational soul and are created in God's image; they have the same nature and origin and, being redeemed by Christ, they enjoy the same divine calling and destiny; there is here a basic equality between all and it must be accorded ever greater recognition.
>
> Undoubtedly not all people are alike as regards physical capacity and intellectual and moral powers. But any kind of social or cultural discrimination in basic personal rights on the grounds of sex, race, color, social conditions, language or religion, must be curbed and eradicated as incompatible with God's design (*Gaudium et Spes* # 29, Flannery edition).

The family is the first and primary context in which we can learn to put aside our discriminatory attitudes and appreciate God's love for all humans. It is the first school where we can be trained to respect people of various races and diverse religious beliefs, and to value our commonalities rather than be divided by our differences.

Finally, the Christian family, like the whole church, has to become conscious of the cosmic dimension of Christ's redemption (see, for example, Edwards 1991). Our dualistic tendencies have inclined us to identify Christ's salvific concern with the "spiritual" (understood as soul vs. matter) rather than with the whole human person and the whole of creation. The New Testament, however, points us toward a cosmic perspective of salvation.

> He is the image of the unseen God,
> the first-born of all creation,
> for in him were created all things
> in heaven and on earth:

everything visible and everything invisible . . . .

He exists before all things
and in him all things hold together . . . .

He is the Beginning,
the first-born from the dead,
so that he should be supreme in every way;
because God wanted all fullness to be found in him
and through him to reconcile all things to him,
everything in heaven and everything on earth,
by making peace through his death on the cross

(Colossians 1:15-20).

In his letter to the Romans Paul speaks of the whole of creation being freed "from its slavery to corruption and brought into the same glorious freedom as the children of God." (Romans 8:21).

The bishops of the Second Vatican Council pursue the same cosmic theme:

The world which the council has in mind is the world of women and men, the entire human family seen in its total environment. It is the world as the theatre of human history, bearing the marks of its travail, its triumphs and failures. It is the world which Christians believe has been created and is sustained by the love of its maker, has fallen into the slavery of sin but has been freed by Christ, who was crucified and rose again in order to break the stranglehold of the evil one, so that it might be fashioned anew according to God's design and brought to its fulfillment (*Gaudium et Spes # 2*, Flannery edition).

The family can participate in this cosmic dimension of Christ's redemptive mission in numerous ways. We can sensitize each other to the sacredness of the human person as the enfleshed consciousness of the material world. Family members can grow in appreciation that we are all "children of the universe," affected by what happens to it, and in turn affecting it by our attitudes and our actions. Finally, we can teach each other to be respectful, conserving, and considerate in the way we treat, consume, and share the goods of the earth.

Summary

In this first part of the essay we have reflected on the potential that the truly Christian family has for being a church of the home. We have attempted to do this by selecting four aspects of what it means to be church, and then exploring how the Christian family is called to incarnate within itself each of these ecclesial dimensions. Like the church universal of which it is a part, the family is challenged to become the sacrament (visible manifestation) of Christ's presence in the world today, a people actively participating in His death and resurrection in the context of their daily lives, a community of persons who become eucharist for others, and a people striving toward the fullness of Christlike holiness. While we have reflected on each of these four dimensions separately, it is clear that they are all interrelated. The family becomes the sacrament of Christ as it shares in his death and resurrection, becomes eucharistic, and achieves the holiness to which it is called.

What has been said so far is applicable not only to the family headed by a first time happily married couple, but also to a variety of family forms. Since every one of these alternative ways of being family present their own distinctiveness, we turn to a brief consideration of some of the aspects of spirituality appropriate to four of these diverse forms..

2. Alternate Family Forms; Churches of the Home
A. The Hurting Family

The family can be hurting for many different reasons. Here I am focusing on the hurt caused by what marriage and family therapist Christopher Reilly calls the critically wounded marriage, namely, one that is in serious trouble, but not beyond repair (Reilly 1989, 1).

The church, the people of God gathered by the Spirit in the name of Christ, is at one and the same time graced and sinful. The Christian family, gathered by the same Spirit is also ever graced and sinful. Hence, the church, as well as the family, are always in need of reform, forgiveness, and reconciliation. The church is a pilgrim people journeying through many peaks and valleys. The family, too, is ever on pilgrimage, travelling through many ups and downs. Some married couples hurt so badly they are on the brink of going their separate ways. Are there particular dimensions of a spirituality that can especially speak to them in their dark moments and in their pain? Several such aspects come to mind.

First, there is hope. The words of the psalmist are particularly relevant here.

> Even when I walk through a dark valley
>> I fear no harm for you are at my side;
>> Your rod and staff give me courage (Psalm 23:4, NAB).

The couple are called to believe and trust in a God who loves them and is with them, even though God may seem so far away, because of the painful distance from each other that is now pulling them further apart. They are also challenged to believe in themselves and trust in the God-given strengths and possibilities that reside within themselves and in a relationship that at least once existed, and, while seriously waning, is not yet dead.

Second, they are called to accept humbly the moment of truth: their relationship is at a critical point and in deep trouble, and they are in need of help. They have to swallow their pride and embrace the help they need from God, from each other, and from "outside" agents, whether non-professional or professional, as the situation demands.

Third, each partner has to own up to the ways s/he might have contributed to the problem, and have the courage and willingness to amend any offensive behavior.

Finally, they need to forgive themselves and one another, work toward reconciliation and deeper unity, and get on with their lives. They cannot cling to past hurts and hostilities. While these may be impossible to forget, they can be remembered with *healed* memory.

B. The Single Parent Family

The hurt and alienation in some cases exceed the limits of possible repair, and the marriage inevitably ends in divorce. In other families a spouse has been lost in death before the children reached adulthood.

Some singles have children. Others adopt. The family, the church of the home, in these situations consists of a single parent unit. There are various ways in which the faith of this community can function.

Where divorce has occurred, there has usually been much pain and disappointment. Divorce is, in a very real sense, a kind of dying. A marital relationship, that once was, is no more. However, where there is death, there can also be resurrection, as Paula Ripple points out in her book on divorce, *The Pain and the Possibility* (1978). The divorced Christian is called to die to bitterness, hatred, unforgiveness, vindictiveness, and to grow as a person through the suffering and trauma of the divorce and post-divorce periods. Where pre-adult children are concerned, decisions about custody and visitation rights need to be made in their best interests, rather than out of a spirit of meanness or jealousy toward the other spouse.

The widow/widower has participated in death as closely as one can, short of one's own. The surviving spouse needs to go through the normal period of grieving; but a mourning that is experienced in light of the Christian hope of resurrection, and the belief that death is not the end of life, but a new beginning. The pain of loss can be situated in the context of gratitude for the years and happiness shared together, and the realization that while death puts an end to the earthbound union and the visible presence, it cannot destroy the love relationship nor the invisible presence. Where children remain to be reared, the widowed parent can give ongoing witness regarding the deceased parent by describing that person with affection and appreciation, and sharing memories of that person's love and care of the children. S/he can also point out that this parent now lives with God, and, hence, continues, though in an invisible manner, to be with us, and to love and be concerned for us. We can pray not only for, but also to that parent, thus allowing that person's parenting role to continue in an important way.

The single parent, as sole head of the family, shoulders the responsibility of both parents. S/he becomes the primary former of faith, the leader of prayer, and the inspirer of the human qualities essential for personal maturity. Where there is grief over divorce or death s/he must cope not only with her own, but must be the facilitator for the children to grow through theirs. While the faith-filled single parent cannot fully make up for the absence of a second loving parent, s/he is empowered to create a well nurtured and nurturing family that is a distinctive expression of what it means to be church of the home.

C. The Blended Family

This term is used to refer to a family that is created when a divorced or widowed person with children remarries. The blend is more complex when the other spouse also brings children into the marriage. The qualities of acceptance and fairness, understanding and communication that are necessary for every family unit are challenged in special ways in the blended family.

Most families grow incrementally. A blended family may double or triple in size overnight. Two familial units, consisting of several different personalities, used to bonding within blood lines, and accustomed to their own distinctive ways, are suddenly "thrown together" with "strangers." If this new conglomerate is to become a community, a family, not to mention a church of the home, an extraordinary degree of acceptance and accommodation is essential. Those not of blood relationship must now be considered among one's daughters and sons, one's sisters and brothers. The normal tendencies of parental preferences and sibling rivalries are exacerbated. Parents and siblings are challenged to treat the new members with the same consideration and fairness which they show their own.

Often in periods of transition we can become so absorbed with our own struggles and problems that we forget the comparable difficulties and pain that others are enduring. In the process of putting together a blended family the couple need to "walk in each other's shoes," so as to understand what the other is going through in establishing meaningful relationships with the "new" children. Both have to be sensitive to the suffering children can go through adjusting to the "new parent" to whom they are now also accountable. As in so many trying situations, the key to this kind of understanding is talking out the difficulties and listening to each other's struggle.

D. The Three Generation Family

The reality of three or more generations of a family living under the same roof, along with relatives that go beyond the parent and sibling relationships, has always been a part of family life in many cultures. As people live longer, and as the economy makes it more difficult for young adults to get started on their own, the multi-generation family may become a more common experience for other cultures as well. Where the multigeneration family is a new experience, much can be learned from intercultural dialogue.

One of the important ways for achieving harmony and peace in the three generation family is the mutual respect and appreciation that the diverse generations have for each other. The stereotypical prejudices that view the young as "all going astray," and the elderly as "over the hill," need to give way to an appreciation of the vitality, ambitions and budding gifts of most children and young adults, and a respect for the proven efforts, achievements and wisdom of most senior citizens.

Each generation must also respect the primary responsibilities and priorities that belong to one another. Parents must assume the major obligations of rearing their children, and not use the grandparents as cheap babysitters and caretakers. At the same time they need to allow opportunities for genuine children-grandparent relationships to develop. Grandparents, on the other hand, have to refrain from interfering with the role of the parents. Occasional advice is appropriate. Pressure to "do it the way we used to do it" is not. It is also important that any married couples living in a multigeneration family be given enough space and privacy to nurture their own marital relationships.

Conclusion

As indicated in the beginning of this essay, there are understandable objections raised against calling the family a church of the home. Though, admittedly, this use of the term could be problematic, I chose to explore what validity this usage could have. The main reason for doing so is my belief that probing the ecclesial dimensions of family can be another way of discovering the Christian vocation of the family, and the kind of spirituality to which family members are called.

In this essay we have focused on four aspects of what it means to be church, and have explored how these aspects can be lived out in various forms of family life. Like the church, the Christian family is called to be the sacrament of Christ, to share in Christ's death and resurrection, to be a Eucharistic community, and to follow the call to holiness. To the degree that family members can do this they become more fully a Christian family, and hence a true church of the home. In this way, like a leaven in the dough, the family has a transforming effect on the wider church, and the broader community of humankind.

References

Abbott, S.J., Walter M., editor. 1966. *The Documents of Vatican II*. New York: America Press. The three documents referred to in this essay are *Gaudium et Spes* (*Pastoral Constitution on the Church in the Modern World*), *Lumen Gentium* (*Dogmatic Constitution on the Church*), and *Sacrosanctum Concilium* (*Constitution on the Sacred Liturgy*). Unless otherwise specified, all quotations from these documents are from Abbott's edition.

Edwards, Denis. 1991. *Jesus and the Cosmos*. Mahwah, NJ: Paulist Press.

Flannery, Austin, O.P., editor. 1996. *Vatican Council II: Constitutions, Decrees, Declarations*. Northport, NY: Costello Publishing Co.

Harris, Thomas A. 1967. *I'm OK, You're OK: A Practical Guide to Transactional Analysis*. New York: Harper and Row.

John Paul II. 1981. *Familiaris Consortio*. Washington, DC: United States Catholic Conference.

Reilly, Christopher C. 1989. *Making Your Marriage Work*. Mystic, CT: Twenty-Third Publications.

Paula Ripple. 1978. *The Pain and the Possibility: Divorce and Separation among Catholics*. Notre Dame, IN: Ave Maria Press.

Roberts, William P. 1988. *Marriage: Sacrament of Hope and Challenge*. Cincinnati: St. Anthony Messenger Press.

Roberts, Challon O'Hearn and William P. 1988. *Partners in Intimacy: Living Christian Marriage Today*. Mahwah, NJ: Paulist Press.

Schillebeeckx, Edward, O.P. 1963. *Christ the Sacrament of the Encounter with God*. New York: Sheed and Ward.

The New American Bible (Saint Joseph Edition). 1992. New York: Catholic Book Publishing Co. Quotations from this edition are indicated by NAB.

The New Jerusalem Bible. 1985. Garden City, NY: Doubleday & Company, Inc. Unless otherwise specified, all biblical quotations are taken from this edition.

United States Catholic Bishops. 1994. *Follow the Way of Love: A Pastoral Message of the U.S. Catholic Bishops to Families*. Washington, DC: United States Catholic Conference.

Contributors

MICHAEL HORACE BARNES, Ph.D. is Professor of Religious Studies at the University of Dayton. He is the author of *Stages of Thought: the Co-Evolution of Religious Thought and Science* (Oxford 2000), and *In the Presence of Mystery: An Introduction to the Nature and Evolution of Religion* (Twenty-Third Publications, 3rd edition, 2002).

JOSEPH A. BRACKEN, S.J., Ph.D. is Director of the Brueggeman Center for Interreligious Dialogue at Xavier University in Cincinnati. He is the author of seven books and many articles on trinitarian theology and process philosophy, including *The One in the Many: A Contemporary Reconstruction of the God-World Relationship* (Eerdmans, 2001).

JOHN A. COLEMAN, S.J., Ph.D. is the Casassa Professor of Social Values at Loyola Marymount University, Los Angeles. Among his recent published essays are "Christianity and Civil Society" in Nancy Rosenblum and Robert Post, eds., *Civil Society and Government*, Princeton University Press, 2001, and "Selling God in America" in Richard Madsen et al., *Meaning and Modernity: Religion, Polity and Self,* University of California Press, 2001. He is currently doing research for a book on Catholic Charities, U.S.A.

WALTER E. CONN, Ph.D. teaches ethics in the Department of Theology and Religious Studies at Villanova University in Pennsylvania. His books include *Conscience: Development and Self-Transcendence, Christian Conversion*, and *The Desiring Self.* He is the editor of *Horizons: The Journal of the College Theology Society.*

LAWRENCE S. CUNNINGHAM, Ph.D. is John A. O'Brien Professor of Theology at the University of Notre Dame. The author or editor of over sixteen books, he writes the "Religion Book Notes" for *Commonweal* magazine, and lectures or teaches widely both in this country and abroad.

JOHN K.DOWNEY teaches in the Religious Studies Department at Gonzaga University in Spokane. He received his Ph.D from Marquette University. Downey specializes in foundational theology and methods. He is the author of *Beginning at the Beginning: Wittgenstein and Theological Conversation* (University of America Press, 1986).

GERALD M. FAGIN, S.J., Ph.D. is Associate Professor of Systematic Theology and Spirituality at the Loyola Institute for Ministry, Loyola University, New Orleans. He also co-directs an internship for spiritual directors at the New Orleans Archdiocesan Spirituality Center.

BARBARA J. FLEISCHER, Ph.D. is Associate Professor of Psychology and Pastoral Theology at the Loyola Institute for Ministry, Loyola University, New Orleans, where she teaches graduate courses in pastoral ministry. She is also faculty coordinator of the Human and Organizational Development Undergraduate Program at Loyola. She holds a Ph.D. and an M.S. in psychology from St. Louis University, and a Master of Pastoral Studies from Loyola University, New Orleans.

JOANN HEANEY-HUNTER has her Ph.D. from Fordham University. She teaches theology at St. John's University in New York, where she specializes in the theology of marriage and family. Her most recent research focuses on developing a sacramental spirituality of the family. She has written and lectured widely on these topics.

WILLIAM J. KELLY, S.J., Ph.D. entered the Wisconsin Province of the Society of Jesus in 1941. He received his A.B. and M.A. from Saint Louis University, and his S.T.D. from Institut Catholique de Paris. He has been a member of the Theology Department at Marquette University since 1961, and since 2001 has been Associate Professor Emeritus of Theology at that institution. His main areas of specialization are systematic and dogmatic theology with a special interest in the theological thought of John Henry Cardinal Newman, and the historical background of contemporary atheism and theism.

MICHAEL G. LAWLER, Ph.D. is the Amelia and Emil Graff Chair in Catholic Theological Studies and Director of the Center for Marriage and Family at Creighton University. He is the author of eighteen books and numerous scholarly articles, many of them on marriage. His latest is *Marriage in the Catholic Church: Disputed Questions* (Liturgical Press, 2002).

BERNARD J. LEE, S.M., Ph.D. is Assistant Chancellor and Professor of Theology at St. Mary's University, San Antonio. His doctorate from the Graduate Theological Union in Berkeley is in philosophical theology, and many of his published works reflect the dialogue between theology and philosophy (e.g., process thought, hermeneutics, postmodernity, etc.), as well as between theology and the social sciences.

WILLIAM P. LOEWE holds a Ph.D. from Marquette University. He is Professor of Systematic Theology at The Catholic University of America where he has served as department chair and associate dean. He is Past President of the Catholic Theology Society.

GARY MACY, Ph.D. is a professor in the Department of Theology and Religious Studies at the University of San Diego. He received both his Bachelor's and his Master's degree from Marquette University where he specialized in historical and sacramental theology. He earned his doctoral degree in Divinity from Cambridge University. Macy has published five books in historical theology as well as numerous articles.

WILLIAM P. ROBERTS, Ph.D. is Professor of Theology at the University of Dayton. He specializes in systematic theology and marriage and family. He is the author or editor of a dozen books and sixty articles and book reviews. His most recent publication is *Thorny Issues: Theological and Pastoral Reflections* (Nova Science Publishers, 2001).

GERARD S. SLOYAN, Ph.D. a priest of the Trenton Diocese, is Professor Emeritus at Temple University in Philadelphia, and presently teaches at Catholic University of America. He is a past president of the Catholic Theological Society of America, and the author of numerous books and articles. He specializes in New Testament and patristics.